THICK MORALITIES, THIN POLITICS

For Judge Richard Posner
in appreciation

Benjamin Gregg

Benjamin Gregg

THICK MORALITIES, THIN POLITICS

Social Integration Across Communities of Belief

Duke University Press   Durham and London   2003

© 2003 Duke University Press

All rights reserved

Printed in the United States of

America on acid-free paper ∞

Designed by C. H. Westmoreland

Typeset in Cycles with Helvetica display

by Tseng Information Systems, Inc.

Library of Congress Cataloging-

in-Publication Data appear on

the last printed page of

this book.

FOR KEQIN

CONTENTS

ACKNOWLEDGMENTS

I am grateful for the thoughtful and sensitive readings, and attendant critical feedback, of David Braybrooke, Joseph Carens, Fred Dallmayr, Dick Howard, J. Donald Moon, and my anonymous reviewers for Duke University Press. I am especially indebted to David Braybrooke, who urged me to consider and then reconsider my arguments in almost all of their parts. My work, whatever its merits, is better for my attempts to respond to all of these critical readings. Expectably, any weaknesses in it go not to the respective accounts of my various interlocutors but solely to mine.

Chapter 5 originally appeared, in a somewhat different version, as "Using Legal Rules in an Indeterminate World: Overcoming the Limitations of Jurisprudence," in *Political Theory* 27, no. 3, pp. 389–410, copyright © 1999 by Sage Publications. Used with kind permission of Sage Publications.

INTRODUCTION

Thick Moralities, Thin Politics constitutes an extended argument for social and political agreement under conditions that discourage agreement. Among those many conditions I speak directly to moral diversity, a normatively heterogeneous populace, and morally and culturally
diverse communities active within modern, cosmopolitan societies.
My goal is a conception of legitimate politics, progressive public policy,
and responsive law that can hold for all component communities even
as they differ from one another. I develop a model of validity for arguments made in the public sphere, of understanding between and
among competing worldviews, and of adjudication of disputes generated by normative differences. My approach considers how social integration, broadly conceived, can be configured to this end. Part 1 of this
book focuses on a certain kind of politics—what I develop as "normatively thin"—in social integration. Part 2 centers on integration more
narrowly, in political judgment or decision or agreement. Together the
two parts of the book urge an integration accommodative of difference via "thin norms." All comprehensive worldviews, from repressive to emancipatory, from benighted to enlightened, are "thick," in
my sense of the term. I argue that a common political regime characterized by normative "thinness" is the best way to allow different and
competing "thicknesses" to flourish side by side in mutual tolerance.
While the goal of thin politics is successful integration and social cooperation, such politics does not preclude or discourage political contestation about moral principles, long a means of social and political
progress. I also develop a notion of "generalized community" that institutionalizes peaceable, rational auspices for carrying out such contestation. Generalized community oversees a society's various concrete
communities in normatively neutral ways, promoting equality among
them through a politics of recognition (as legal equals) or through a
politics of difference (as carriers of unique identities). Each concrete
community, in taking the attitude of generalized community toward
itself, commits to respecting the different, even competing orientations of other concrete communities. Each concrete community can
expect to be tolerated by the others in return. If the different concrete
communities relate to one another in terms of generalized commu-

nity, their mutual tolerance will allow each to flourish, in part because generalized community's thin normativity needn't "infect" or elide the normatively thick commitments of these concrete communities. Nor does it surrender either the poor or the otherwise marginalized. Not to surrender means not to forsake efforts toward political and social progress, not to forego contestation over moral principles, not to preclude any role for the state in implementing policies toward social justice and equality among citizens.

My theory draws upon particular disciplinary debates but always within the broader focus of my own, autonomous project (which for the most part foregoes *explication de texte*). The philosophical warrant for my position is a notion of pragmatism; mine is a pragmatist model of how competing worldviews might understand one another. One strand of this strain of pragmatism is the claim that all knowledge and judgments are fallible. Another is the claim that the theory, although abstract, is at all points concerned with practical implications: how people in fact cope with normative diversity and how they might cope better. The theory seeks to identify and develop the various elements of a pragmatist approach to social integration under conditions of moral diversity. These are the elements necessary for social integration within cosmopolitan societies, among diverse communities, and in the personality structures of individual citizens. I apply the theory in three salient contexts for political judgment: critique of ideology, decisions about how best to interpret indeterminate legal norms, and genuine understanding between competing systems of cultural values.

My goal is systematic not historicist: to provide a critical account of social structure and human agency with respect to the grounds and formation of legitimate political judgment, in my threefold sense of critique (chapter 5), interpretation (chapter 6), and understanding (chapter 7). Beyond the scope of this theory, at least as developed to this point, is some general procedure for political judgment. Beyond its scope is the design of specific institutions that would accomplish the goals of normatively thin social integration. And beyond its scope is the design of tests that would allow a society to distinguish appropriate from inappropriate norms.

My theory approaches issues of social and political theory as they are shaped by epistemology and sociology, rather than, say, ethics or comparative politics. It is more interested in questions of actual social and political process than in the ultimate requirements for a just society. Its pragmatist orientation rejects the foundational project of first philosophy and its abstract universality.

The theory draws on intellectual currents quite beyond pragmatism. Thus it analyzes the relationship between thick and thin norms in microsociological ways, through several kinds of interactionist approaches (compatible with yet distinct from philosophical pragmatism). These approaches focus on face-to-face relationships between and among persons, in distinction to the mediation of persons through social institutions. But the theory also applies this approach to communities and groups interacting with one another, not only to interacting individuals. It shows that social interaction and negotiations of meaning across the various communities I discuss (including social critique, judicial interpretation, and the efforts of one value system to understand another, competing one) take place within institutional parameters which themselves are not open to complete negotiation. It looks to various kinds of community to understand shifts in the direction of institutional change in cosmopolitan societies.

A third element of my approach is the influence of critical social theory, of the Frankfurt school, although, save in the case of Jürgen Habermas, this element is less explicit. My theory of normatively thin, general social norms seeks to contribute to integration not only within any given community but also among many different communities. It also seeks to formulate a justifiable and useful notion of critique in heterogeneous societies, as a theory of the unique nature of modernity and the challenges modernity poses to traditional forms of social theory and political philosophy. It argues that modern integration can only occur through a self-reflective and critical understanding of political life. The book's title (*Thick Moralities, Thin Politics*) attempts to make this point: that social integration in complex modern societies depends not on thick moral norms but on the capacity of citizens to configure and be bound by thin norms, examples of which I elsewhere analyze as indeterminate norms.[1] The subtitle (*Social Integration Across Communities of Belief*) asks the reader to reflect on social integration in the contemporary context of normative diversity. And my theory of thick moralities, thin norms shows how dependence on thick norms banks on a nongeneralizable form of critique, a form that reliance on thin norms replaces with a critique more subtle, more flexible, more participatory, and hence better able to contribute to social integration in a diverse society.

Clearly my theory does not lie in the Anglo-American tradition of analytic philosophy. But it does draw directly on the work of a number of American thinkers, including George Herbert Mead, Talcott Parsons, Erving Goffman, Harold Garfinkel, and a considerable number of American feminists. It also draws on the "classical" Europeans G. W. F. Hegel, Karl Marx, Emile Durkheim, Max Weber, and Georg Simmel, as well as on the contemporary contributions of Niklas Luhmann, Pierre Bourdieu, Anthony Giddens, and Jürgen Habermas.[2]

Finally, my theory's emphasis on the political advantages of normative thinness is in many ways compatible with liberal thought. At the same time I distinguish my approach precisely from what I call "political liberalism," a term associated prominently with the work of John Rawls. I offer my theory as an unusual form of political communitarianism, which, while certainly inflected with elements of political liberalism, can be defined in part over against Rawlsian liberalism (even as I am sympathetic to some of its claims, as later chapters show). Above all with respect to "liberal neutrality" (what I shall develop as "normative thinness"), my theory is more radical than Rawls's. And I arrive at my position not, in Rawlsian fashion, via moral theory but rather through an epistemological approach. Consider four points in particular.

First, Rawls (1993:147) posits for liberal democratic societies a specifically moral form of justice: political virtue is moral virtue where justice derives from principles "embodied in human character and expressed in public life." On this account (to employ a topical example), an evangelical Christian opponent of legalized abortion and a secular supporter of abortion rights would have to seek justice in putative principles embodied in their characters as human beings, hence in principles universally shared, hence universally valid in the eyes of those who recognize them. (On this account, everyone holds such principles, but not everyone may realize that he or she holds them, in which case such persons hold false beliefs about themselves. This move only compounds the explanatory problems of Rawls's approach.) The approach presupposes fundamental agreement among persons on both sides of the issue; it assumes that all persons share the same thick morality, as the content of those principles. But were this the case, how would one account for the fact that there continue to be two robust sides to this issue, each intractably opposed to the other? On Rawls's account, one would have to conclude that some people simply do not realize what their own, true fundamental beliefs are. This conclusion is unsustainable because it presupposes what cannot be shown (or at least I know of no plausible account): that these principles actually exist at some universal, perhaps ultimately anthropological level. By contrast, my approach presupposes no empirically unverifiable "fundamentally shared principles" held by all human beings. In fact, my approach does not even work toward normative consensus but rather toward the less ambitious, more realistic goal of "accommodation." It is not deep or broad agreement but is political cooperation all the same.

My proposal of normatively thin politics of mutual accommodation has to do with contending political, or cultural, or social groups recognizing one another as having the status as every other group. To that extent my proposal constrains all groups to respect one another as an aspect of their right to advocate their position peacefully and within the bounds of law. No one of these groups has the right to impose its position on another, unless those positions "win" in terms of legislation or judicial interpretation. "Losing" groups retain the right to maintain their contrarian viewpoints and to continue to advocate them. These groups, which may be normatively thick, are related to one another in the various normatively thin ways I develop in the course of the book. Justice in normatively thin terms is not moral (normatively thick) but political (which I develop as normatively thin). Justice occurs in the normatively thin relations among groups within a constitutional order that applies to all normatively thick groups equally. To be sure, the losing side of the abortion debate will experience moral anguish at its defeat, but it need not be politically violated: anguished as Christians but not as citizens (or, if the secularists lose, anguished as secular humanists but, again, not as citizens).

Individuation under terms of normatively thin politics refers to the creation of individuals as bearers of rights, as legal persons: a status that can be generalized to all citizens. Political socialization into a constitutional order is distinct from individuation in normatively thick groups, which refers to the creation of individuals as bearers of identities, as members of distinct ways of life that—in the face of rival groups and competing thick normativities—cannot be generalized politically and legally to all members of society. Rights provided by normatively thin politics pertain to all individuals in all normatively thick groups, and cannot be trumped by rights internal to these groups.

Of course, the politics of thin norms must expect constant disagreement at the moral level, but it seeks political cooperation in the face of enduring disagreement. After all, it does not elide differences among normatively thick groups or standpoints as a condition of recognizing them in its normatively thin way. Nor need it abandon the individual-istic formulation of the rights of the citizen. On the other hand, norma-tively thin politics "protects" normatively thick groups by recognizing their members within the normatively thin political order but not by guaranteeing the survival of any particular thick normativity (where a guarantee would amount to privileging that normativity over others).

The two sides to the abortion debate will not agree at the end of the normatively thin day, but they can cooperate as citizens with each other if they are constrained to make their pitches for their respective views in thin terms—terms therefore potentially acceptable to the op-posing side—rather than in thick ones, which will always shipwreck on the rocks of the opposing thick view. What are those thin terms? Prominent in the mix is legalism: the notion that the abortion issue be regulated by a set of rules that apply equally to all citizens. For example, if the Supreme Court defines the unborn fetus as a "person" in the sense of the Fourteenth Amendment,[3] then abortion is unconstitutional and the secular pro-choicers must accept that only a constitutional amend-ment, or a later ruling by the Supreme Court overturning the earlier ruling, can be a politically acceptable means to establishing their view as the legally binding one. If the Court does not so define the unborn fetus, then the pro-lifers stand before the same desideratum: change the rules (amend the Constitution) or change the legally controlling interpretation of the rules (by appropriately influencing the selection of future authoritative interpreters).

Second, I break radically with Rawls not just in rejecting thick mo-rality as a point of departure, but in rejecting his notion that humans as such possess a fundamentally moral personality, certain "powers of moral personality" that generate a "sense of right and justice" as well as a "capacity for a conception of the good" (1993:302). The problem with this view is that it is politically meaningful—in the sense of adju-dicating divisive issues of public policy—*only* if we assume what we cannot assume: that every relevant person possesses more or less the same moral personality. The evangelical pro-lifer may well doubt that the secular pro-choicer has a moral personality, and perhaps vice versa. We get ourselves into these sorts of problems with normatively thick assumptions such as that of a "moral personality." The normatively thin alternative is *not* to set the issue up as one between *my* moral personality against *your* immoral one (which is how the two sides might view each other on Rawls's scheme). The alternative is to set the issue up as one having nothing to do with the personality of the individual but only with his or her public persona, as a citizen bound by rules that strive to neither favor nor disfavor any particular morality, but to be neutral toward all moralities. This is the approach of positive law, and in democratic contexts the opponents of any particular law seek new legislation, rather than spiritual condemnation or spiritual conversion of the opposing side.

Note that the individual's membership in the normatively thin constitutional order need not threaten his or her simultaneous membership in a normatively thick group if it does not threaten that group's thick normativity. Membership in such groups needn't threaten membership in the normatively thin constitutional order as long as normatively thick groups abide by the constitutional order's thin normativity. In this way the constitutional order uncouples thin and thick levels of social integration—or thin normativity from thick, or generalizable ways of life from nongeneralizable ones. It allows normatively thick groups to interrelate on the basis of thin normativity, without having to forsake the thick normativity constitutive of their respective identities.

Third, I reject the notion of an altruistic rationality or the idea that rationality is somehow inherently altruistic. While Rawls (1993:51) does not entertain such a notion,[4] he does imply that normal human agents are not solely preoccupied with benefits to themselves. Normatively thick is the assumption that "rational agents approach being psychopathic when their interests are solely in benefits to themselves." A self-regarding or even selfish logic is no more or less "rational" than an other-regarding or even altruistic logic. The normatively thin alternative is *not* to invest rationality with this or that normative valence. And it rejects Rawls's normatively loaded concept of "public reason," a concept normatively loaded because it seems to presuppose its own correctness in matters of justice, as in the unsustainable assumption that public reason and the Supreme Court "more or less overlap" (Rawls 1993:231) as they do the work of justice. The evangelical pro-lifer likely will reject any "public reason" that claims both to be normative and to have found for the pro-choice side. Correspondingly, the secular pro-choicer will reject any "public reason" that claims both to be normative and to have found for the pro-life side. This impasse follows from a normatively thick conception of reason. By contrast, a normatively thin conception allows that reason, including public reason, may well lead to conclusions that one rejects from one's moral standpoint. Hence the grounds for accepting unwanted outcomes of rational deliberation or rational processes has to be a willingness to accept (as an obligation of citizenship, that is, of membership in the legal community) the possibility that rational deliberation in the public sphere will not confirm, but sometimes may well disconfirm, one's moral commitments. And one must be prepared to place (in the public sphere, on matters of public policy) one's faith in rational deliberation above one's own moral commitments, when those commitments are not sustained by rational deliberation or rational process in the public sphere. If one finds oneself on the "losing" side in such a process, one seeks to "win" the next round of deliberation, or to prevail in other rational—but not moral—terms. Here one persuades fellow citizens of the merits of one's arguments not by converting them to one's own thick worldview, but by providing reasons that are both persuasive on rational grounds and at least not violative of the addressee's thick worldview. After all, an evangelical Christian is not *as such* pro-life, any more than a secularist is *necessarily* pro-choice. The Christian might affirm his or her faith with the following argument: even where abortion is an inexpensive and safe option, a woman's community that took responsibility for the physical and emotional welfare of mothers and their children (by making adequate medical care unproblematically available, for example, and by not discriminating culturally or otherwise against single mothers) would provide that woman a powerful alternative to abortion.[5] So phrased, the Christian's argument, if persuasive at all, is equally persuasive to Christian and non-Christian alike. By the same token, the argument that abortion is murder can be made from a secularist viewpoint, for example in the claim that the unborn fetus is a legal person and as such enjoys equal protection of the laws. If addressed to persons of religious faith, the secular argument so phrased would not require the addressees to abandon or otherwise compromise their religious beliefs.

Groups that refuse these means of contestation are, by my lights, "dogmatic." Dogmatic is a normative thickness closed to all normative thinness. Without self-contradiction or violation of its own principles, the normatively thin constitutional order must be intolerant of intolerant, normatively thick groups. Dogmatism's normative exclusiveness is its accommodation only for converts, or its coercion of others to assimilate to its normative thickness. Against such thickness I would note that individual rights flowing from membership in the normatively thin constitutional order allow the individual a right of exit from any normatively thick group, including dogmatic ones.

Fourth, I reject Rawls's (1993:71) notion of the fundamentally moral identity of citizens. He regards public norms as "inhibiting self- or group-centered tendencies," that educate citizens to the "ideal of citizenship" and elicit in them "an effective desire to be that kind of person." Normatively thick are these sorts of efforts to change or form the individual's normative self-understanding. Certain self- or group-centered tendencies need to be inhibited in democratic societies, but this can be done in normatively thin ways, in ways that do not seek to change the citizen's normative self-understanding or his or her moral self-regard. Evangelical pro-lifers and secular pro-choicers alike can regard basic political rules (for example: popular majority rule, or the authoritative interpretations of controlling documents) as legitimate despite their personal moral disdain for some of their outcomes. Here there is no talk of transforming people's hearts and minds; the thick normative alternative to Rawls's theory allows evangelicals to be evangelicals and secularists to be secularists. For both, adjudicating rules needs to be politically legitimate, not necessarily morally acceptable. Politics in a normatively thin mode does not do away with moral disagreement; it brackets it (in the public sphere) and works around it as much as possible. At the same time, because diversity can be consistent with a normatively thin constitutional order, normatively thick groups can thrive within the thin constitutional order, because the rights of thick groups derive from that order and from nowhere else.

Part 1 of this book consists of four chapters, in the course of which I develop my basic theory of normatively thin ways of coping with normative diversity in complex modern societies.

Chapter 1 argues that normative thinness best allows different and competing thicknesses to flourish side by side: (1) Thin norms tolerate difference: agreement on points of public policy despite differences in the participants' specific ways of life, or particular religious faiths, ethnic identities, or socioeconomic statuses. They are neutral toward most of the competing worldviews and ways of life in liberal democratic polities, although not toward positions intolerant of liberalism's tolerance. (2) Despite their heterogeneity, modern societies display common cultural practices, on which either a thick or a thin normativity might draw. Among the characteristics of a thin core, several are at odds with thick normativity: a thin core is not consensual; it emphasizes individual rights; it embraces diversity; it is relatively "neutral" in a political sense; and it is tolerant of social differences. (3) Sociality through thinner forms of normativity does not conflict with the need for rules to regulate society but with the notion that such rules need be moral in kind. Social and political understanding, even agreement, can be normatively thin in various ways: groups and individuals can be integrated socially in part through a variety of nonmoral media of exchange, and in part through language where description can be morally neutral or normatively uncommitted; and some legal structures can motivate without appealing to morality. (4) One could know if this or that thick norm were needed in a given context and could not be replaced by a thin norm, only with reference to the logic of the institution, legal order, or public policy in question. One could then identify abiding social needs for thicker levels of morality without invoking some a priori standard.

Chapter 2 claims that recognition and tolerance of difference within a community, or among communities, poses problems for overarching normative agreement. Toward securing greater popular agreement on critical communal issues, it proposes social integration through "normative thinness." (1) I show that normativity has gradually withdrawn from many areas of social life, leaving a normativity both "thin" and "local." (2) I argue that normative thinness is possible both where the kind of contexts needed to adjudicate disputes need not be particularly moral, and where successful social integration need not be based on solidarity or sincerity or overarching values. (3) I identify several features of thinly normative integration: validity that is local and context-dependent; merit-based norms rather than convention; and community in terms of strangers whose otherness is not absorbed by the relationship. And (4) I draw on Erving Goffman's work to argue for social integration as "agonistic pluralism," a kind of interactional modus vivendi, which, while not unproblematic, offers welcome possibilities for social integration in heterogeneous societies. It can lead beyond social coordination to social cooperation because it does not preclude a social order stabilized through a widely shared notion of justice.

Chapter 3 analyzes, in modern liberal societies, two kinds of community: the ideal of the "generalized community" of the constitutional state, and various "concrete communities," each committed to a particular way of life or worldview. The notion of generalized community is one of normative neutrality. Where most political theories treat neutrality individualistically, I transpose the problem to a higher level: to the relation of a general community to its component subcommunities. In this way I develop a notion of communitarianism among communities, in distinction to a notion of simply *the* communitarian community.

Here the issue of normative neutrality returns with some force. Building on similarities between George Herbert Mead's analysis of the individual's socialization into the group and the relationship among communities in a democratic constitutional order, I explore a politically communitarian relationship among various concrete communities in modern liberal states. This theory of the similarities between mental structure in individuals and social structure in communities proceeds in four steps: (1) *a basic model of social integration in heterogeneous societies:* in dealing with each other, concrete communities assume the attitude of generalized community's normatively thin social framework, on which most normatively thick communities can agree; (2) *the major prerequisite for integration:* separating thick from thin normativity, which allows concrete communities to interrelate on the basis of thin normativity, without having to forsake the thick normativity constitutive of their respective identities; (3) *integration through the thin normativity of legal rights,* where generalized community establishes equality among concrete communities in one of two ways: through the "politics of recognition" (formal equality) or the "politics of difference" (recognizing the unique identity of the concrete community, its distinctness from all other concrete communities); and (4) *the limits of integration:* dogmatic communities that practice exclusiveness to the point of an intolerance incompatible with generalized community.

Chapter 4 develops, more fully than the preceding chapters, a theory of the person as entailed by my overall theory of thick and thin normativity. It approaches the individual as a political agent in terms of three mutually constitutive dimensions, as three interlocking "systems": the social system, the personality system of the individual, and the cultural system instantiated in the individual's behavior. These systems correspond, respectively, to *society,* which integrates the individual into the patterns of its institutions, including the legal, administrative, and economic spheres; to *culture*, which integrates the individual into the cognitive patterns of the various groups to which he or she belongs; and to *personality*, which integrates the individual as an individual, as a unit in itself. Culture, society, and personality are held together through their carriers' normative behavior. They are constitutive of that behavior. Normative action is one kind of purposive activity, whose purposes are regulated by values. It can be normatively thick, but it can also be thin. I argue that in a normatively heterogeneous populace, normatively thin forms of culture, society, and personality better serve social integration than do thick forms. This claim resonates with the notion that social integration in modern, heterogeneous societies has a certain "negative" character. Incisive analysts (including Ferdinand Tönnies, Emile Durkheim, and Georg Simmel) concerned with the historical transition to modernity in the West examine modern societies as moral orders from which moral consensus is absent—and in this sense, as "negative" orders. What such authors diagnose as "negativity" in social integration in modern societies I develop as thin normativity, specifically as thin forms of social solidarity, at the level of society; thin forms of shared cultural understandings, at the level of culture; and thin forms of individual identity, at the level of personality.

Part 2 comprises three chapters, each of which applies the theory developed in part 1 to specific areas of contemporary social life.

Chapter 5 argues that, to apply a norm whose meaning and application are indeterminate, one must draw on knowledge or competence or interpretations not contained in the norm itself. Norm-guided behavior generates aspects of social order, but in the case of indeterminate norms we cannot explain the generation of order in normatively thick terms but only in thin ones. Taking my cue from the way (according to Harold Garfinkel's ethnomethodology) humans work with indeterminate rules in everyday situations, I argue that such norms, in the form of laws, can be made determinate in normatively thin ways (1) where we can focus on the "competent" use of laws rather than on their "correct" or "incorrect" application (to distinguish between "correct" and "incorrect" is to presuppose a standard that holds across cases of correct rule-application, but where application is ad hoc because indeterminate, each case of application must have its own, unique standard of correctness); (2) where the relevant question is not whether the action in question is legal or illegal, but whether the problem and solution are known or unknown (after all, when problem and solution are indeterminate, rule-application itself can be a means to define both); (3) where we can employ rule-autonomous procedures rather than rule-needy procedures (where "correct" procedure does not require clarification by rules); (4) where we can exercise creative noncompliance rather than narrow compliance (where not to invoke the law is a more useful way to approach a particular legal issue); (5) where our concern must be with practical methods because abstract principles provide no guidance (where we are guided by the methods or ways in which indeterminate rules are actually applied or have been applied in the past); and (6) where we can apply situations to rules, rather than rules to situations (where laws are themselves resources to determine how a context should be approached). In short, where rule users do not passively follow rules and roles but actively manipulate them, even instrumentalize them, toward achieving their goals, they can draw on thinly normative ways to render those rules and roles meaningful and applicable. A normatively thin approach offers more scope, because more flexibility, than normative thickness for constructing agreement in the face of contested interpretations of the meaning and proper application of otherwise indeterminate laws.

Each system of cultural values displays a peculiar set of thick norms defining its identity and guiding the individual's behavior in ways appropriate to that system. Chapter 6 studies the efforts of one system—the "scientific" study of religion—to understand another—religious faith—in the work of Karl Marx, Emile Durkheim, Max Weber, and Talcott Parsons, generating proposals for a nonreductive relationship between competing value systems. The relationship can avoid reductionism (1) by allowing for more than one "world" or sphere of valid values (thus sociological claims and counterclaims about religion can be evaluated only if the sociologist assumes the reality of religion beyond all discourse about religion, as the external or independent referent of discourse); (2) by allowing an abiding autonomy to some spheres or forms of nonrationality; (3) by not collapsing evaluative questions into factual ones, that is, by allowing at least some socially legitimate values to be autonomous of truth. And (4) a thin relationship is possible where one value system shares both distance and proximity with another value system, a kind of solidarity beyond cultural differences. These four proposals attempt to confront the epistemological difficulties of understanding another person as he or she understands himself or herself, by seeking a thin understanding between competing value systems, where understanding is not corrigible to the observer. Moreover, (5) any given system should evaluate the validity of the claims of any other system in nonimmanent (or external or detached) terms, rendering the observed system corrigible by the lights of the observer. Thick cultural values would seek justification in ways thin not thick, but only in those thin ways that did not thereby misconstrue those thick cultural values.

Chapter 7 works out a notion of normatively thin ideology critique, as the critique of claims asserting universal validity for the interests and experiences of only one social sector or group: Thin critique can avoid being itself a form of ideology by avoiding a "hegemonic" approach. A hegemonic approach absolutizes the particular social situation of some persons or some groups and thereby denies or ignores differently situated persons in that group or in other groups. Here I explore a range of examples concerning women in contemporary American society. Thin critique engages ideology at the macro level of structure (where it identifies ideology-spawning social structure in social expectations internalized by the individual in the course of socialization, as well as in the patriarchal family), and at the more micro level of agency, as deep repression, internalized by individuals and rendering them agents of their own domination, yet who are unable to grasp their dominated status and their roles in perpetuating it. In this context thin critique has two socially generalizable goals: equality, both as "women equal to men" and as "equal freedom of individual choice"; and autonomy, both as the private autonomy of individuals who, as the addressees of the relevant social arrangements, receive equal treatment, and as the public autonomy of citizens who, as the makers of these arrangements, must themselves decide how best to structure them toward the goal of individual autonomy. When treating equals equally in all relevant respects, only the participants themselves can determine which respects are relevant.

Finally, in a brief coda, I argue that the normative diversity and fragmentation this book responds to is not a phenomenon of moral decline but of an increasingly porous social structure. And I argue that my theory of thin normativity, as a response to normative diversity and fragmentation, furthers normative engagement on the part of citizens in the public sphere, not moral abstinence or disengagement, let alone decline.

PART I

Thick

Moralities,

Thin Politics

in Social

Integration

THICK AND THIN

1

As complex modern societies become increasingly heterogeneous in terms of the worldviews and lifestyles of their inhabitants, agreement among citizens on many issues with normative dimensions becomes correspondingly difficult. These issues include welfare and housing for the poor; the financing and provision of medical care to the middle classes as well as to the poor; the legal status and social treatment of groups often marginalized because of race, sex, alienage, disability, or sexual orientation; problems of equal access to meaningful participation in the political process; the free exercise of religion (especially minoritarian or nonmainstream faiths); policies to counter the scourges of drug abuse, homelessness, and violent crime; "social engineering" by public policy and judicial opinion to deal with ethnic, racial, religious, or other divisions within pluralistic societies; and immigration and the legal status of immigrants in the host society. Even as agreement becomes more difficult, some significant level of agreement among the citizenry in areas of public policy and other forms of politics remains a major goal for any democratic polity. And normative agreement in particular remains a foremost goal: agreement on norms that might best guide decisions in political and social life and that could guide the resolution of conflicts on issues of public policy.

This book focuses on the politics of social norms. I understand "norms" as rules of right conduct and right living, where "rightness" derives from a comprehensive worldview rather than, for example, considerations mainly legal, procedural, technical, or strategic. Such considerations are narrower than comprehensive worldviews; they are also less constitutive of personality structure and individual identity. Thus the legal rule "Congress shall make no law respecting an establishment of religion, or prohibiting the free exercise thereof"[1] can be neutral over against the specific norms of any given religion. The individual's identity is less likely to be constructed around an abstract rule of governmental neutrality toward religions than around his or her religious convictions. In everyday usage "norm" sometimes means "rule" and sometimes "standard"; in both senses norms may be morally, politically, or ethically indifferent. I shall use "norm" to mean rules eliciting behavior that is morally committed or politically, theologically, or ideologically committed as well, often self-consciously so, within an overarching perspective on right and wrong behavior.

As much as norms are necessary to the functioning of society, they are inevitably problematic in multiple ways. Often they are imprecise: for example, can "equality before the law" ever mean one group's public accommodation that is "separate but equal" to the public accommodation of other groups? Often they are ambiguous: do "family values" preclude any form of sexuality other than married heterosexual relations? They are always open to slippage: Thomas Jefferson's "self-evident truth" that "all men are created equal" slipped, over two hundred years, from referring only to landed white Protestant men to many other kinds of men as well as women and children; the norm of "equality" didn't change—only its referent did. And even if the meaning of a particular norm could be pinned down to the satisfaction of all affected persons, it may still serve as the basis for disagreement rather than as a practical guide to resolving this or that issue. Many debates about norms appear to be intractable because they revolve around the relative merits or appropriateness of a given norm ("Should physicians seek to preserve life at all costs, regardless of circumstances?") and the concerned parties cannot agree on a particular norm's merit or appropriateness. Debates about norms easily arise over the best way to realize a norm without questioning whether the norm itself is valuable, justified, or desirable ("Is racial equality advanced through affirmative action in higher education, or does affirmative action perpetuate another form of racial inequality?"). Many important social norms are problematic because a community or society cannot agree about which are appropriate or desirable or just; cannot agree on what they mean; cannot agree on how they should be applied.

In the last quarter-century a great deal of scholarship has wrestled with advancing a deep or rich common understanding of social and political obligation under circumstances that discourage agreement on norms, or agreement that might be reached on the basis of shared norms. Such efforts cannot succeed, I suggest, because they seek or presuppose a moral community no longer feasible over the whole extent of complex modern societies. This book provides a distinct alternative and with it one way out of a significant impasse in contemporary social and political theory. It argues that public policy may be the more feasible, and the more effective, the more it is crafted as "thin" or detached rather than "thick" or invested normativity.

I shall use the terms "thick" and "thin" relatively, with different lines of division in relation to different topics, but always to contrast *more* comprehensive demands for normative commitment with ones *less* comprehensive.[2] But there can be no definite threshold dividing "thickness" from "thinness." The threshold can only be somewhat indeterminate, given that the terms "thick" and "thin" can only be relative. In a particular case the degree of determinacy increases by means of specific interpretations in light of concrete circumstances and specific contingencies. But these interpretations may not always possess validity beyond the particular case. Members of any given group, a particular community, or a whole society may well differ about where thin stops and thick begins, yet still agree on a scheme of terms that lends itself to different applications with different interpretations.

Social Integration Challenged by Social Differences

I distinguish between thick and thin norms as a way of getting at some of the problems generated by differences among the members of a community, or among communities within a society. Some of these differences, I shall show, challenge integration within the community or across communities. My concern is with social integration in modern, politically liberal societies, and here integration depends (I shall show) on not eliding many of the differences within the populace. Some of the most important of these differences are enduringly normative. For example, the shift of Christianity in the West from a state religion to the somewhat "privatized" institution officially "outside" the secular state did not mark the wholesale triumph of secularism over faith but the transformation of religiosity from one form—one religion identified with the state and articulating a unified national vision—to another: the legal protection of freedom from any imposed religious belief and practice, and of the right to religious belief and practice, with no particular religion privileged or deprivileged politically or legally, at least officially. Both ways of dealing institutionally with faith facilitate forms of social integration, but differently so. What are the differences between a religiously legitimized state and a secular, legally legitimized one? General, society-wide trust based on shared religious faith is thickly normative, unlike the thinly normative general trust based on legally grounded and legally enforced norms of justice understood in terms of equality, fairness, and impartiality. Law and religion both facilitate social integration in that both provide reasons to trust in abstract institutions (such as church or state) that make claims on people's beliefs and behavior. Both offer those institutions an important source of legitimacy. Both regulate certain kinds of disputes and adjudicate certain kinds of controversies; both define legitimate reciprocal expectations, including support for the social order. Both provide sanctions for noncompliance. But each does so in ways very different from the other. Above all, religion links legitimacy to thick norms, ethical ideals, and cultural values, whereas much of modern law links legitimacy to the normatively thin nature of procedure, to procedural regularity, and to formal continuity (such as the interpretive principles of precedent and *stare decisis*). The practical upshot: private autonomy is better protected by law, as is a plurality of ways of life, whereas a homogenizing normative vision is better realized by religion, as is an integration of private life and public creed. (I devote a chapter each to homogeneity and religion: chapter 5 develops a notion of ideology as a homogenizing vision, and chapter 7 suggests ways of understanding, as an outsider, systems of religious values.)

This book argues for a kind of social integration that can accommodate normative difference by distinguishing between "thick" and "thin" kinds of norms and by pursuing integration through thin norms as much as possible. It explores how, on issues of politics, public policy, law, social critique, and even religion, modern societies might better cope with moral heterogeneity by making as few appeals to morality as possible—and by making remaining appeals to thin morality rather than thick. To make as few appeals to morality as possible means to frame issues in nonmoral terms wherever possible. To make remaining appeals to thin rather than thick norms means that, wherever issues cannot be reformulated in nonmoral terms, they should be formulated in terms of a thin morality, a morality that can be generalized to almost all of society without violating the integrity of concrete ways of life or political commitments or worldviews (in the way that a law that does not violate the federal Constitution might be considered thin). It means not to frame a moral issue in terms of thick norms, norms that, if generalized to all of society, would damage the integrity of other ways of life and worldviews. Thus a norm that specifies freedom of religious belief and religious practice, as well as freedom from religion, is thin in that it favors neither religion nor nonreligious belief systems. Any specific religion, like atheism, is thick: to generalize one is to violate the integrity of others. By "morality" I mean a certain kind of normativity, as should become clear in the following discussion; my larger concern in this book is with a variety of normativities, with the moral kind receiving heightened scrutiny.

Social Integration through Thin Norms

Social integration is impossible in the absence of all normative input whatsoever, as is agreement in the public sphere. Modern, heterogeneous societies can better pursue as much integration as is practical by distinguishing between thicker and thinner levels of normativity, and exploring possible political and social advantages of thinner levels. We find thicker forms of normativity where individuals more or less passively internalize the norms of their environment, so that their normative orientation corresponds with the orientation of the institutions they inhabit. (Think of an observant Catholic whose opposition to abortion is based solely on the authority of the pope.) But we also find thick forms of morality that are mediated by self-reflection, as in sincerely held and well-understood political or religious doctrines. (Think of an observant Catholic's opposition to abortion on the basis of her thoughtful, reasoned, nondogmatic religious convictions.) Thickness can be a product of unquestioning and unreflective adherence just as much as it can be a product of fervent, thoughtful attachment. In many cases (in the most important and interesting ones), "thickness" is no synonym for self-blinding fundamentalism. Thinner levels of morality follow from citizens sidelining to some extent some of the norms they nonetheless thickly possess; here groups and individuals assume a calculating approach to the more moral aspects of social life. "Distancing" and "calculating" include choosing from several norms which to obey, as well as modifying norms as needed for possibly nonnormative ends. (Think of the observant Catholic whose opposition to abortion is conditioned on the contingencies of any given pregnancy: whether the pregnancy was a product of rape or incest, whether the pregnant woman lives in circumstances of violence or poverty, and so forth.) This book argues for the possibility of political agreement within a heterogeneous population by constructing forms of social stability, integration, and solidarity that do not require thicker levels of normative commitment or moral consensus. It argues for the possibility of social integration within a heterogeneous community and across communities different from each other, by developing thin forms of social solidarity, thin forms of shared cultural understandings, and thin forms of individual identity. It argues for the possibility of agreement on the basis of thin norms.

Again, as a means to social integration in normatively heterogeneous societies, this book marks out ways of *reducing* overall levels of normativity in the public sphere. It seeks to work the following hunch into an insight. In cosmopolitan societies such as those in North America or Western Europe, public policy may be the more possible, and the more effective, the more it is crafted as "nonnormative," or of "lower" rather than "higher" normativity. Why? Because society-wide agreement about citizens' highest ends, and the appropriate goals for the collective weal, is increasingly unlikely. Modern societies have become far too complex for their unity to be guaranteed by ethical or otherwise normative beliefs. They should avoid or minimize moralizing or otherwise "normativizing" issues of politics, public policy, and law. Human flourishing in cosmopolitan societies urges lower rather than higher levels of normativity. But this claim in no way entails that normative thickness is necessarily pejorative or problematic. The argument rather is that a political regime and a social milieu characterized by normative thinness is the best way to allow different and competing thickness to flourish side by side, in the interests of each.

Tolerance of Difference through Thin Norms

Citizens' normative viewpoints can be highly relevant to their political and social behavior. Consider agreement among citizens on public matters. To agree thickly means to agree on very particular ways of life, or specific worldviews, or distinct identities. To agree, say, on a liberal democratic way of life is to exclude a restrictive, authoritarian one. To agree that almost all women should be homemakers and caretakers of children is to exclude a view of women as careerists or political activists. To agree that race is a socially constructed category is to exclude race as a biologically determined trait (with profound consequences for how groups of different skin pigmentations view one another). In each of these examples, thick agreement privileges one kind of commitment (democracy, a woman's "proper" place in society, "raceless" identity) over alternative commitments (authoritarianism, feminism, racialism).

To agree thinly means agreement on points of public policy *despite* differences in the participants' specific ways of life, or particular religious faiths, ethnic identities, or socioeconomic statuses. To agree thinly does not mean the complete absence of all thick agreement whatsoever. Any thin agreement necessarily presupposes at least some basis in thick agreement. For example, a commitment to proceduralism is itself thick. But this particular thick commitment then facilitates thinness, in the sense that proceduralism does not predetermine specific outcomes beyond satisfying the dictates of proceduralism. Thus only persons legally authorized to vote may participate in elections, a procedural requirement that does not itself decide the election's winners and losers. Another example: a political order committed to certain thick values—to its citizens' security, physical safety, personal freedom, health, economic prosperity, family stability, equality of opportunity, and common law equity—can still be thin in the sense of not imposing on its citizens this or that political conviction, economic philosophy, aesthetic preference, moral value system, or comprehensive worldview. To agree thinly is not to privilege one way of life, or worldview, or identity, over others—other than, of course, the approach I shall develop as thin normativity, an approach to tolerating competing approaches.

This strategy is neutral toward most of the competing worldviews and ways of life in liberal democratic polities—*most* but not all. It is neither neutral nor indifferent toward criminal or belligerent behavior, nor toward persons or communities that would harm their members (harm as defined from a normatively thin standpoint), nor toward persons, groups, or belief systems intolerant of the liberal tolerance entailed by thin normativity. In a society that practiced thin normativity, none but those intolerant of that society's constituent communities would regard normatively thin public policy as violative of its integrity. Yet normative thinness allows each concrete community (other than those intolerant of normative thinness) an identity of such integrity that it would be violated if some other concrete community were to impose its own identity on it. And a normatively thin political order precludes such impositions. Normative thinness is a form of liberal tolerance of difference, of difference within a normatively heterogeneous political and social order.

For example, a normatively thick approach to governmental regulation might allow regulation on the basis of this or that thick worldview (say, a politically conservative or liberal one) or perhaps no regulation at all (as in a libertarian view). The conservative view might disallow any program of affirmative action, whether in admissions to public colleges and professional schools, or in the granting of governmental contracts, or in the state's distribution of a limited number of broadcasting licenses. The liberal position might embrace affirmative action to the extent such a strategy responsibly attempted to compensate for past systematic discrimination. A libertarian view might reject affirmative action as illegitimate governmental engineering. Then again, it might readily allow it, at least for private institutions, on the claim that private enterprises should be free to pursue their interests with as little governmental intervention as possible—even in the context of the heavily regulated modern welfare state.

How does my approach differ? A normatively thin approach to governmental regulation would not privilege one thick view over another. Thicker forms of normativity often imply lower levels of tolerance for difference. For example, a completely conservative and a completely libertarian viewpoint are both morally thick, and for that reason each might rule out the other. Thinner levels of normativity require some tolerance, because to limit any viewpoint is to compromise it, in the sense of an outsider denying some of its claims, or of an insider renouncing some of its claims. To deny or renounce some of the claims of any one viewpoint ideally encourages openness to some of the claims of other, competing viewpoints. To choose a thicker morality might be to choose either very strong governmental regulation (if that morality were conservative, advocating no affirmative action, but also if that morality were liberal, advocating a robust program of affirmative action) or none at all (if it were libertarian). To choose a thinner morality would allow for a mix of moralities, which, taken in the aggregate, might be to choose weak regulation. In the case of affirmative action, this approach suggests neither no affirmative action whatsoever nor an unmediated form of affirmative action but rather a program mediated by factors in addition to race. This would broaden the exclusively racial focus of the program to include factors flowing from legacies of nonracial forms of systematic discrimination. Here one thinks of religious persecution, economic deprivation, marginalized status as an immigrant, or marginalization because of one's handicap or sexual orientation.

We might approach this question from a different perspective. Some debate over affirmative action concerns how best to attain shared principles of legal equality, democracy and the rule of law, not whether equality, democracy or the rule of law are desirable. For these participants—including some who oppose affirmative action—the debate is not over the merits of equal opportunity but over how best to pursue it. A normatively thin approach would seek out that option of pursuing equal opportunity that imposed or entailed the smallest degree of thick normativity. For example, a procedural approach that configured equality not in terms of making culturally, racially, or ethnically different kinds of people somehow more similar, and in that sense more equal, but rather one that would seek equality while allowing the participants to maintain those aspects of their unique identities that should be irrelevant to legal and political equality. A different version of the same debate revolves around the question of whether affirmative action, predicated as it is on the basis of a person's ascribed characteristics, such as his or her race, subordinates one thick value—the rule of law—to another (such as the value placed on a society more just because some groups heretofore marginalized have attained or might attain, via affirmative action, greater equality in social life vis-à-vis society's more privileged groups). Someone who holds this view will construe the debate over affirmative action as one over the very desirability of the rule-of-law norm. Here a normatively thin approach will favor a thick norm that issues in thin normativity—the rule of law, and equality before the law—over a thick norm that issues in thick normativity, say, privileging one way of life or one social group or one religious commitment over another. And it will disfavor any thick norm that violates the integrity of a thick norm that issues in thin normativity (such as the rule of law, or the equal treatment of legally equal persons).

A different example again shows how a normatively thin approach to political judgment would not privilege one thick view over another. One debate over multiculturalism in the United States today is not whether topics about formerly marginalized or underrepresented groups should be included in the curriculum of public schools. The debate is over how to include them and with what consequences for topics about groups already included. The real debate is not between racists or xenophobes and enlightened cosmopolitans but rather between two or more sides of well-intentioned, thoughtful citizens each with plausible arguments. Imagine a school board—and beyond the board, an entire school district and its families—confronted with the decision of how best to present, in a required textbook for a mandatory course in American history or social studies, the role of different peoples in the course of American history. Hard choices have to be made with regard to a text that can only have so many pages to be studied by pupils in one or two semesters. Women, black Americans, Native Americans, and non-European immigrants will find a presence in the ultimate choice. But what kind of presence? As the publishers of this and all books know, space is sorely limited, as is classroom time and time for study outside the classroom. One option would be to privilege, with respect to number of pages, the role of the elites: for example, the ways in which James Madison and Thomas Jefferson learned from, and expanded upon, the cultural heritage of Europe in fashioning an American republic much more progressive than its former English colonial master. Another option would be to recount, in many pages, the—for many contemporary Americans—potentially inspiring untold stories of the various nonelites, including the various subaltern groups subjected to centuries of legal discrimination and political exclusion. Should the school board choose the text that gives more space to John Locke's influence on Madison or the one that gives more pages to the role of the slave-based economy in the development of American capitalism? Should the school district prefer a book that gives more space and thereby informs young Americans—including today increasing numbers of young citizens of non-European heritage—about the roles of indigenous peoples and African slaves, or one that shows that a political system ultimately capable of responding to slavery, discrimination, and cultural genocide feeds off a European cultural tradition that, in the twenty-first century, may still outpace African and Asian and Middle Eastern cultures in terms of encouraging democratic practices, cosmopolitan tolerance, and Enlightenment rationalism? Would the school district think its young clientele intellectually and morally more inspired (and, in a political sense, more "profitably" inspired) by an extended account of slavery in the South or by the nascent development of political liberalism in the former colonies? Pages are scarce; shall we spend more on George Washington, perhaps an unusually well-qualified occupant of the first presidency of the United States, or on women, who, as the primary socializers of young human beings, powerfully shape the intellectual and moral capacity of youth to become citizens of a democracy? Shall we spend more time on the fact that the Founders deeply influenced the shape of twenty-first-century America or on the fact that many were slaveholders?

Which text the school board selects is of considerable political importance to a polity (and culture and way of life) that reproduces itself with respect to certain shared values and beliefs. Why does it matter which text the school board selects? The standard for making such decisions will impact directly the moral nature of the polity's citizens. This book argues that the politically best standard for such decisions is one of thin, not thick, normativity. But what is the standard for making such decisions? A thin approach might concede uncommitted respect for (and sometimes the partial merit of) one or more competing approaches, and in that sense may be open to compromise among approaches. A mix—for example, of a multicultural-friendly and a multicultural-skeptical approach—would certainly compromise both approaches but need not preclude the integrity of either. Both political conservatives and liberals might agree that, in the composition of required textbooks for elementary and secondary students in public schools, some significant attention to formerly historically marginalized groups is desirable. In a mix, both viewpoints might be present, but only thinly, for example where textual presentation acceptable to political liberals allows conservative viewpoints as legitimate and authentic expression of some interested or affected persons yet treats them as viewpoints not binding on all participants but only on those who freely embrace them.

So the presence that black Americans, Native Americans, and immigrants from non-European countries find in the ideal textbook will be "contrapuntal," as will the presence of Locke, Madison, and elites generally: both will be present, in tension with each other, sometimes even as counterarguments to each other. Thematic counterpoint is possible in two forms. In some cases equal space will be given to starkly contrasting aspects of related topics—say, the roles of indigenous peoples and African slaves, on the one hand, and a political system ultimately capable of outlawing slavery, on the other. And in some cases one topic—say, the ways in which the Constitution profoundly influences the shape of contemporary American society—will receive more space than others, such as the fact that many of the authors and ratifiers of the Constitution were slaveholders. In this second sort of thematic counterpoint, balanced arguments might be advanced in the text for devoting more space to one aspect of a topic than to another. In the present example the student might consider (but not therefore simply embrace) an argument that the significant fact that some of the Constitution's authors were slaveholders ultimately did not vitiate the document's capacity to outlaw racial and other forms of systematic and institutionalized discrimination. On this argument, given the scarcity of textbook pages, proportionally more pages would be devoted to the successes and failings of the Constitution than to the moral and political successes and failures of its authors. Students should be invited not only to read the text but to debate the merits of the arguments advanced there in defense of the tough choices made in organizing the text. Such exercises would display two features conducive to thin normativity: self-reflexivity (the text would encourage its readers to regard the text as one possible approach among other plausible approaches, with specific benefits and disbenefits when measured against competing approaches, about which the text would encourage the students to speculate) and fallibilism: the text would not present itself as gospel truth but as an exercise in critical pedagogy and historiography, as theses to be defended discursively with good arguments and likely to be revised in subsequent editions of the textbook, in light of new information, or new forms of social awareness, or new theses that could be defended rationally as superior to those in the current edition.

Not all relevant persons (parents, students, and teachers, but also citizens concerned about public education) will agree on any one format or any one edition of such a textbook. But all relevant persons should be able to agree in part, and where they disagree, they will be able to disagree in ways that do not violate in wholesale fashion their normatively thick convictions (because the book will not rule out in wholesale fashion any one normatively thick perspective). And where the relevant persons agree, they will agree in normatively thin terms: on a text that is nondogmatic, self-reflexive, and fallibilistic about its choices—a text that engages youthful readers (and their parents) of different moral positions while urging them to refrain from pressing their respective positions to the very end in the interests of open debate, considered tolerance, and a robust, student-participatory education.

The Normative Core of Society: Thick and Thin Alternatives

Despite their tremendous heterogeneity, complex modern societies are exposed to common cultural practices, and such sharedness constitutes a kind of continuum. The continuum itself suggests various possibilities for areas on which either a thick or thin normativity might draw, as thick and thin are (imprecisely delimited) areas on a continuum. A normatively thick core would differ of course from a normatively thin one, in ways I shall address, but the point is that both kinds of normativity can draw on some kind of common social core.

In what might such a vital center consist? In modern Western societies today it probably includes everything from a belief in democracy to a belief in the inherent dignity of the individual and his or her right to freedom and liberty (of some sort). It probably includes everything from the desirability of the best possible system of primary and secondary education to the importance of stable families. Politically, a common core entails that citizens who "do not affirm the same comprehensive doctrine" can still "affirm the same political conception of justice," sharing "one that has high priority," "supporting just institutions and . . . giving one another justice accordingly, not to mention many other ends they must also share and realize through their political arrangements" (Rawls 1993:202). Culturally, a common core means that commercial or mass culture is shared in part because it homogenizes a great deal of popular culture—that is, creates general patterns of preference and consumption within a population. Carried by mass marketing, television, and other homogenizing media, culture of this sort is often shared across racial, ethnic, religious, economic, and political divides. Indeed, "although ethnic and racial minorities demand economic goods that reflect their particular lifestyles and tastes, these preferences are expressed as variations on mass-produced and widely consumed popular commodities" (Smelser and Alexander 1999:9). For personal spheres, a common core entails, for example, that people who are "divorced still express support for marriage and typically remarry, . . . [that] homosexual men and women legitimate their choices by stressing their ability to sustain stable monogamous relationships . . . [and that] stepparents, separated parents, and other members of 'affinal' family networks assert in words and deeds that their primary concern remains their children's well-being" (ibid.).

Some aspects of a common core might be thicker and others thinner. Thick is the moral obligation of communal members to uphold society-wide institutions embodying nongeneralizable ways of life—that is, embodying shared ways of life peculiar to one community. Talcott Parsons (1964:99) claims that all social institutions are normative and, more often than not, thickly normative: "*All* institutionalization involves common moral as well as other values. Collectiv[e] obligations are . . . an aspect of every institutionalized role," and social roles sustain various structures for collective life. By performing their respective roles, physicians, accountants, and janitors (among many other personnel in a hospital) make medicine possible as an ongoing institution. For Hegel (1996) a person can behave normatively only in the context of such institutions as the family, the occupation, and the state. But Parsons and Hegel miss the extent to which complex modern societies, especially liberal democracies, do not rely on thick norms in all aspects of public life. In many cases they rely on the thin norms of procedural guarantees, and on the thin norms of individual rights—which are thin in the sense that they hold for all individuals, regardless of differences, and in the sense that they allow great diversity with respect to all individuals' worldview, way of life, religious conviction, and so forth. To be sure, a thick core is always found in various forms of social obligation. Some social institutions live through or are carried by the behavior of those humans who play the various roles appropriate to it. Professionals, as they behave in accordance with their occupation, are carriers of that institution. The physician's behavior in a hospital differs from the teacher's behavior in a school precisely in the ways that the institutionalized roles prescribed by hospitals differ from those prescribed by schools. Physicians as physicians are not autonomous from the thick norms of hospitals (such as healing rather than harming patients); scholars as scholars are not autonomous from the thick norms of universities (in research, such as acknowledging contrary findings). The individual is less than autonomous where he or she is embedded in a profession, where he or she is constrained to abide by general rules and procedures and understandings that define that profession. At the same time, however, obligations to sustain institutions and ways of life can also be normatively thin, but only as obligations that, if generalized, could be freely recognized as valid by diverse groups that reject one another's thick norms. Obligations of this kind would include the rule of law, proceduralism, and formal rights. The norms that found expression in public institutions could, because they were thin, still correspond more or less with the norms by which individuals choose to guide their communal behavior.

Beyond the fact that, in modern societies, a common core displays a mix of thick and thin norms, some authors—for example, David Hollinger (1995) and Michael Lind (1995)—claim that only a normatively thick core can sustain social integration. Others, including John Rawls (1993) and Jürgen Habermas (1995), assert—as shall I—that a normatively thin core is best suited to the demands of social integration in complex modern societies. A thick version of solidarity and social integration refers to shared, deeply held norms; a thin version asks for no such commitment. A thick core is less tolerant of social differences seeking legal and social recognition. It is more comfortable than a thin one with a public role for religion, and it regards the moral convictions of individual citizens as relevant to the debate over public policy. A thin core, by contrast, tends to "privatize" the individual's moral convictions and religious beliefs (and perhaps some of his or her cultural traditions as well). And it tends to "privatize" substantive values and to make procedural ones public. Proceduralism is normatively thin because its validity is tied not to the outcome of a procedure but to its formulation; if the procedure is correctly formulated, the outcome should be acceptable to the participants. By such means persons of different and competing worldviews can nonetheless agree on the thin principles of proceduralism and on its results. Proceduralism is normatively thin because it reduces an issue to the formal correctness of its formulation.[3] We can know if a procedure is "correctly" formulated by considerations of a more formal or technical nature, such as internal consistency.

Among the various characteristics of a normatively thin core, five are immediately at odds with major claims of thick normativity. First, a thin core is not entirely consensual or free of internal tensions or inconsistencies—which, *pace* thick core, is not problematic. Normatively thin social integration requires no society-wide consensus on a set of public and private norms. It requires no "soulcraft," molding hearts and minds in thick normative agreement. Neither thick norms nor thin ones are concerned solely with the self-realization of the individual, any more than they are concerned solely with the interests of a group or community or of an entire society. But thin normativity, unlike thick, does not regard the goal of individual self-realization as antithetical to communal responsibility.

Second, a thin core emphasizes individual rights—which, *pace* thick core, need not undermine social solidarity. Where a society is organized in thinly normative ways, there an emphasis on formal legal rights need not be antithetical to social responsibility, communal solidarity, or political legitimacy. Thin political rights can protect groups and associations as well as individuals. To recognize, in normatively thin fashion, some of the rights of individuals in no way precludes the simultaneous recognition of some of the rights of groups large and small. In each case recognition protects "all from one another in an appropriate balance specified by its guiding principles of justice" (Rawls 1993:221 n. 8).

Third, a thin core embraces diversity—which, *pace* thick core, need not threaten social integration. In a society organized along normatively thin lines, social diversity—and political and legal recognition for some kinds of diversity—need not threaten social integration and communal solidarity. Civil society is certainly possible in nontraditional forms—one can imagine virtual "town meetings" taking place over the Internet. Cultural life is possible amid diversity and difference in heterogeneous forms (which is just what the term "multiculturalism" means). And state-based identity is possible despite diversity and difference in unreconciled, plural forms—for example, in a Germany that allows for the everyday, institutionalized recognition of Islamic cultural and religious practices of its citizens or permanent residents of Turkish origin. Thin normativity threatens none of them.[4]

Fourth, in a political sense, a thin core is relatively "neutral"—which, *pace* thick core, need not compromise the freedom of citizens to pursue, in fair and legal ways, their thick political commitments. That is, normatively thin public policy allows for a great deal of freedom *from* thick normativity. Of course, if the thin implies a more limited conception of what politics embraces, it is still political. Thus the neutrality of thin normativity is only relative: it is normatively more neutral than thick, to be sure, but it is never completely neutral. Achieving pure neutrality in matters of politics, public policy, and law is impossible. Most social or political principles are committed to this or that normative substance (think of the principle of legal equality, or social justice, or economic fairness). Commitment occurs already at a linguistic level (which is why opponents of the legalization of abortion call themselves "pro-life" rather than "anti-choice" and advocates of legalized abortion call themselves "pro-choice" rather than "anti-life"). While a normatively thin language is by definition less biased than a thick one (thickness is a greater normative commitment, hence is more "biased," than thinness, a lesser normative commitment), thick and thin both employ vocabulary laden with at least some normative substance. Neither offers a normatively neutral language of radically distanced and neutral observation, or some other guide to completely unbiased behavior.[5] Still, a thin core has certain advantages over a thick core, where a liberal democratic polity would have reason to prefer the relative neutrality of thin normativity to the substantive normativities of comprehensive worldviews and concrete ways of life. For example, neutral in the sense of thin normativity is that conception of justice that "avoids taking sides in the contest of [some range of] competing forms of life and worldviews" (Habermas 1996:60). Or neutral in the sense of thin normativity is a formulation of the prerequisites for inclusion in various domains of public life: for example, compulsory primary and secondary education where "every *person* (whether . . . [wealthy or poor], Christian, Jewish or Muslim, infant or adult) has the same legal status" (Luhmann 1982:243).

Fifth, a thin core is quite tolerant of social differences—which, *pace* thick core, need not threaten social cohesion or successful social integration. Thin normativity is a minimalist vision: for example, social solidarity through procedural agreements, through the far-reaching recognition of differences, or through a robust respect for cultural and personal autonomy. To respond thinly to society's normative fragmentation is to require citizens to tolerate many normative differences among themselves. Given its tolerance for normative difference, thin normativity can tolerate normatively thick ways of life. Thin normativity supports an "inclusive view" in which a member of a community lives or practices or perpetuates his or her personal thickness yet does so in support of communal thinness—and thereby pursues a kind of "public reason."[6]

The relation of a community to its component subcommunities might be configured in a democratic constitutional state in this sense. Here a "generalized community"[7] would encompass all individuals and social groups while still allowing for each of the various "concrete communities" of the various social groups to follow its commitment to a particular way of life or worldview. The generalized community would be normatively neutral vis-à-vis each of the various concrete communities (neutral except for intolerant communities, as I show in later pages). Concrete communities need to assume the attitude of generalized community's normatively thin social framework, on which most normatively thick communities should be able to agree. The major prerequisite for integration is the separation of thick from thin normativity, which allows concrete communities to interrelate on the basis of thin normativity, without having to forsake the thick normativity constitutive of their respective identities. Generalized community establishes equality among concrete communities in one of two ways: through a "politics of recognition" (formal legal equality) or through a "politics of difference" (legally recognizing the unique identity of the concrete community, its distinctness from all other concrete communities).[8]

Nonmoral Rules in the Public Sphere

The notion of politically successful sociality through thinner forms of normativity does not conflict with the need for rules to regulate society but rather with the notion that such rules need be moral in kind. In a variety of ways, social and political understanding, even agreement, can be thinly rather than thickly normative. Reflect on three examples. First, groups and individuals can be integrated socially in part through a variety of nonmoral media of exchange, including the monetary media of the economy, as well as the medium of power that courses through the bureaucracies that administer so many aspects of life in modern societies. Both media can influence the decisions of participants strategically, thorough the end-means rationality of calculating amounts of value (thus homeowners and utility companies are "integrated" through monthly exchanges of the homeowner's money for a consumed supply of gas, water, and electricity; and where the price of the commodity is not subject to bargaining, integration is not subject to normative claims or considerations). These media replace linguistic communication (that is, processes of communication oriented toward reaching understanding) with a symbolic generalization of rewards and punishments (one can purchase a loaf of bread without taking a stand on the justness of capitalism, and one can meet a legal obligation to pay income tax without taking a position on the fact that the government spends a much larger proportion of tax dollars on military defense than on public education). After all, economic transactions are oriented to exchange, not to placing into question the justice of the overall economic organization in which the exchange is embedded. Similarly, bureaucracies seek the formulation of means to the realization and enforcement of pregiven goals rather than their critical review.

Second, groups and individuals can be integrated through language where description can be morally neutral or normatively uncommitted. Descriptive language of this kind provides an alternative to morality where, for example, the criteria of rationality need not conform to moral norms (an argument for national health care could be made in terms of overall economic efficiency: a workforce that receives adequate health care is more satisfied and more productive than one that doesn't). Another example: in the realm of politics in its narrower sense, specific criteria of rationality (for instance, rules for winning elections) need not conform with the generally liberal or generally conservative morals of a specific society or with the specifically bureaucratic ethos of consistent decision making.

Again, descriptive language is an alternative to morality where the unity of society need not be represented through moral claims. Thus a society organized around legal protections of civil rights may tolerate a diversity of mutually incompatible worldviews, whereas a society organized around the supposed moral superiority of one worldview may well discriminate against persons holding any other. (This example assumes a nonmoral foundation for civil rights: for example, equal rights justified by the notion that no rational person would choose to live in a society where he or she had fewer civil rights than other citizens.) In these and other ways, linguistic communication can be independent of moral factors. Then social breakdown would not be moral breakdown but a kind of technical failure that might be restored by the technical means of communication. (I say "might": language can easily be a means not only to agreement but equally to sharpen disagreement. No medium can guarantee outcomes; any tool can be used to defeat a goal as well as to achieve it.)

Third, some legal structures might also provide generalized or common motivation without appealing to morality. Sometimes nonmoral legal rules can compensate for divisions and disagreements about moral rules. A law providing freedom of expression may settle, on

nonmoral grounds, such potentially moral disputes as: Is pornogra-
phy legally protected expression? How about flag-burning? Monetary
contributions to a political campaign? Hate speech? In such cases, law
obligates in ways that morality cannot. And where morality is impo-
tent as a means to social integration and cooperation, law, standing in
reserve, offers practical and effective recourse. Even if the idea of limiting governmental power has its origins in moral thought, or even if,
historically, a religious conception of the person preceded the notion of
government protecting the individual's integrity, neither limited government nor individual rights require a moral foundation for their
practice or justification today. (One can oppose murder because one
feels bound by the Ten Commandments. But one can oppose murder
for many other reasons as well, including a secular belief in the worth
or dignity of the individual, or the utilitarian Hobbesian calculation
(Hobbes 1985) that one might protect oneself from murder by agree-
ing not to murder others.) The absence of morality—to the degree it
is absent—in the context of contemporary liberal democratic polities
need not threaten constitutional norms, or the principles of democracy, or legality itself.

Constitutional norms, or the principle of democracy, or legality itself, all have moral aspects. The notion of limiting government through
a constitution is normative; the idea of democracy makes a normative claim about the worth and dignity of the individual citizen; and
legality is characterized by what Lon Fuller (1977:42) calls the "inner
morality of law," including normative imperatives that we "make the
law known, make it coherent and clear, see that your decisions as an
official are guided by it, etc." Fuller is not advancing "higher law" in
the full traditional sense, for example, of natural law (which is normatively thick in its advocacy of substantive moral positions). Rather, he
describes metarules, or rules about rules: conditions that rules must
always meet as one source of their validity. Metarules are normatively
thin because they do not specify the moral content of the particular
rules they govern. Constitutional norms, or the principle of democracy, or legality itself may well draw upon the various moral aspects
they possess to motivate citizens' respect for and willingness to be
guided by the Constitution, democracy, or the law. But in doing so constitutionalism, democracy, or legality appeal to the thin normativity
of procedural metarules—and beyond, to (still thin) law-abidingness—
and not to the thick norms of a substantive worldview quite beyond all

proceduralism. The self-legislation of a community or society can satisfy Fuller's procedural imperatives without being, and without needing to be, moral self-legislation; constitutional rights need not imply or imitate moral rights (even as they follow Fuller's metarules); normatively thin principles of democracy (guided by Fuller's "inner morality of law") need not be normatively thick principles of morality. Legality need not be a limitation on thick morality but rather could supplement or sometimes even relieve it. It might accomplish some social tasks better than thick morality, such as achieving political equality among citizens or compensating through the welfare state for maldistributions of social wealth or adjudicating disputes among rival religious or ethnic groups.

Abiding Need for Thicker Norms Even in Normatively Thin Societies

A theory concerned with tensions between moral and nonmoral forms of social integration must remain sensitive to possible abiding social needs for thicker levels of morality. This claim does not presuppose a politics of the Right or the Left. In formal organizations of public administration and economy, for example, "compensation" for market failures or maldistribution of social wealth is ultimately a moral imperative rather than an economic or legal one. From the perspective of political liberalism, the welfare state must not impose any particular normative worldview on the recipients of welfare. From a politically conservative stance, the welfare state might well employ faith-based institutions, including churches, synagogues, and mosques, as a means of reaching recipients. The liberal perspective would be concerned that such institutions not proselytize welfare recipients; the conservative view might argue that faith-based institutions could provide, in addition to the state's material provisions, emotional and even spiritual succor, which might be offered to welfare recipients in ways that do not proselytize. Another example: a democratic polity is centrally devoted, in a variety of ways, to the goal of self-determination in politics. Conviction in the desirability of political self-determination (by person or group) is ultimately normative. Even if it does not entail, imply, or impose any particular outcome of self-determination, it is itself a normative value not shared by monarchists or communists, or the theocrats of Iran or the market-oriented authoritarians who run Singapore. Religiously oriented communitarians and secular liberals can equally embrace this value, if for different reasons. The former group might seek through political self-determination the moral improvement of its members, whereas the latter may pursue maximum individual liberty over against all manner of groups and organizations. A final example: one can imagine an abiding need for thick morality as the ultimate justification for the citizen's recognizing the validity of a legal regime or constitutional order. Normative convictions, such as the inherent dignity and value of all human beings as such, might serve as the final basis for legal validity, even in positive law. On the one hand, an abiding need for a normatively thick foundation does not necessarily entail a normatively thick legal or political order, which might function in largely procedural or in other nonnormative ways. On the other hand, some values claiming a transcendental or otherworldly or otherwise thick validity are not irrelevant to modern societies and not corrosive of secular government or secular humanist values.

I don't know that there is some a priori standard by which to distinguish between a real need for thick morality and where no such need exists. In any given case criteria for establishing the need for a thick norm would follow from the logic of the institution or legal order or public policy in question. The welfare state can be normatively thin in the sense of not imposing any particular worldview on its citizens, which means that it can provide welfare to the needy without making adherence to any particular worldview a prerequisite for receiving welfare. But the rationale for providing welfare to the needy in the first place cannot be deduced from the liberal tolerance of many differences that animates a normatively thin approach. But it does follow from the very idea of the welfare-state, which, after all, does not exist for itself, but for the broad masses of its members (whereas an oligopoly or a dictatorship exists for a small group of privileged persons, or even just for one privileged person—where the thick norm of providing welfare to the broad masses does not follow). Again, much of a democratic order can be configured in normatively thin ways (as in procedures for determining who receives which powers, for what periods of time). But the notion of political self-determination itself does not follow from democratic proceduralism; rather, democratic proceduralism would seem to presuppose the value of self-determination. Likewise, a constitutional order guaranteeing rights presupposes the thick norm of the individual's inherent dignity and worth. Such an order can be normatively thin where it grants the right of individuals to decide for themselves, but this thinness only makes sense with the assumption of the individual's value as such. In each of these examples, a normatively thin approach presupposes this or that thick norm; in each case, the thin approach needs this or that thick norm as an ultimate justification. And in each case, the relevant norm follows from the logic of the enterprise or institution or policy in question.

Society is itself an ongoing enterprise, and societies reproduce themselves through the social integration of their members. Chapter 2 sketches the contours of a normatively thin form of social integration. Thin integration, I argue, is best suited to the enterprise and policies and institutions of a morally diverse or cosmopolitan society. Those policies and institutions confront significant differences in the normative commitments of the population they serve, or supposedly serve, or aspire to serve. In chapter 2 I develop the argument begun in this one: that a normatively thin approach is better able than a thick one to deal well with difference.

SOCIAL INTEGRATION WITHIN COSMOPOLITAN SOCIETIES

2

As we saw in the previous chapter, complex modern societies increasingly pursue social integration tolerant of normative differences among the populace. This is especially true of liberal, democratic societies whose communities more and more reflect the multicultural makeup of a fluid, global economy. As I argued in chapter 1, heterogeneity may threaten understanding and agreement among the populace in such normative areas as politics, law, public policy, culture, and systems of values. Recognition and tolerance of difference within a community or among communities threaten the bases for overarching normative agreement. Often, normative differences cannot be reconciled without one side or the other forsaking its position, conviction, practice, or identity. Where this is unacceptable, as it often is in tolerant polities, citizens may find themselves unable to agree with one another—which makes democratic politics difficult—or find little reason for participation in communal concerns, which discourages the participatory designs of democracy. To resolve this problem this chapter proposes various ways of securing greater rather than lesser degrees of popular agreement on critical communal issues, despite differences within a heterogeneous society. Popular agreement encourages group and individual participation in communal concerns. Participation of this sort is possible in a competitive social structure in which politics and citizenship are based not on formal neutrality (as in many forms of political liberalism) but on a nonneutral normativity. For this structure I propose social integration through what I introduced in the last chapter as "normative thinness," in citizens' interaction both cooperative and competitive.

My argument runs orthogonally to the debate between liberalism and (conventional types of) communitarianism, in that I regard communitarian thinking as a critical perspective within the larger context of liberal thought, rather than as a complete alternative to it.[1] Thus if communitarianism emphasizes the need for shared conceptions of the good, liberalism stresses the desirability of individual autonomy to opt in or out of such shared conceptions, and the right to challenge them at any time. Still, thin communitarianism differs importantly even from what might be described as a normatively thin liberalism. I specify several differences with respect first to Habermasian proceduralism, then with regard to the political liberalism of the later Rawls.

Normatively thin are various procedural rules, rules for obtaining fairness *in process*, for assuring fairness *in outcome*. Such rules constitute deontological constraints on the process of argumentation. Jürgen Habermas (1998:44) proposes four: "(i) that nobody who could make a relevant contribution may be excluded; (ii) that all participants are granted an equal opportunity to make contributions; (iii) that the participants must mean what they say; and (iv) that communication must be freed from external and internal coercion so that the 'yes' or 'no' stances that participants adopt on criticizable validity claims are motivated solely by the rational force of the better reasons." The normative thinness of this conception (and of proceduralism in general) is its freedom from entailing specific outcomes. Proceduralism then appears as a kind of reciprocity among deliberating citizens. It is like socialization as a relationship of some reciprocity between society and individual. For proceduralism as for socialization, the individual is most relevant as a member of one or more social groups. Commitments and communities are constituted, and constitute themselves, through the mediation of others; commitments and communities are group activities. The communitarian will underscore that individuals also "socialize" the community and thus may well regard the community that socialized them with some degree of moral concern. But thin communitarianism will claim against thin liberalism that even normatively thin deontological constraints presuppose a community or society in which such rules are available, understandable, and acceptable as a viable means of problem solving. As Charles Larmore (1987:56–57) notes, "[W]hat we consider optimal conditions for justifying a belief or action can never depart entirely from our historical circumstances. 'Ideal' conditions of justification are a function of our general view of the world and what we believe are the best ways of acquiring knowledge about it."

The thin liberalism of proceduralism thus makes various substantive assumptions about participants' personality structure, educational background, and cultural disposition. These include the postconventional normative stance that embraces only those norms it understands and freely accepts, only those obligations it understands and finds legitimate, and only those social roles it chooses for itself (or at least it does not conflate its own unique identity with the identities of the roles it plays). Such assumptions describe the personality structure of citizens as social critics, or at least as critical citizens, with the psychological and cultural disposition to question the status quo and to distinguish between truth and dogma for themselves and to attempt to understand other persons as they understand themselves. In short, even formal, deontological constraints on the process of discussion and justification may not be equally plausible to most participants, most of the time, at most venues. Even debate over functionally equivalent alternatives to these formal constraints itself presupposes those very constraints. Proceduralism is normatively thick in its derivation from the political culture of complex, modern democracies, and political proceduralism is perhaps inconceivable outside of democratic culture. In liberal democracies, not all such constraints will be controversial. But some citizens may sometimes reject them, and when they do so, formal processes dedicated to democratic ideals of fairness, justice, and participation are threatened.

Unlike Habermas, John Rawls (1993:192) acknowledges that his notion of liberalism—"justice as fairness"—is not procedurally neutral, that its "principles of justice are substantive and express far more than procedural values, and so do its political conceptions of society and person." Yet in various ways Rawlsian liberalism makes normative assumptions that are difficult to sustain. To begin with, Rawls (ibid., 147) proposes normative conviction as the basis of liberal society. The "object of consensus, the political conception of justice, is itself a moral conception" and is "affirmed on moral grounds, that is, it includes conceptions of society and of citizens as persons, as well as principles of justice, and an account of the political virtues through which those principles are embodied in human character and expressed in public life." Second, Rawls assumes a robustly moral nature on the part of socialized individuals, that "while citizens do not have equal capacities, they do have, at least to the essential minimum degree, the moral . . . capacities that enable them to be fully cooperating members of society over a complete life" (183). He understands persons "so far as possible solely as moral persons" (ibid., 273), attributing to them distinct "powers of moral personality" (which he defines as a "sense of right and justice" and a "capacity for a conception of the good") (302). Third, he invests rationality with an other-regarding valence. Thus "rational agents approach being psychopathic when their interests are solely in benefit to themselves" (51). And "public reason" is "guided by a political conception the principles and values of which all citizens can endorse" (10). Rawls (231, n.11) assumes that, in a well-ordered constitutional regime with judicial review, public reason and the supreme court "more or less overlap" as they do the work of justice. Fourth, Rawlsian liberalism is strongly consensual, though in empirically unlikely ways. It assumes a substantive normative identity among the members of a community or society, allowing them to "live politically with others in the light of reasons all might reasonably be expected to endorse" (243). And in the "well-ordered society of justice as fairness citizens do have final ends in common," because in affirming the "same comprehensive doctrine, they . . . affirm the same political conception of justice" (202). Rawls (71) regards public norms ambitiously as "inhibiting self- or group-centered tendencies," which educate citizens to the "ideal of citizenship" and elicit in them "an effective desire to be that kind of person."

In four steps I propose a thin communitarianism. First I show how normativity has gradually withdrawn from many areas of social life, leaving a normativity both thin and "local." Then I differentiate between two senses of normative thinness. Third, I identify several necessary features of thinly normative social integration. Finally I draw on Erving Goffman's work to sketch out social integration as "agonistic pluralism," a kind of interactional modus vivendi, which, while not unproblematic, offers distinctly welcome possibilities for social integration in heterogeneous societies.

Sources of Thin Normativity

Thin normativity derives from those areas of social life from which thick normativity has withdrawn over the course of the modern age. We see this especially with morality, one of the most significant and easily problematic forms of normativity. In complex modern societies, thin normativity becomes possible in part as morality contracts. Law, for example, becomes differentiated from morality in those cases where it impedes the resolution of conflicts. While both law and morality serve to stabilize the expectations each person has of other persons' behavior, and while both depend on generalizations of behavioral expectations, they do so in very different ways. To be sure, differentiation of one from the other does not preclude their mutually influencing each other. Pressures of a moral nature can effect changes in the legal sphere, just as legislation and legal enforcement can alter moral understandings. Law and morality are analogous means toward socially useful cooperation among groups and individuals. In some respects the moral code aligns a person's self-interest with the law's social interest, reinforcing the legal code (Posner 1999:39). Nonetheless, these overlaps are too limited to align two very different techniques of social control. When law is differentiated from morality, legal questions cease to be moral questions wherever moral claims cease to be claims to truth. (That is, answers to legal questions, but not to moral questions, can be claims to cognitive truth.) Law no longer backs up morality, and judges properly decide the former, not the latter (ibid., 108). Law does not enforce morality, nor is it guided by moral intuition (ibid., 109). Law can be indifferent to morality where it finds morality the irrelevant form of normativity. Above all, morality cannot be the primary goal of social integration. Social integration no longer proceeds on a moral basis, and the values of functional systems are no longer moral values, as Niklas Luhmann (1994:28–29) points out. In these ways, among others, normativity withdraws from the functional systems of modern society.

Where individuals are bound to each other socially, yet now by ties that are more loose than strong, more temporary than permanent, there, too, normativity has withdrawn to some extent. Social bonds of this sort capture only an aspect of the person, so that different bonds have different purchases on the individual, and no one bond has a purchase on the individual in his or her entirety. Thus no one is only and entirely a citizen, an employee, a parent, a consumer, a neighbor. Accordingly we speak of groups and communities in the plural: no one is a member of just one group, and everyone has allegiances to multiple communities. Even as individuals, our identities are not singular but plural, just as our loyalties are not one-dimensional but multifaceted.[2] While the various communities are differentiated from one another, they are not differentiated out from some overarching entity—which is why modern society has no moral or structural center.

With increasing specialization in everything from labor to social roles, people are actively interrelated but only as fragments, as the fragment relevant to a particular role or function or goal. Normatively oriented interaction among citizens recedes as humans are increasingly mediated by generalized media of exchange, such as money or administrative power: "One exchanges labor, according to specific demands, for wages in a certain amount. Here the inclusion of a human being's full complexity in that of another is not only unnecessary but is even avoided as a disturbance factor" (Luhmann 1995:239). The normative category of "esteem can be dispensed with, and the assessment of capacities for work and wage suffices" (ibid.).

Normativity withdraws from functional systems where, say, health is no longer judged to be morally superior to illness (where disease is no longer regarded as chastisement, for example). Normativity withdraws from functional systems where ownership of property is no longer adjudged morally superior to nonownership. It withdraws where simply being the party in political power is no longer considered to morally eclipse the party out of power. It withdraws where successful scientific research is not regarded as moral success. Normativity withdraws from functional systems where winning in sports is not considered a moral triumph (Luhmann 1994:29). In each of these spheres, the criterion against which the preferred state is measured is no longer moral: the health in terms of which illness is defined has no moral aspect; ownership in contrast to nonownership is not a moral status; a political party successful at the polls does not measure the election returns in moral terms; the function of democracy is not normative in the sense of realizing moral values, indeed politics is morally open-ended; progress in scientific experimentation is not regarded as morally superior to failure; athleticism and gamesmanship are viewed as morally neutral. Each of these functional spheres defines itself according to its own criteria, rather than to otherworldly moral criteria. In modern societies a political system operating along moral lines is no more plausible than a system of scientific research, or economics, or even artistic production, operating according to moral measures.

Consider, for example, the ways in which contemporary Western culture celebrates wealth (where poverty is stigmatized not simply as an undesirable state for practical purposes but as a moral failing) and health (where some homophobes regard AIDS as divine punishment for sex between men) and success (where sports stars are accorded measures of general social respect and influence quite beyond the athletic sphere; hence the common expectation that superior athletes be moral role models for youth). But I further claim that such linkages in our culture today are increasingly weaker than in earlier times. People who regard AIDS as divine retribution are proportionately much smaller in number than persons who, in the European Middle Ages, regarded pestilences as signs of heavenly disfavor.

Indeed, says Luhmann (1994:36), at least "individuals in particular can feel relieved as they come to realize that today nobody who takes a moral point of view can claim to speak for the whole of society." In this sense law differentiated from morality can provide security against moral pressure and immediate normative regulation of daily life, affording a significant cooling-down of law's more moral aspects (Luhmann 1978:68). Property rights protect against moral claims as to sharing and just distribution; contract law protects against direct normative regulation in everyday life; rights of freedom protect against pressures of both church and state, where either makes moral claims on the individual. Law secures the individual's freedom to choose from among competing moralities. In cases of conflict between morality and law, the latter trumps the former in local settlement.[3]

Accordingly the normativity appropriate to, say, education will differ from that appropriate to economics or politics. By this process normativity becomes increasingly local, more and more a matter internal to any given functional system. Behavior within each system may be evaluated as to its conformity with the norms of that system, but one system can hardly judge the norms of another. By this process normativity becomes socially contingent: the norms of any one system are not backed by generalized ideas (such as religious ones). The norms of any one system are not universally binding. The differentiation of the respective normativities of society's various functional systems leaves each normativity socially contingent: contingent upon the nature, requirements, and experiences of its own system. This holds for morality as a functional system as well: morals in modern society are contingent on various spheres of morality but not on other, nonmoral spheres.[4]

Two Forms of Thin Normativity

The "thinness" of thin normativity captures two distinct (but not incompatible) senses of thin: (1) where the kind of contexts needed to adjudicate disputes need not be thick and (2) where successful social integration need not be based on solidarity or sincerity or overarching values.

(1) "Thin" means "nonmetaphysical," that is, not invoking, presupposing, or otherwise relying on otherworldly sources of validity. It presupposes no collective consciousness, even where communal normativity is forged, identified, and legitimized internally and collectively by the participants themselves. One might object that thin normativity can only be a small-bore optic on social and political issues, but precisely therein lies its capacity for cosmopolitanism: in the relative simplicity and minimalism of its commitments, claims, and perspectives. An approach that bears little normative baggage can better accommodate the often substantial normative baggage of its various clienteles. Simplicity renders a thin approach capable of embracing significant difference. Here also lie the distinct limitations of thin normativity: it cannot inform us about the plethora of details and richness of thick normativities. In other words, it cannot address many social and political questions on the thick level, nor can it win access to many meanings at that level, much like the distance that separates the outside observer from the local participant. But normative thinness need not be normatively weak, irrelevant, or marginal. In one sense the thin is more essential than the thick, for it represents a pared-down form of the thick, the thick shorn of most of its features.[5]

By contrast, a "thick" normativity is one that tends to reduce individuals to the communities from which they spring or in which they work or reside. Significant authors whose thought betrays aspects of a normatively thick conception of social integration include, at the end of the nineteenth century, the Frenchman Emile Durkheim and, in the middle of the twentieth, the American Talcott Parsons.[6] Toward the end of the twentieth century the German Jürgen Habermas, on the other hand, offers a political conception of thin normativity. Whereas Durkheim (1947) and Parsons (1954) argue that social integration is possible only on the basis of an unconscious, society-wide normative consensus, Habermas (1985) urges a social integration ideally through a rationally achieved consensus in the public sphere.[7]

On thick conceptions, the "product" resembles the "producer": the individual is like a social product, such that where there is no social constitution of the individual, there is no individual. Correspondingly, ways in which individuals define themselves over against the social—in individualism and personal autonomy, for example—are themselves deeply social products. Even highly individualistic individuals are created as such by an environment that values individualism. Community makes individuality possible in the first place, just as individuation is possible only through community. On thick conceptions, the individuality of individual realization should not confuse us as to its common source. The source of the individual's autonomy is not primordially private (as is so strikingly the case in Hobbes, Locke, and Rousseau) but ultimately public. Private good has public good as its source: the good of "private" is a good only in a society that commonly values the "private" and "the individual." The individual who pursues his or her private good thereby affirms common values: shared understandings that are public not private. Autonomy, no less than equality or liberty, benefits individuals in their self-understanding as those individuals understand themselves—even as autonomy's source is mainly the public good, the commonweal, or shared understandings.

The thicker the normativity of social integration, the more it renders individuals' orientations and worldviews coeval with the communities they inhabit. Thick forms too easily assume harmony and understanding, concern and sympathy, via shared subjectivities. They refer to a more assimilationist solidarity that absorbs individuals into the group, in relatively high degrees of understanding and agreement. They easily elide differences within the community. At the extreme, thick in this sense is normativity with a totalizing impulse, or social integration with authoritarian implications.

The stronger the unity within a community, often the weaker the difference among its members. In cases of thick normativity, an individual's identity and worth often lie less in his or her difference from others than in his or her similarity to others. Important for communal unity is less the degree to which individuals are equally unique and more the extent to which they can be taken to be similar. A thickly normative desire for community stresses an understanding of others not as "they" understand themselves but as "we" understand ourselves. To agree thickly is to look more at the consistencies than at the inconsistencies of members' internalized norms; to agree thinly is to agree on points of public policy despite (yet cognizant of) differences in comprehensive worldviews, as I show. For these reasons a thick strategy is more likely than a thin one to privilege one worldview over others in its normative commitments. A thin one is better able to concede at least the partial merit of competing approaches and in this sense can be more open to compromise among them.

Varieties of thick normativity correspond to the diversity of social relations marked by reciprocity, for example in tradition and convention. Tradition and convention are significant reservoirs of background information more or less uncontested by their carriers. Society reproduces itself where the same patterns are sustained from one social context to the next, a reproduction less likely where patterns are contested. Patterns are sustained where individuals do not contest characteristics already regarded as belonging to them, where individuals behave reliably in terms of these characteristics (Goffman 1967b:239). The sharing of a great deal of background information is crucial on a constant, everyday basis to any community or society because it enables cooperation as well as the peaceful noncooperation that disagreement sometimes becomes. Necessarily some aspects of normative thickness are constituents of any ongoing community, even thinly normative ones.

Christopher Lasch (1986:67) stresses the particularity of any given community's uncontested background information. In its particularity it makes shared understandings possible as more than mere conformity: "Tradition, and tradition alone, is precisely what makes it possible for men and women to disagree without trying to resolve their disagreements by the sword." By contrast, Michael Oakeshott claims that tradition and convention necessarily preclude any form of normative thinness. He rejects any notion of politics that is thin, on the argument that political conceptions and goals can be evaluated solely from within an already existing tradition of political sensibilities and ways of evaluation. According to Oakeshott (1984:229), politics amends "existing arrangements by exploring and pursuing what is intimated in them," namely, patterns and sympathies for hidden or unapparent aspects of community. Political activity explores that sympathy and political reasoning, "present but not yet followed up," and demonstrates that "now is the appropriate moment for recognizing it" (ibid.).

In their different ways Lasch and Oakeshott both point to conventional kinds of thick normativity. Conventionalism means that local bonds are valid simply by virtue of being local. Validity of this sort is indispensable to intersubjectivity, whatever form it takes. Again, convention is some part of any intersubjectivity, indeed its very precondition. Convention contains various norms latent within intersubjectivity, reflecting some of the norms held by some of the persons who now carry it (or who carried it in the past). We see this, for example, in the rules governing correct usage of the medium of communication. Successful communication depends on the participants' ability and willingness to use correctly the same set of rules, such that communicative competence refers, at a basic level, to the same skills (communicatively competent persons are competent in the same way). Intersubjectivity resonates with its human carriers the more it reflects their convictions, value preferences, and need interpretations. In turn, intersubjectivity finds expression in norms: socialized individuals recognize themselves in norms intersubjectively valid, norms that individuals can freely adopt because, in a sense, these norms already are their norms.

At this point a significant political problem emerges into view. These communal obligations are locally valid norms, and their recognition will often generate principles. But whatever else they may be, such principles are unlikely to promote social criticism. Conventionalism regards the sheer facticity of such norms as their primary merit, their source of validity, and our foremost reason to accept them. Standards wholly internal to a community easily preclude justification valid across different communities and societies. Where norms are legitimate by the sheer fact of their existence, localism can excuse or self-servingly rationalize local power merely on the basis of its being local. In pluralistic communities this lack of critical capacity poses significant problems. After all, rational and democratic adjudication of disagreements and competing visions in public policy, as elsewhere in politics, depends on rationally persuasive, hence critical and self-critical dialog among the participants and other affected persons. A claim that survives critical scrutiny is rationally more persuasive than an unexamined claim. Here a normatively thin perspective is superior to a thick one. From a thin perspective, no belief or particular way of life can be justified by appealing solely to the values, norms, and ideals embodied in the cultural conventions and practices of any given community. Otherwise, parochialism becomes a predicate of truth. The liberal criticism of self-validating communal norms applies to conventionalist understandings of argumentation, localism, and normativity. Validation must exceed the norms inherent in the community under evaluation, because nothing in the community can be valid—at least rationally valid—simply because it is communal.

But not all forms of thick normativity are conventionalist, nor are all forms of conventionalism incapable of self-criticism. Both points are made by Hegel's (1996: paras. 150, 151, 156) notion of *Sittlichkeit*, an exceptional example of thick normativity as lived, organic, normative community. The self comes to be what it is, and to understand itself, by fulfilling its communal obligations, the moral obligations of social life. These are larger than the individual and precede him or her. He or she realizes him- or herself normatively by freely and consciously participating in them and so sustaining them. This normatively thick relationship is anything but static or passive: the individual's participation in communal practices and institutions involves developing normative patterns and realizing their potential. Participation both preserves a normative complex and refines it, as well as fostering the participant's normative development. Through communal institutions the individual realizes universal conditions of freedom; here the parochial can be a route to the cosmopolitan. In *Sittlichkeit* the conventional can be a means to the postconventional. Because interests and preferences are embedded in history, tradition, and locality, a community that embraces only abstract principles—normative thinness—threatens its moral integrity. Where thin principles have some purchase, they have it only in addition to, but never in exclusion from, the local, embedded, thick normativity. Even then, thickly embedded thin principles can transcend the thick. In Kant such principles are self-reflected, and while Hegel criticizes Kant for not being able to make those abstract principles concrete in any way that would motivate people's behavior, he does not reject them in their critical function.

My argument against parochial forms of localism is simply that localism must be able to identify and reject objectionable social practices and defeat their claims to legitimacy, if localism is to redeem any positive normative claims.[8] This claim finds richer expression in a related argument against parochial forms of normativity. The argument here is that a rationally plausible normative system must be able to entertain criteria of truth distinct from its own, to transcend its culture at least partially, to abstract from itself and exceed its own situatedness to develop criteria for choosing among rival norms and among competing normative commitments. (I develop this approach in chapter 6, with respect to competing cultural values.) A capacity to adjudicate among, and choose from, competing views of normative commitments and social goods must be able to reject some perspectives and some communities on the basis of its own understandings. After all, the goal of community cannot be to entertain difference to the point of extinguishing a community's own identity. Absolute tolerance implies a complete lack of identity on the part of the tolerant community; a community that tolerated everything would have no identity (would not be a community). Less than absolute tolerance is tolerance within limits, toward some goal, guided by a self-identity not negotiable in all of its parts.

But how can thin normativity redeem such claims to critical perspective? How can it entertain criteria of truth distinct from its own, or how can it partially transcend its culture? How can it abstract from itself and exceed its own situatedness to develop criteria for choosing among rival norms and among competing normative commitments? The following section of this chapter ("Three Features of Social Integration through Thin Normativity") shows that a critical perspective is possible even under normatively thin conditions. The final section ("Agonistic Pluralism as a Modus Vivendi") attempts to show how a critical perspective is not impossible in daily life even under the ordinary circumstances of widespread deception and manipulation. But first consider another form of thin normativity.

(2) This form concerns the mediation of human beings. Communities are constituted, and constantly constitute themselves, through the mediation of their members. Where the individual's social integration is mediated through complex webs involving large numbers of people over great distances—mediation typical of complex modern societies—mediation can alienate in various ways. It alienates, for example, where it robs the agent of his or her agency by encroaching on it directly, or indirectly by colonizing its conditions and consequences (Habermas 1987)—where, for example, persons are integrated less and less through a civic activism that involves the to and fro of discussion and debate among participants and increasingly through economic exchange (where the imperatives of the market, rather than the affected citizens, decide issues of public import) or administrative power (where the imperatives of the bureaucracy, rather than the affected citizenry, adjudicate matters of public policy). Mediating institutions like these discourage the individual's participatory competency, his or her capacity and ability to participate in the public sphere.

Yet the notion of thin normativity allows us to see that some institutions also have the capacity to enhance political and social participation. Some forms of mediation can realize degrees of solidarity among the mediated. And where mediation and its institutions can facilitate civic participation, there mediation need not alienate. Consider, for example, patterns of cooperation that arise among individuals, or in large groups, or within small communities. The institutionalization of such patterns in legal codes and administrative directives, and in other institutions of governance, might preserve some of these originally spontaneous patterns—yet at a higher, though more rigid, level. The unionization of workers is a potent example, as are changes in the workplace that in the United States followed from the political successes of the civil rights movement or the women's movement half a century ago. Yet spontaneous provenance is no precondition for nonalienating mediation. Civic cooperation knows many forms. It can be spontaneous, or it can be encouraged by political, administrative and other means. It can work in small-scale collectivities, but in large ones as well. It is possible in direct, face-to-face exchanges, as well as in mediated ones. It need not be thickly normative, and it can be normatively thin.

Thin normativity offers a further argument for nonalienating mediation. In fact it urges the counterintuitive claim that a type of thinly normative social integration also occurs between and among persons whose linkages are tenuous at best (as increasingly is the case for many relationships in modern societies). A thinly normative communitarianism is possible even among strangers. Indeed, this condition makes communitarianism *more* likely than conditions often desired by normatively thick models of communitarianism: conditions of strong bonds among persons. Consider also that face-to-face relations are local but not therefore superior to mediated, nonlocal, relations. Face-to-face relations are not "more pure, authentic social relations than relations mediated across time and distance. For both face-to-face and non-face-to-face relations are mediated relations, and in both there is as much the possibility of separation and violence as there is communication and consensus" (Young 1986:16). Further, political community conceived as predominantly face-to-face relationships among members (a notion typical of normatively thick communitarian theories) can grasp neither the potential, nor the problems, of relations often centralized, indirect, anonymous, or large-scale. Yet these are just the sorts of relations that mark complex modern societies, where the closely knit neighborhood or the harmonious workplace is not often the sort of unit that mediates communities and the individuals who compose them. Among communities, exchange—of personnel, resources, products, but also of culture, politics, and education—likely will not share the characteristics of smallness and decentralization prized in some self-determining communities and prized by thick communitarianism.

With this argument about a "communitarianism among strangers" I would urge that political, cultural, and economic institutions can create forms of social cohesion without participants needing to agree on worldview, moral conviction, or other matters of normative import. Cohesion of this sort is an example of thin normativity. Politics, conceived in thinly normative terms, is a way not of making participants virtuous but of allowing participants of differing views on virtue to cooperate in the public sphere—where the common and public interest is not widely shared virtue but widely acceptable policy. The theory of thin normativity rejects competing models of thick normativity for insisting on stronger or deeper or more meaningful relationships among persons. Thin normativity suggests that communitarianism is possible under conditions of weak relationships among persons, indeed, is much more likely there than under conditions of strong relationships.

Three Features of Social Integration through Thin Normativity

Thinness is constructed out of thickness: we put together a particular thinness out of pieces drawn from a variety of thicknesses. (Consider a social practice that finds different expression across a variety of communities and cultures, such as salutations: all cultures know forms of greetings, yet the simple acknowledgment of another person's presence need not commit the acknowledger to a close or sincere or moral relationship with the acknowledged.) Members of a community can apply thinness only with reference to thickness because the particular circumstances—the local significances, the contingencies—are the sole terms in which we can flesh out thinness in a particular case. And the particular tends to be thick. The thin can be realized only in a particular place, at a particular time. This embeddedness of the thin, its realization through various particularities like place and time, does not render thin into thick, although it does highlight their enduring connection.

Despite this connection, thin normativity cannot substitute for thick; each functions in ways distinct from the other. Thick normativity can powerfully inform the collective identity of groups and individuals, whereas thin normativity best serves groups and individuals in instances where they are pressed to solve problems with people who do not share their thick convictions. The thin then represents the non-negotiable aspects of the participants' respective thick normativities, those aspects of the encumbered self that he or she cannot or will not shed. While the thin contains aspects of the thick, it cannot be deduced (or induced) from the thick. The thin does not constitute recognition of the thickness of the opposing side, but only of those aspects found mutually acceptable. The thin does not represent mutual recognition of differing worldviews but mutual acceptance of a few features possibly continuous between two or more competing worldviews—as degrees of conviction in, say, democracy might be continuous across differences separating liberals and conservatives, or across differences separating proponents of a strong welfare state and advocates of a relatively noninterventionist one. In this way it allows for agreement in the midst of significant disagreement.

From the discussion so far one might think that thinly normative social integration possesses no necessary features, or that thin qualities can only be teased out of thicker ones, or perhaps that they can only be products of compromise. In fact, normative thinness displays at least three necessary features: "particularity," rationality, and "fragmentation" (as a form of thin communitarianism).

(1) Particularity: As local and compromise-driven, shared understandings are context-dependent, their validity relative to the collective understandings (cultural, historical, political, economic) that produce and preserve them.[9] Their validity expires at those points where those same collective understandings reject them. Possibilities for agreement then depend on the extent to which those contexts can be "shared" (made plausible, sometimes even persuasive, to outsiders), and shared in processes of negotiation. The very negotiability of contexts and their boundaries opens up possibilities for greater sharings[10] because, through negotiation, differences can be addressed and compromises forged. Thin normativity can accommodate negotiation more easily than can thick. This feature of thinness I call "particularity."

We observe "particularity" no less in normative thickness. The social world is thick in the sense that participants (but not observers) have immediate access to it because it is both constituted by and constitutive of the participants' convictions and expectations, experiences and practices, language and lifestyles.[11] Thickness reflects particularity, that which makes this community or that one the particular community it is. Particular is both what the collectivity is as well as how it perceives itself (and misperceives itself). These ways of being and perceiving are contingent, local, embedded; they are encumbered with memory, a defining feature of culture.

The location of particularity in both thin and thick social integration indicates once again how thick and thin are tied to each other inextricably. Even to describe the thin requires us to draw upon the thick. Any definition of the thin reflects in part the definer's circumstances and thick identity, an identity without which the definer could no longer recognize his or her life as his or her own. No neutral, uncommitted, presuppositionless standpoint exists from which one might articulate the thin (or the thick). Only in terms of the definer's identity and circumstances can the thin find expression. Thinness is an abstraction carried out under circumstances of thickness.

(2) Rationality: Rationality is a feature also of social integration through thin normativity. A political community is rational only if it can find norms acceptable on their rationally accessible merits rather than simply because they are already accepted. Merit-based norms (which are more likely to be thin than thick) are open to critical examination more readily than tradition-based ones: we embrace the former precisely because they have sustained rational scrutiny.[12] By contrast, tradition-based norms are often significant sources of thick normativity. To the extent an aspect of thick tradition is reflected thoughtfully and embraced critically, it might become available to merit-based norms as well. This capacity for critical reflection—a rational quality— is more likely in normatively thin social integration than in its thick alternatives.[13]

Rationality can facilitate political participation and political access: after all, self-determination is as much a cognitive act as a political one. It has a cognitive element in the self-conscious construction of identity, as well as a political element, for example, in the public sphere where identities of various sorts may guide political activity. Under democratic circumstances, access to politics means access to public discussion and public decision. In all political processes power is present, yet its presence does not entail that differentials in access to power must be wide, or concentrations of power narrow. Where wider access to power means that more persons can more easily participate in politics, there power is more likely to aid than hinder democratic self-realization. Thin normativity offers itself as one version of wide access.[14] The rationality of argumentation, the reasoned competition among different arguments, interpretations, and claims, can facilitate thinly normative social integration. Such competition is possible only where it is cooperative, and cooperation can bind participants in thin agreement for strategic purposes of solving problems through discussion and adjudication of competing arguments.

(3) Fragmentation: In earlier pages I proposed a communitarianism that is more realistic, especially in heterogeneous political communities, because less ambitious in its normative presuppositions and goals. Normatively thick conceptions of communitarianism presuppose far-reaching equality among members of the community. By contrast, I argue for a communitarianism possible under the more likely conditions of social inequality. Whereas most versions of communitarianism cannot deal well with the social facts of coercion and deception, my model recognizes the pervasiveness and endurance of both and can cope with these problems even under communitarian conditions. This approach does not advocate inequality, nor does it preclude efforts to criticize or ameliorate it. Social critique is still possible under conditions of thin normativity, which, to remain thin, need not distance itself from the normativity of social criticism. But my approach can function in the face of inequality: it does not presuppose the greater equality still to be achieved in constitutional democratic states.

Nor need it surrender the poor or otherwise marginalized: it can be inclusive of more persons, persons heretofore excluded, "silent voices," and others. Thin communitarianism is capable of what Seyla Benhabib (1989:385) identifies as a "participatory" strain in communitarian thought. From a thin perspective, political modernity is characterized not by High Normativity—by "belonging, oneness and solidarity" (ibid.)—but by Low Normativity, by "political agency and efficacy" (ibid.) that doesn't require oneness or even significant solidarity among participants. Thin communitarianism does not seek to reconstitute old value commitments and personality structures or to create new ones (although it doesn't preclude change, either). It is oriented on existing ethics and politics, and on critical assessments of given value preferences and social structures. The goal of assessment is not to make friends out of strangers but to enhance the structures and conditions of political participation, above all participation that nonetheless respects differences among participants and their various memberships.

Thick communitarianism mistakenly supposes that individuals in community cannot be exterior to one another in any robust sense. It conceives community more as totality than as a composite of differences. Thin communitarianism, by contrast, can grasp the empirically more likely community based not on face-to-face associations but on affiliations among strangers. Thin communitarianism conceives of community as affiliation among others whose otherness is not absorbed by the relationship. Iris Young (1986:21) describes this possibility: "Strangers encounter one another, either face to face or through media, often remaining strangers and yet acknowledging their contiguity in living and the contributions each makes to the others." On this view people are related externally and "experience each other as other, different, from different groups, histories, professions, cultures, which they do not understand" (ibid.). Fragmentation remains.[15]

Indeed, politics and other forms of civic participation cannot overcome normative fragmentation, where participation is still possible in a thinly normative sense, one that doesn't commit each participant to the thick normativity of each of his or her coparticipants. Participation by all possible participants may be possible, but only thinly. Cooperation of this sort, as in so much of modern life, cannot presuppose or require unity. Nor does it require normative thickness, nor even social and legal equality. Joint action for mutual benefit is sometimes a question of proportion or balance among the participants—but it needn't be. The principle of equality, and of equal participation in particular, says Charles Taylor (1985:414), "shakes men loose from their traditional communities, but cannot replace them as a focus of identity," cannot reconstitute normative thickness out of thin principles.

Modernity has brought us community under conditions of normative fragmentation rather than normative unity. Fragmentation marks the fact that, in complex societies, the relation of individual norms to one another is often broken. A person's political beliefs, for example, may reject the practice of capital punishment, yet he or she nonetheless may support a judiciary that has interpreted the Constitution as allowing the practice. Or a person's religious views may reject the practice of abortion, but he or she may strongly agree that a woman should have the right to decide for herself. Many norms can be splintered within themselves: an antiracist orientation may regard race consciousness as necessary to combat racism, as in affirmative action programs in higher education or hiring by public institutions, even where some persons may not be hired or receive the governmental contract or receive admission to an educational program precisely because of their race. Even shared understandings, like all products of compromise, are sometimes fraught with internal tensions as the price of mutual adjustment of opposing claims, reciprocal modification of demands, and concessions on all sides. Under these circumstances many norms of modern community are unlikely to be simple, homogenous, uncontroversial, or unchanging.[16] They more likely result from repeated compromises among competing interests and the various groups that carry them. Even then not all members of the community will embrace compromise. For this and other reasons, many persons' purchase on such norms can only be partial. The compromise-driven generation of norms is itself a source of normative fragmentation.[17]

Agonistic Pluralism as a Modus Vivendi

Many communitarian theories presuppose or seek conditions of public consensus. Not thin communitarianism.[18] Normative consensus in pluralistic societies is an increasingly unlikely goal. Difference and disagreement—political but also social, cultural, religious, and economic—is so chronic within them as to be part of their normative architecture. Even in a public sphere built around deliberation, discussion, no matter how enlightened, may not coalesce into the same conclusions, understandings, or norms—let alone definitions of facts, needs, and wants. Thin communitarianism seeks social integration that can accommodate citizens and other participants who disagree, so that integration does not collapse under the weight of constant difference and disagreement. Accommodation is not deep or broad agreement, but it is cooperation nonetheless. Communitarianism of this sort recognizes that even formal, deontological constraints on the process of discussion and justification may not be equally plausible to most participants, most of the time, in most venues. Debate over functionally equivalent alternatives to such formal constraints presupposes those very constraints. In liberal democracies some of these constraints often are not controversial. But in venues where they are rejected, formal processes dedicated to democratic ideals of fairness, justice, and participation are unlikely to work.

Because it rejects the notion of some prior, comprehensive, community-wide consensus of normative rules offering cultural meanings as well as practical guidelines for daily behavior, the notion of thinly normative cooperation offers a solution to an old impasse in social theory.[19] Groups and individuals make their behavior contingent on the behavior of other groups or individuals, yet the one side often does not, often cannot, know in advance what the other side thinks or plans. Action is predicated on each side's calculations of the possible thoughts and behaviors of others. How is social action possible where parties must act in light of what they think other parties are thinking about them, yet where none of the parties can be certain that what they imagine is in fact correct? One solution is fundamentally communitarian, in my "thin" sense. We can draw out the normative minimalism of thin communitarianism, as a kind of "agonistic pluralism," by considering aspects of Erving Goffman's analysis of everyday behavior as strategic interaction. The analysis approaches ordinary, face-to-face interaction in terms of "players" who present themselves to an "audience," that is, individuals and groups who, through the way they present themselves, attempt strategically to manage or otherwise control the impressions of others. Further, the individual determines that he or she often has more to lose by challenging the status quo than by conforming to it and voluntarily avoids topics or behaviors that he or she knows would challenge the order. By saving face the individual also contributes to maintaining social order (Goffman 1967a:43). Here normativity and manipulation are intertwined. The socialized individual seeks to abide by the normative standards of social life yet that seeking is, often as not, an amoral engineering of behavior to create an impression for the benefit of others that the individual is in fact behaving in accordance with moral standards. The engineering of one's own behavior is simultaneously an engineering of others' behavior, as the manipulation of information (think of consumer advertising), or as competition in defining a situation (think of a lawyer's construction of evidence to the benefit of his or her client), or as succeeding at the expense of the other (think of the "spin doctoring" of politicians and their handlers— or of ordinary people just trying to "get ahead" at work or in other venues). Yet this very behavior serves to reinforce the status quo, to affirm the social order, and might well be described as amoral rather than immoral.

From the perspective of agonistic pluralism we can analyze political power as control over the definition of social reality and its values. We then approach politics as the struggle to have one's definition trump competing definitions. The problem of indeterminacy in social action—each side depending on, yet often ignorant of, the other side's thoughts and plans—appears as a political problem, not just an epistemological one. Here impression management, in its concern with the power of definitions, relates to social integration. Defining political or social reality offers one way of coping with both cognitive and normative indeterminacy. The notion of normatively thin, agonistic communitarianism opens up this perspective. Yet Goffman's theory is not generally regarded as particularly communitarian (or in any other sense collectivist). On the contrary, it is usually read as an account of atomistic individuals exercising significant levels of agency.[20] Against a conventional reading I would emphasize how Goffman (1959:254) focuses on the "structure of social encounters" that "come into being whenever persons enter one another's immediate physical presence." While agency is certainly prominent in this model, I argue that it shows how collective social structure ultimately subsumes individual agency. To begin with, information control may be analyzed as a collective concern with indeterminacy; structure is one means by which we cope with it. Impression management is the engineering of communications, which "belong to a less punitive scheme than do facts, for communications can be by-passed, withdrawn from, disbelieved, conveniently misunderstood, and tactfully conveyed" (Goffman 1967a:43). Impression management concerns the "individual's capacity to acquire, reveal and conceal information. The perspective here is that of an organizationally committed observer who needs information from another person" (Goffman 1969:4).

Goffman analyzes the politics of information management as a group's effort to maintain, in the face of possible challenges, its desired definition of the situation. We can read Goffman's (1959:141) concern with information control as a collective concern with achieving determinacy: "One over-all objective of any . . . [group] is to sustain the definition of the situation that its performance fosters,"[21] involving overcommunicating some facts and undercommunicating others, so that, for example, "outsiders" do not acquire information contrary to the situation as defined by "insiders." The important point here is that normative claims are modest (or "thin") but nonetheless adequate to instances of social integration where people conceal their true objectives and needs behind claims about values that participants acknowledge superficially—but often merely for purely strategic purposes of social cohesion. Consider: a group can mislead others on the basis of having defined reality itself. In that case the work of defining reality is collective not individualistic. This teamwork of impression management enmeshes the individual participants in collective forms of behavior. Collective behavior displays institutionalized norms, generalized ways of behavior, a distribution of roles, and a division of resources, molding the individual in communal ways, in the shared understandings and expectations of both participants and outsiders. Teamwork is a type of communal activity. Community, so understood, attempts to establish its interests over against those of other communities by attempting to have its definitions dominate the political construction of their shared realities. (Similarly a group within a community attempts to establish its interests over against those of competing groups in the community.) Communal work needn't presuppose constant communal unity; within any community (and within any group within a community) individuals may compete to have their definition of the community (or group) dominate rival definitions.

On this conception much of social integration is highly strategic. For example, the effectiveness of a performance depends on cooperation among the performers, a cooperation part of whose effectiveness may lie in its being well concealed from the eyes of third persons (Goffman 1959:104). Indeed, a "degree of deception may be essential to getting along in the social-political milieu; . . . the success of the deception will correlate only weakly with the degree to which others are actually deceived; . . . the populace itself plays a major contributing role [in deceiving itself]. Subtle but pervasive contractual elements may contribute to the process . . . [in the form of] tacit agreements among the populace as to what can and cannot be discussed openly (e.g., what is 'politically correct')" (Beahrs 1996:4). Communal agreement is more a veneer: individuals and groups suppress actual beliefs and intentions to achieve cooperation and understanding. This is social integration without consensus, where participants nonetheless contribute to the overall definition of the situation—and in that sense cooperate.

Here community-wide harmony, as a kind of "consensus that arises when each individual present candidly expresses what he really feels and honestly agrees with the expressed feelings of the others present," is "not necessary for the smooth working of society" (Goffman 1959:9). Successful social integration, the "smooth working of society," requires only so much cooperation among the performers that definitions proffered by various performers not openly contradict each other. Social integration requires only that each participant "suppress his immediate heartfelt feelings, conveying a view of the situation which he feels the others will be able to find at least temporarily acceptable" (ibid.), while each hides his or her true beliefs and intentions behind the norms minimally acceptable for communal association. Social integration in complex modern societies requires only an interactional modus vivendi.[22]

An interactional modus vivendi has an ambivalent normative status, apparent in contexts both public and private. On the one hand participants, not the state, generate a great deal of social order, including the public sphere; indeed, participants do so sometimes even despite the state and its massive authority. On the other hand, rights and privileges, risks and disadvantages are distributed unequally in the order established through interaction, yet most participation in that order tends to reinforce the status quo and so legitimizes the social and political powers that be. After all, participation constitutes at least passive acceptance of the social order's norms and conventions. Here an interactional modus vivendi is normatively problematic (1) with respect to the deceptive behavior that it allows to serve the selfish interests of one group at the expense of another, or even to repress the self in pathological ways (as in some forms of self-deception). But it would seem everything other than problematic (2) with respect to the social cooperation that it furthers. An agonistic, pluralist order might successfully realize (2) without generating (1), or at least might attempt as much.

(1) A modus vivendi can be socially dysfunctional. The greater the extent to which interpersonal experience is based on deception, the greater its complexity and the greater the possibility for social breakdown. Where, for example, mutual deception leads to the exclusion or corruption of information necessary to the solution of social problems, there community or society suffers. Of course it also suffers where shared deception exacerbates social conflicts, or where a society can be unified only by taboos and rules that dare not speak their name.

Further, a modus vivendi can be oppressive for the individual where it renders him or her a merely hollow carrier for larger social purposes. One needn't believe that individuals have essences waiting for social expression to believe that individuals are much more than their social roles. Even where they actively participate in the constitution and modification of the roles they play, they are oppressed by those roles where the individual is possible only by submitting to hierarchy and power. In other words, roles are oppressive where they subordinate the individual to a hierarchy, where the only socially accepted presentations of self are status-reinforcing ones and where the only politically tolerated performances are ones perfectly homogenous with the dominant culture.

Third, a modus vivendi would seem pathological where it encourages individuals to *want* to be deceived, that is, where social cooperation and stability encourage self-deception—perhaps where the self seeks to avoid responsibility, or to circumvent unpleasant realities, or to cope with uncertainty, or to avoid retribution. "Whatever his position in society, the person insulates himself by blindnesses, half-truths, illusions, and rationalizations. He makes an 'adjustment' by convincing himself, with the tactful support of his intimate circle, that he is what he wants to be and that he would not do to gain his ends what the others have done to gain theirs" (Goffman 1967a:43).

Finally, the benefits of a modus vivendi that accrue to participants are not always (and not for everyone) greater than the cost of participation. Indeed, what from one perspective appears to be socially beneficial orderliness appears, from a different perspective, to be socially unnecessary repression. Where one person sees inclusion, others may see exclusion. Goffman (1983:5–6) notes how, "over the short historic run at least, even the most disadvantaged categories continue to cooperate. . . . Perhaps behind a willingness to accept the way things are ordered is the brutal fact of one's place in the social structure and the real or imagined cost of allowing oneself to be singled out as a malcontent. . . . [T]here is no doubt that categories of individuals in every time and place have exhibited a disheartening capacity for overtly accepting miserable interactional arrangements."

(2) At the same time, the notion of an interactional modus vivendi opens up perspectives for thinly normative social integration. First, a modus vivendi can facilitate social cooperation. Even as an agreement more on the distribution of power than on claims to truth, it can still be socially productive in avoiding the projection of conflicting definitions of the situation. Here participants would together "contribute to a single over-all definition of the situation which involves not so much a real agreement as to what exists but rather a real agreement as to whose claims concerning what issues will be temporarily honored" (Goffman 1959:9–10). A modus vivendi then functions as a system of

enabling conventions that, while of no intrinsic value in and of themselves, serve social coordination much the way the rules of a game make the game possible or the way grammar and syntax make possible linguistic communication. Such conventions work only where all participants are similarly constrained. No doubt one could find among participants quite a range of personal reasons for accepting such constraints. Yet regardless of the diversity of their reasons, participants can still accept the identities and meanings proffered by one another. Doing so needn't violate the participants' self-respect; it can also allow for considerateness in social interaction. Of course, in some cases this may mean reciprocity in deception: where each respects the deceptions of the other, that one's own deceptions may be respected in turn. In that case the pursuit even of self-serving goals may contribute to some measure of social cooperation.

Second, the collective orientation of an interactional modus vivendi may be practically effective in the politics of daily life, even in its normative thinness. Here the individual finds some degree of freedom in the management of information, namely, in the manipulative presentation of self to others and in the engineering of others' impressions of oneself. I say "some degree of freedom" because that freedom will be restricted by social context; individuals are always constrained in choice of roles and statuses. Some members of society will find a measure of individual freedom precisely in participation: "if the person is willing to be subject to informal social control—if he is willing to find out from hints and glances and tactful cues what his place is, and keep it—then there will be no objection to his furnishing this place at his own discretion" (Goffman 1967a:43). Such "freedom" from strong normative commitments likely enhances rather than detracts from possibilities for successful social integration, especially under the integration-discouraging conditions of modern, normatively heterogeneous communities.

So conceived, the modus vivendi of an agonistic pluralism seeks community in which members experience detachment (but not necessarily indifference) rather than union, where they find affiliation without collapsing difference into identity, and where strangers remain strangers even as they engage in various forms of cooperation as well as competition. Integration here is loose, a matter of apparent agreement despite significant misgivings. A working consensus means a level of cooperation sufficient for successful interaction, which requires of par-

ticipants a measure of self-control adequate to maintaining that cooperation. Agreement may grow out of impression management and
information control, where some information may be emphasized and
other information suppressed; cooperation may flourish where groups
and individuals engineer idealized impressions. Agonistic pluralism
can still be normative: "any projected definition of the situation also
has a distinctive moral character" to the (limited) extent one can assume that "any individual who possesses certain social characteristics
has a moral right to expect that others will value and treat him in an appropriate way" (Goffman 1959:13). After all, we commonly have "moral
expectations about the behavior not only of our fellows but of strangers
too" (Walzer 1994:17).

Agonistic pluralism can still be democratic and does not necessarily
preclude or hinder increased equality. Within it, definitions and interpretations of shared understandings are open to debate. Debate
itself can achieve closure, if only temporarily, in turn only through
shared understandings. Understandings, so shared, allow for meaning
to be forged communally, even as it allows for individuals to pursue
those meanings privately as well as in common: public origins allow
for private applications (including, of course, deception and strata-
gems). While agonistic pluralism may not be strong in the area of critical self-reflection, it doesn't preclude critical reflection either. As a
political entity, community still engages in self-interpretation; it still
takes itself as its own interpretive object. Even under these normatively
fragmented circumstances, self-understanding might sometimes, in
some ways, be a platform for a rational, self-critical community, even
if not strongly encouraged by its normatively thin and often strategic constitution. On the other hand, it is precisely thin normativity
that holds out the greatest promise for a rational and tolerant relationship among various concrete communities in democratic constitutional states. The following chapter shows that where thick normativity can be separated from thin, there a politically communitarian
relationship among diverse communities is possible. In other words,
where normatively thick communities can relate to one another in normatively thin terms, tolerance of the other communities' differences
becomes tied to other communities' guaranteeing the integrity of one's
own community's identity and practices. The fabric of social stability
is woven with strands of both thick and thin normativity.

SOCIAL INTEGRATION

AMONG DIVERSE COMMUNITIES

3

The preceding chapter's model of social integration within a normatively heterogeneous society aims beyond social coordination to social cooperation. The normatively fragmented circumstances of late Western modernity do not preclude the possibility of rational, self-critical communities in which various ideals of justice can be realized. The three chapters of part 2 of this book flesh out concrete versions of justice in communities and societies open to normatively thin ways (specifically in the areas of interpreting and applying legal rules, in the relationship between competing cultural values, and in efforts to identify and combat discrimination against women). The present chapter extends my general theory of thick and thin to justice between and among heterogeneous communities making up a modern society. I argue that modern liberal societies display two kinds of community. The liberal constitutional state is a kind of "generalized community"[1] inhabited by citizens most of whose characteristics (such as race, religion, and socioeconomic station) should be irrelevant to citizenship. This state proffers few common goals beyond security, physical safety, personal freedom, health, economic prosperity, family stability, equality of opportunity, and common law equity. It is neutral on most of the competing worldviews and ways of life of its citizens—most, but not all. The state cannot be neutral or otherwise indifferent toward criminal or belligerent behavior, nor can it be neutral to communities that would harm their members:[2] it cannot be indifferent toward communities that reject generalized community. A second form of community is "concrete," committed to, say, particular ways of life, or worldviews, identities, or cultural values. Unlike generalized community, concrete community intentionally privileges some of its members.[3] Generalized community eschews particularist identities, conceiving citizenship as a formal identity, whereas concrete community is guided by the identities and normative commitments of these particular men and women. Within generalized community there is no "foreignness" or "otherness," whereas each concrete community is an "other" to every other community.[4]

Picking up from the previous chapter, this one explores a politically communitarian relationship among various concrete communities in democratic constitutional states. A communitarian relationship cannot accommodate any concerns and viewpoints of one concrete community that cannot be translated into those of another. To recognize one another as communities, each must be able to recognize that the concerns and commitments and understandings of other communities possess a meaning and reference for it (including meaning and reference that the community of the first instance may repudiate for itself). To do this each concrete community must take the attitude of generalized community toward itself. In doing so, each concrete community commits itself to respecting the different, even competing orientations of other concrete communities. In return, each concrete community can expect to be tolerated by other concrete communities. Where different concrete communities relate to one another in terms of generalized community, their mutual tolerance of one another allows each to flourish, in part because generalized community's thin normativity need not "infect" or elide the normatively thick commitments of these communities. Thin normativity can recognize the legitimate claims of thick communities, even as it understands itself as normatively thin. In this way I develop a notion of communitarianism *among* communities, in distinction to a notion of simply *the* communitarian community.[5] This approach builds on similarities between George Herbert Mead's analysis of the individual's socialization into the group and the relationship among communities in the democratic constitutional state. It builds on similarities between mental structure in individuals and social structure in communities.

I construct the approach in four steps: a basic model of social integration in heterogeneous societies; the major prerequisite for integration: separating thick from thin normativity; integration through the thin normativity of legal rights; and the limits of integration: communities that reject generalized community and cannot be integrated.

Basic Model of Social Integration

Mead (1967:47) describes interaction as a "conversation of gestures," whose meaning is collective not individual, social not private: symbols possess the "same meaning for all individual members of a given society or social group" because they "respectively arouse the same attitudes in the individuals making them that they arouse in the individuals responding." Gestures enmesh the individual's behavior—in all its contingency—in the social network of shared symbols of communication, such that self-consciousness is social consciousness, consciousness as a member of a group with shared meanings. I apply this model to concrete communities belonging to one generalized political community, where the self-understanding of any one group includes understandings of other groups. By allowing one concrete community to take the perspective of another, generalized community facilitates the recognition of concrete communities among themselves. It also aids self-recognition, the capacity of one concrete community to see itself as others see it.

Consider by analogy the notion of human rights, or rights possessed by each of the members of diverse groups all of whose members are human. Problematic though this notion may be (which rights, whence?), its logic is analogous to my model in two respects. First, just as everyone possesses the same human rights as everyone else, so in my model each concrete community possesses through generalized community the same status as every other. Second, just as the possession of human rights need not collapse or violate communal and individual identities in all their distinctness—except where they deny or circumscribe human rights—so in my model membership in generalized community needn't infringe upon the identities of the various concrete communities, except where the latter communities violate the provisions of generalized community (such as: no concrete community may foist its identity on any other concrete community). Consider a different example: just as citizenship can mean that each citizen has certain rights within his or her country, so in my model each member of a concrete community has certain rights within that community. Citizenship can also mean that each country recognizes the citizenship of other countries, so that a citizen abroad is subject to the rules of the host country—but also is protected as a foreign national in the host country, just as the host country's citizens residing abroad are protected by their hosts in turn. "Protection" does not require the guest to abandon his or her identity, even as some of the host's rules circumscribe it in some ways (the foreign carnivore may not eat beef in India, the foreign Christian may not proselytize in fundamentalist Islamic states, foreign practitioners of ritual female genital mutilation must desist once they become residents of France).

On this model members of different concrete communities interact with members of other concrete communities—through the rules of generalized community—without having to abandon their identities, yet constrained by generalized community to respect the identities of other communities.[6]

Taking the Attitude of the Other

Mead views communication and understanding among persons as a process of each participant taking the viewpoint of others—not converting to those viewpoints but imaginatively considering "various possible viewpoints and courses of action" (Collins 1989:10), rehearsing behavior toward others, anticipating others' behavior. For my purposes a community "takes the attitude" of other communities toward itself and so can adjust itself to other communities and modify its interaction with them.[7] To understand is to acknowledge and give status to "what is universally present—everyone has an identity—through recognizing what is peculiar to each" (Taylor 1994:39), to presume that each has value. To find meaning in something, to grasp meaning, is to interpret it. Interpretation proceeds from the understandings of the interpreter. What is coherent and plausible to the interpreter is a basis for understanding what is coherent and plausible to the interpreted. Communication among different communities is a matter of each being able to take the attitude of the others, anticipating how each might react to a given action by the instant community, and imagining (in what Mead calls an "internal conversation") how the instant community might, by its own lights, best act in any given situation. For example, each of the different ethnic groups in a multiethnic society, as in the former Yugoslavia, communicate in this sense when Serb can take the attitude of Croat, when a Christian can anticipate how a Muslim might react to a given action by the Christian community, and where Serb and Croat, Muslim and Christian each observes him- or herself from the perspective of the other and is guided in his or her behavior in part by that perspective. Ethnic cleansing or religious persecution is less likely where potential perpetrators can see themselves from the perspective of their potential victims. "To take the attitude of the other" means that a concrete community develops and articulates its own identity by becoming an object to itself in the way other concrete communities are objects to it.[8] It means that a concrete community experiences itself indirectly, from the standpoints of other communities in the same society, viewing its own history or public postures or common opinions not from its own viewpoint but from the viewpoints of others.[9]

Concrete community also experiences itself indirectly[10] from the standpoint of generalized community. Concrete communities learn from other concrete communities about their respective thick normativities, and from generalized community they learn about the thin normativity that allows concrete communities to interrelate. Kent Greenawalt (1988:200) shows how the liberal secular state, and a religious community within it, might understand each other's standpoint with respect to religiously based claims to exemptions from general rules of military service:

> [I]f one believes that there exists an objective religious truth whose moral demands may well come into conflict with the state's requirements, one may be more disposed to think that conscience should be accommodated than if one does not believe in transcendent sources of moral truth. Further, if one believes that religious truth actually requires action that is contrary to what is demanded by present state requirements, as a religious pacifist would feel about a general conscription law, one would be likely to rate the need for accommodation very high. The pacifist who derives his views about war from religious premises is not required by liberal principles to put his religious convictions out of his mind when he thinks about whether pacifists should receive an exemption.

Accommodation by the state requires sensitivity to concrete communities, to the sincerity of beliefs and their role in the life and culture of affected persons. Accommodation by the religious community requires sensitivity to the different, yet equally sincerely held beliefs of other communities. And it requires understanding of how the secular state's occasional impingements on the actions of some religious communities is an unintended consequence of attempting to provide freedom of religious belief and exercise under conditions of competing beliefs. Thus might concrete community understand the standpoint of generalized community: mutual respect among concrete communities, and recognition of limits that such respect places on all communities' behavior.

Community Identity through Taking the Attitude of the Other

A community's identity emerges precisely where it differentiates itself from other communities; it develops within social processes involving other communities. A community forms its relationship to its environment of other communities through the particular sensitivities of the communities involved.[11] For example, some Euro-Canadians (say, of Greek or Polish heritage) regard themselves as members of the concrete community of anglophone Canada in which the national heritage of one's forbearers is no longer one's primary cultural identity. Another group of Euro-Canadians, the Québécois, constitute the concrete community of those francophone Canadians for whom the forbearers' linguistic heritage is a primary locus of identity. And some of the various indigenous peoples of Canada (such as the Cree or Déné) regard themselves foremost in terms of their non-European heritage. Each of these groups is distinct from the others, yet distinct in a manner mutually constitutive of each as fellow Canadians. Québécois define themselves principally as distinct from the "mosaic" Canadians (rather than, for example, the French, Belgians, or Americans) and by implication as distinct from certain aboriginal peoples as well (Canadian rather than other American or Australian native peoples, for instance). "Mosaic" Canadians identify themselves in terms more of their undifferentiated Canadian identity than their various European or Asian heritages. The indigenous peoples distinguish themselves from both the "mosaic" Canadians and the Québécois. But all three groups are Canadian in the sense of generalized community: citizens of the same constitution, neighbors of the United States, beneficiaries of the country's nationalized health care, and so forth. All three can be Canadian in the sense of generalized community, even as each has a relationship to generalized community somewhat different from the others' (some regard themselves as Canadian by virtue of their membership in their respective national communities; others regard themselves as Canadian in terms of their relationship as individuals to the federal state).[12]

Concrete Communities Possible Only through Generalized Community

Generalized community determines the norms that govern society in general. In dealing with other concrete communities, any concrete community assumes the attitudes of generalized community's normatively thin social framework, on which most normatively thick communities can agree, and on which all are expected to agree (as a condition of membership in generalized community). The thin framework facilitates agreement because it includes the rule that most concrete communities have equal rights vis-à-vis the national government.[13] The framework of each concrete community includes the rule that our community cannot treat any other concrete community in ways different from how generalized community would treat it.

Correspondingly, a public policy unacceptable to generalized community cannot be available to any concrete community. If the policy is normatively thin—as it must be to satisfy the requirements of generalized community—then it is likely to be acceptable to the various concrete communities to which it applies. Indeed, the pursuit of normatively thick policy is excluded by generalized community and would be unacceptable to most concrete communities anyway. Thus to the extent sexual orientation is constitutive of a particular concrete community (as constructed through public policy in provisions of certain legal rights of spouses or domestic partners, such as those involving health, insurance, inheritance, and the adoption of children), persons in a heterosexual relationship have (through generalized community) no more right to impose a "heterosexual lifestyle" on the homosexual community than the latter has a right to impose a "homosexual lifestyle" on the heterosexual community.

Concrete community is possible only as a member of generalized community.[14] Accordingly new immigrants are immigrants first to generalized community, the community that admits them to the constitutional order, and only secondarily are they immigrants to other concrete communities. A concrete community's rights—embedded in legislation and political culture alike—depend for their realization on common attitudes with other concrete communities, shared through generalized community.[15] For example, "Because American identity still inheres in the abstractions of the civic culture, citizens who seek a more inclusive definition of our national community can draw on two valuable resources. First, it is consistent to express both a strong ethnic identification and a strong attachment to the nation. Second, tolerance of other groups is itself proclaimed as a national ideal" (Karst 1989:183). If diversity can be consistent with community, then concrete community can be consistent with generalized community, because the rights of concrete community derive from generalized community.

Rogers Smith (1997:31–32) makes a related claim in his discussion of citizenship as a feature of generalized community. Inclusion within generalized community defines the normatively thin portion of any given concrete community's identity:

> [C]ontestation over laws defining membership is ongoing in most societies. Sometimes these disputes take place quietly, at the margins of major political conflicts, while most civic rules are left intact because they do not disturb the leading political forces. But at other times, especially when old regimes are being toppled and people are building new ones, battles over membership take center stage, as they have in many parts of the former Soviet bloc. Yet even when they are not venues of great struggles, citizenship laws are essentially but potentially incendiary institutions that mirror and shape politics in obvious and subtle ways. Their importance and volatility stem from the fact that the fundamental task of fostering a "people" is today a difficult challenge in most societies. Almost every state contains many people whose political history, religious or political beliefs, ethnicity, language, or other traits give them reasons to decide that their primary political identity and allegiance is to some group other than that defined by the regime governing the territory in which they reside. All modern political boundaries are products of long periods of struggle which have left members of losing sides still living in regimes they can potentially be mobilized to oppose.

Efforts of any group to define generalized community (for example, as "citizenship")—with the aim of having one group's definition trump competing definitions—are highly contested because the stakes are so high. Generalized community as the locus of citizenship is the condition for the existence of concrete community (as defined perhaps by "political history, religious or political beliefs, ethnicity, language, or other traits"). While citizenship is a feature of generalized community, its content for any given group or individual may be influenced by membership in this or that concrete community. Canadian citizens living in Quebec and the rest of Canada's citizens are both participants in the argument about the extent to which Quebec is like, and unlike, the rest of Canada and the extent to which it should be treated similarly and differently. But in that debate Canadian citizenship may not have precisely the meaning for Québécois that it has for anglophone Canadians.

Prerequisite for Social Integration of Diverse Communities: Uncoupling Thick from Thin Normativity

The individual's membership in generalized community need not threaten his or her simultaneous membership in concrete community if it does not threaten the latter's thick normativity. And membership in concrete community needn't threaten membership in generalized community as long as concrete community abides by generalized community's thin normativity. In this way generalized community uncouples thin and thick levels of social integration, or thin normativity from thick, or generalizable ways of life from nongeneralizable ones. It allows concrete communities to interrelate on the basis of thin normativity, without having to forsake the thick normativity constitutive of their respective identities. The thickness of one community recognizes, but need not adopt, the thickness of another, where this relationship is mediated by generalized community's thinness. "Recognition" is not merely an acknowledgment of the recognized community's existence; it acknowledges that the community has this or that particular normative content.

Avishai Margalit (1996:153) illustrates how two concrete communities, each marginalized in its respective society, appeal (and appeal differently) to generalized community: "Palestinian Arabs claim that they are second-class citizens in Kuwait, and Israeli Arabs maintain that they are second-class citizens in the state of Israel. These are two different claims. The claim regarding Kuwait is that Palestinians who were born in Kuwait, and have lived and worked there all their lives, are denied Kuwaiti citizenship even though they are entitled to it. The Israeli Arabs, in contrast, possess formal Israeli citizenship, but they are denied various civil rights, and others are not applied to them." Indeed, says Margalit (ibid.), the "majority of Israeli Arabs do not perceive Israel as an encompassing group that they need for their self-definition, and for some of them belonging to it is even quite embarrassing. Nevertheless, their insistence on equal civil rights is not merely a demand for just distribution of whatever goods and services are distributed to citizens, such as government housing mortgages on easy terms; the fact that they are denied these goods, even by a society they do not identify with, is perceived not only as injustice but also as humiliation." The concrete community of Israeli Arabs appeal to generalized community even as it feels rejected by it. Israeli Arabs do not claim that their community's thick norms should be adopted by the whole society. Rather, they claim that their community should be included on the same footing as other concrete communities, above all the majoritarian Jewish community (which from a particular Arab perspective must appear monolithic, though to its members may appear rent with such sharp divisions that members distinguish within it a plethora of concrete communities). The just and equal inclusion of diverse communities can occur only through generalized community. Diverse communities can recognize one another through generalized community if they are willing to uncouple their respective thick normativities from their relationships to other concrete communities and relate through the thin norms of generalized community.

Reflexiveness

Self-reflexivity is a concrete community's capacity to call out in itself a set of responses shared by a society's other concrete communities. Generalized community's thin normativity allows each of the concrete communities to consider truths claimed by other concrete communities, without any of the concrete communities thereby sacrificing its own claims to validity. The "ethical integration of groups and subcultures with their own collective identities" are then "uncoupled from the abstract political integration that includes all citizens equally" (Habermas 1994:133–134). A community achieves identity through reflexiveness, so that its internal perspective reflects its normatively thin relationships with other communities: by turning back upon itself its experiences with other thin communities, by "bringing into itself" its experiences with them.[16] In other words, through reflexiveness a concrete community opens itself to the normatively thick attitudes of other concrete communities and does so precisely through the normatively thin attitudes it exhibits in generalized community and among concrete communities. Thus any one community will find, in itself, the thin attitude of any other concrete community.[17] Through the normatively thin attitudes of other concrete communities, each can acknowledge the content of the others' normative thicknesses. Each can do so because the thin relationship mandates recognition of the equal rights of other concrete communities—equal rights for their thick normativities. For example, an arbitration agreement between employees and management (both as concrete communities) might require that opposing groups "take the roles of their opponents, recognizing the other's perspective . . . to find a new social practice acceptable to all and beneficial to a reconstructed social order. They should not . . . involve the imposition of authority or the imitation by subordinates of prescribed habits" (Feffer 1990:244).[18]

Generalized community's normative thinness provides a platform for discussing public issues of common concern among the various concrete communities. Here "all persons must also be recognized as members of ethical communities integrated around different conceptions of the good" (Habermas 1994:133), where "one party can recognize the other parties as co-combatants in the search for authentic truths without sacrificing its own claims to validity" (ibid.). The platform need not "infect" the topic of discussion, nor need it prejudice the normative thicknesses under discussion. In this way members of a concrete community can observe themselves critically. Here "self-criticism is essentially social criticism, and behavior controlled by self-criticism is essentially behavior controlled socially"; here, "social control, so far from tending to crush out the human individual or to obliterate his self-conscious individuality, is, on the contrary, actually constitutive" of it (Mead 1967:255). But members of a concrete community can do so only as long as they are not dogmatic, for dogmatism's intolerance and normative exclusiveness precludes this capacity (as I show in later pages). Generalized community can enter critical dialog with a concrete community, where "critical" means evaluative, along the lines, for example, of accepting some aspects of the concrete community's self-understanding and rejecting others.

Integrating Diverse Communities through the Thin Normativity of Legal Rights

Concrete communities are embedded, in generalized community, as members of a constitutional order that applies to all concrete communities equally. On the basis of the constitution, each should treat the others in terms of the organized attitudes of society as a whole (in the form of generalized community), to which each is related as a subaltern. In this way generalized community proffers and protects a (normatively thin) right to normative thickness on the part of concrete communities. Generalized community makes possible a concrete community's right to normative self-determination. Thus immigration, however regulated, is possible only through generalized community, whereas it may run up against limits on the concrete community's right to maintain its integrity as a culture, or way of life, or worldview, or a particular system of cultural values. Generalized community, by giving each concrete community the right to affirm its identity as an aspect of its self-determination, allows each the right to refuse immigrants.

Consider two forms of assimilation. All immigrants need to assimilate to generalized community; this is normatively thin assimilation. Some immigrants may also assimilate to one or more of the existing concrete communities, in an act of normatively thick assimilation. Normatively thin assimilation preserves and protects the autonomy of the various concrete communities, an autonomy provided by the constitutional order. In this sense all concrete communities are assimilated to generalized community. For this reason generalized community can accommodate all manner of immigrants, regardless of whether they also assimilate to concrete communities. By contrast, normatively thick assimilation touches on the immigrant's deep and idiosyncratic identity. Thick assimilation has far greater implications for individual identity than "merely" political socialization, in the sense of normatively thin socialization within the constitutional order. Thick assimilation involves integration at the level of nongeneralizable norms, values, and cultural traits.

A concrete community can insist that all other concrete communities recognize its particular identity, such that (with exceptions I identify in the final section of this chapter) to refuse any community recognition is to violate that community's equal rights and entitlements. Here concrete community does not masquerade as generalized community: where, for example, the community of Québécois might insist that the community of anglophone Canadians recognize its francophone way of life, just as the Inuit might insist that nonaboriginal Canadians (including anglophone and Québécois alike) recognize the non-Western aspects of its way of life. But concrete community does masquerade as generalized community where it imposes its thick normativity on other concrete communities.

Each concrete community defines itself; each decides what characteristics "qualify" someone for membership, and generalized community supports this right of self-determination. Disagreements about such definitions are inevitable, but they are adjudicable in terms of generalized community's thin normativity. Consider the difference between concrete communities as public, and as private, organizations. A public school might constitute a concrete community in terms of its embeddedness in the local culture of its locality but not in terms of its admission criteria. A public school in Florence will have an identity and some interests different from the identity and interests of a public school in Kyoto, but both are equally governed by their respective generalized community's norms regarding admission: factors such as the applicant's race or sex or socioeconomic status are impermissible criteria of admission. By contrast, a private organization may deny membership precisely on the basis of such ascriptive criteria: in France the xenophobic Front National may refuse membership to Arab French citizens, and the Boy Scouts of America may reject homosexuals as scoutmasters. A gay man who identifies with what he takes to be the organization's "authentic" worldview and believes that the Scouts' official self-definition as homophobic is in fact a mistaken interpretation of the organization's "true" identity is nonetheless constrained by the official self-definition. Generalized community upholds the right of existing concrete communities, over against would-be "immigrant" individuals, to define themselves and to regulate membership accordingly.

Still other concrete communities cannot be classified in terms of public or private, and in some of them membership is inevitably problematic. The concrete community of "all women," for example, is plausible with respect to gynecology but implausible with regard to political persuasion. Thus any given concrete community of "feminists" is unlikely as a monolithic singularity but quite plausible as several communities of differently oriented feminisms (as I show in chapter 7). Likewise race: we can expect diverse concrete communities of black Americans of varying political, economic, cultural, or other self-definitions but no concrete community of "black Americans as such." One such community might refuse membership to this or that man not as a "black man as such" but, for example, as a black man with political views or economic commitments or religious beliefs incompatible with the particular community in question (where compatibility is judged by the community and not by the would-be "immigrant"). Generalized community's thin normativity protects the individual's right to be free of any concrete community and to exit any concrete community of which he or she is a member, but it does not recognize any individual's putative right to be a member of this or that concrete community.

Individual and Collective Rights

Generalized community, understood ideally in the form of the constitution itself ideally understood (for example, in ways that defeat racial and sexual hierarchies),[19] proffers to each of the concrete communities equality in dignity, rights, and entitlements. Equality is a predicate of generalized community, not of any particular concrete community. This is also true at the level of individuals. Consider the individual citizen in two (complementary) respects. On the one hand, she or he is a bearer of individual rights that are normatively thin. Here the individual appears as a member of generalized community.[20] On the other hand, he or she possesses one or more normatively thick identities. Here we observe the individual as a member of concrete community.

Both thin and thick aspects are generated intercommunally: normatively thin individual rights obtain, just as a normatively thick identity finds recognition, through the recognition of others. Mutual recognition is a political and legal form of intersubjectivity at the level of community. As members both of generalized community and of one or more concrete communities, individuals are products of socialization. Through socialization they are "individuated." Individuation in generalized community means that individuals are constitutionally created as bearers of rights, as legal persons: a status that the constitution generalizes to all citizens. Political socialization into a constitutional order can be distinguished from individuation in concrete community, or "ethical-cultural integration," or habituation to the "way of life, the practices, and customs of the local culture" (Habermas 1994:138). The latter refers to the creation of individuals as bearers of identities, as members of distinct ways of life that—in the face of rival communities and competing thick normativities—cannot be generalized politically and legally to all members of society.[21]

Rights provided by generalized community to concrete community have nothing to do with most merits of any particular thick normativity—yet everything to do with such generalizable merits as a community's readiness to practice peaceful coexistence. The rights making possible the peaceful cohabitation of various concrete communities are not entirely independent of rights that obtain within the various concrete communities. Rights provided by generalized community pertain to all individuals in concrete communities and cannot be trumped by rights internal to the community. In this sense, rights are constructed as applicable to individuals only, not to collectivities. Liberal societies construct legal rights individualistically, as in rights to due process, bodily and decisional autonomy, privacy in behavior, and equality in the pursuit of such social opportunities as education or voting. A state tailored to individual rights is a state that structures freedom individualistically, not collectively. It recognizes collective rights, and protection for collective ways of life, never as such, but only where it recognizes this or that kind of person, as a bearer of this or that right.

Yet a "politics of identity"—which values difference in and of itself—asserts and pursues collective identities, based, for example, on race, ethnicity, or religion. Sometimes collective identity rejects individual liberty; cultural differences of local validity easily conflict with an abstract system of rights claiming general validity; the state, conceived as normatively neutral, clashes with the state conceived as promoting a specific way of life. These charged relationships are examples of the perpetual tension between thick and thin forms of normativity.[22] Generalized community can cope with this tension. It need not elide differences among concrete communities as a condition of recognizing them in its normatively thin way. Nor need it abandon the individualistic formulation of rights in generalized community, even where other rights internal to a concrete community are formulated collectivistically. Nonetheless generalized community might take a differentiated approach to communities under certain circumstances: for example, where particular communities are threatened by cultural extinction. I turn now to such circumstances.

Generalized Community Facilitates the Self-Preservation of Endangered Concrete Communities

Sometimes concrete communities, in their normative thickness, will be able to preserve themselves, or something of their selves, only by changing and adapting to a changing environment and other new circumstances, such as immigration. Normative thickness may be able to preserve itself only if it is open to transposing its thickness and perhaps sometimes even thinning it out. "Transposing" means "change" in a variety of ways: replacing some traditions with others, revising some practices and finding alternatives for others, being open to some beliefs and practices foreign to the community and ready to engage in exchanges with some of them.

Generalized community distinguishes among concrete communities to facilitate the preservation of those communities facing unwanted dissolution in the larger or mainstream or majoritarian society. It does not privilege a particular concrete community where it facilitates the latter's efforts to preserve itself or where it helps a concrete community compensate for disabilities. Generalized community protects concrete communities by recognizing their members within generalized community, not by guaranteeing the survival of any particular thick normativity, where a guarantee would amount to privileging that normativity over others. Generalized community in some ways can support a concrete community's efforts to persuade its members to preserve its own way of life and normativities. Facilitating the survival of a way of life need not involve thick normativities; it can be accomplished in normatively thin ways. But the survival of a concrete way of life can be guaranteed only in normatively thick ways. Facilitating a way of life need not privilege the concrete community in question over other concrete communities, whereas guaranteeing a way of life does privilege the community in question. Generalized community might facilitate a particular concrete community's efforts to preserve itself in the manner of the federal Canadian government's support of francophone Quebec's preservation through a federal policy of bilingualism.

Generalized community can also view concrete communities in context-sensitive ways and in this way preserve differences among concrete communities. We might distinguish between aboriginal and nonaboriginal cultural communities threatened by unwanted disintegration in culturally plural societies. Will Kymlicka (1989:182) does so when he advocates differential citizenship rights for indigenous minorities, a "special constitutional status that goes beyond equal rights and resources." Generalized or constitutional community, in this sense, is context-sensitive; it allows the concrete communities of indigenous minorities, threatened by cultural extinction, special rights vis-à-vis the national government. Concrete communities not so favored might still agree to the normatively thin framework of generalized community because they recognize that, in this case, formal equality among all communities might in fact disadvantage certain specific communities, such as aboriginal ones, for whom the country as a whole might feel some sort of unique responsibility.

On the other hand, generalized community cannot be in the business of guaranteeing the survival, by administrative fiat, of any particular thick normativity. The members of concrete communities—not generalized community—must have the ultimate say in questions of preserving or not preserving that community. Preservation is possible not through governmental engineering but only through the will of the community as expressed in the beliefs, commitments, or even the personality structures, of its members. Else, generalized community would be robbing the concrete community of the very autonomy it otherwise possesses through the normatively thin laws and regulations of generalized community. No concrete community should be preserved against its will, and every community is ultimately responsible for its own survival.

Concrete community is like an individual person in that, as a unity, it possesses rights over against other communities, but unlike an individual in that it is made up of a multiplicity of individuals who differ from one another and whose attachment to the community may be diverse. Thus sometimes the question of whether a particular concrete community should survive or not will be controversial among its membership, with some members supporting and others opposing its continuation. Generalized community's thin normativity supports those members who prefer continuation over those who oppose it. While generalized community may not foist a particular concrete community on anyone who does not want it, it also may not deprive members of their concrete community who favor its continued existence. Generalized community protects the rights of dissenters to abandon the concrete community whose preservation they oppose, but also requires the dissenters to tolerate that community's continuation.

The Politics of Recognition and the Politics of Difference

Generalized community establishes equality among concrete communities in one of two ways. It grants what Charles Taylor (1994:38) calls an "identical basket of rights and immunities," where every citizen merits the sort of legal recognition and cultural capital conferred by equal citizenship. This is a "politics of recognition." Or generalized community engages in a "politics of difference," an insistence on particularism, on the inherent value of being different, on viewing areas of public life that do not respect such difference as being potentially violative of the integrity of the differences denied recognition.[23] In a politics of difference, generalized community recognizes the unique identity of the concrete community, its distinctness from all other concrete communities. A politics of recognition is a thin view—and the politics of difference, a thick view—of concrete community.

A principle of universal equality characterizes generalized community whereas a politics of difference plays out among concrete communities. A principle of universal equality is relevant to a politics of difference but cannot be assimilated to it, just as generalized community is relevant to but cannot be assimilated to concrete communities. A concrete community may enjoy universal recognition within society despite its differences from other concrete communities.

A politics of equal recognition, the insistence that generalized community recognize all concrete communities, is one kind of nondiscrimination: blindness to difference. "Blindness" means that generalized community neither favors nor disfavors any particular concrete community or unique identity. This is a problematic notion of nondiscrimination: if it ignores all differences among the various concrete communities (and so displays a principle of political liberalism), it cannot then recognize any community's unique identity. Through a politics of equal recognition, a marginalized concrete community may appeal to a notion of generalized community that is "fuller" or "richer" than the current notion:

> In each historical period, Black Americans have been faithful to a Constitution that looked very different from the versions espoused by contemporary courts. It is a Constitution that abolished slavery prior to the Civil War, that provided freed slaves with forty acres and a mule during Reconstruction, that invalidated separate but equal facilities prior to *Brown v. Board of Education*, and that continues to mandate a radical dismantling of discriminatory structures despite the Supreme Court's adherence to the doctrine of color-blindness. Surely Black people are America's chief constitutional idealists, conforming the Constitution's terms to their own sense of justice. No self-respecting person could commit to a covenant that denies her humanity. But why have most Blacks not rejected the Constitution altogether? I think that the answer is that fidelity to the Constitution offers practical advantages to Black people's struggle for full citizenship. (Roberts 1998:227)

Here members of the concrete community of African Americans appeal to a notion of generalized community—inclusion in first-class citizenship—from which the concrete community is excluded: the robust citizenship of fundamental rights and fundamental dignity granted by the Constitution. The concrete community appeals for greater inclusion in generalized community, that is, toward receiving legal and social recognition from other concrete communities, above all from the racially majoritarian community, parts of which have systematically discriminated against the black community. But nondiscrimination as a blindness to difference cannot be part of that appeal. To withhold recognition of difference is to practice a form of oppression.[24] Nondiscrimination so conceived is possible only among communities already equal to one another in terms of legal status and cultural capital. The politics of equal recognition presupposes that equality already obtains among the recognized communities, whereas the politics of difference is "full of denunciations of discrimination and refusals of second-class citizenship" (Taylor 1994:39).

A politics of difference is practiced among concrete communities that insist on how each differentiates itself from others. It offers a second notion of nondiscrimination: consciousness of difference. To be conscious of difference means that generalized community does not regard the difference as something alien, something to be extruded. Generalized community's refusal to privilege the thick normativity of any concrete community over any other does not deny equality to that community; rather, it secures the equality of concrete communities vis-à-vis generalized community. A community's equality with other concrete communities is violated only by the absence or denial of abstract rights (notably civil and political rights), which derive from generalized community and not from any concrete community. According equality of abstract rights to each concrete community implies that the thick normativity of each concrete community deserves equal respect by other communities, as well as by generalized community.[25] Where generalized community recognizes the thick normativity of one community but not of another, there it denies equal recognition. Where it recognizes the thick normativity of each concrete community, there it practices nondiscrimination as consciousness of difference.

Limits of the Model: Communities That Cannot Be Integrated

I shall call "dogmatic" any concrete community that rejects generalized community in the sense of insisting on relating to other concrete communities exclusively in terms of its own thick normativity. Rogers Smith (1997:508 n. 5) discusses "ascriptive Americanism" as an often dogmatic vision of community, intolerant in its multiple exclusions of other groups from generalized community, in the form of citizenship:

> Adherents of what I term inegalitarian ascriptive Americanist traditions believe that 'true' Americans are 'chosen' by God, history, or nature to possess superior moral and intellectual traits associated with their race, ethnicity, religion, gender, and sexual orientation. Hence many ascriptive Americanists have believed that nonwhites, women, and various others should be governed as subjects or second-class citizens, not as equals, denied full individual rights, including many property rights, and sometimes excluded from the nation altogether. Because ascriptive positions stress the significance of involuntarily acquired traits that differentiate people, they always have the potential to support exclusionary and hierarchical citizenship policies.[26]

Not dogmatic is a community that, for example, simply advertises that all other communities are damned. Dogmatic is a community that insists that other communities accept or otherwise recognize such pronouncements as a condition of interacting with the dogmatic community (it insists that they accept that they are damned but regards them as still eligible to visit and trade with the righteous). Dogmatic is fundamentalism if fundamentalism means the rejection of pluralism throughout society, or intolerance of diversity in any community. Dogmatic is not simply the refusal to recognize alternative communities' right to exist, or their right to perpetuate themselves. It is the view that one's belief or way of life is so threatened by alternative beliefs or ways of life that those alternatives must be repressed: dogmatic is the claim that one's belief or practice justifies discrimination against competing beliefs or practices. It is the belief that one's beliefs cannot be true unless they are exclusively or necessarily or eternally true, whereas Thomas Kuhn's (1992:14) account of natural science—that all "past beliefs about nature have sooner or later turned out to be false," hence that the "probability that any currently proposed belief will fare better must be close to zero"—need not defeat the practice of science any more than it need reject a notion of truth in scientific development. Dogmatic is the conviction that religious faith is impossible if some members of the community are secularist, and the refusal to have anything to do with them unless they recognize this objection. (Or dogmatic is the conviction that secularism is impossible if some members of the community are theists, and the refusal to deal with them unless they accept this condemnation.) The Ku Klux Klan and the Nation of Islam are both dogmatic, not simply because each is racist but because their racism is virulently intolerant. Like private clubs that exclude Jews or blacks or women, or private universities that prohibit interracial dating among their students, their normative thickness entails intolerance toward others. Intolerance of this sort insists or entails, however unrealistically, that those shown intolerance somehow accept that they should be shown intolerance. Where the first openly gay couple moves into a small, backwater town, it is not dogmatic if the townsfolk continue to reject homosexual unions for themselves; they are dogmatic if they insist that the couple abandon its convictions as a condition of receiving the respect due fellow citizens (to refuse, for example, to sell goods to them). But a family with a room to rent would not be dogmatic if it refused to rent to the couple on grounds of its normatively thick convictions, whereas a hotel would (hotels, unlike families, are in the business of publicly accommodating differences within the populace). Dogmatic communities practice exclusiveness to the point of an intolerance incompatible with generalized community. Theirs is a normative thickness closed to all normative thinness. Without self-contradiction or violation of its own principles, generalized community must be intolerant of intolerant concrete communities.

Dogmatism's normative exclusiveness—its accommodation only for converts, or its coercion of others to assimilate to its normative thickness—signals a belief by the dogmatic that they are right and that they are justified in believing that they are right. Where the dogmatic cannot concede that they, like everyone else, may be wrong, there they are blind to their own fallibility. Generalized community practices the normative thinness of coexisting with competing points of view, of tolerating rational disagreement among competing normativities in the same "universe of discourse" (Mead 1967:156). "Competition" means that the various positions advance their best claims and thoughtfully entertain what competing positions take to be their best claims. Claims are advanced on the basis of reasons, and the competition presupposes the participants' openness to reasoned argument. The reasons articulated may well reflect the particular normative thickness to which the speaker is committed, but the speaker's openness to competing arguments, and his or her fallibilism toward his or her own claims, provide scope for participants to revise their views—certainly to the extent that the rational acceptability of any given reason cannot be reduced entirely to the accepter's normative thickness. Fallibility characterizes generalized community, and concrete communities able to assume a fallibilist stance thereby facilitate their capacity for tolerance (to recognize that one may be mistaken might make one somewhat more open to the plausibility of a position one nonetheless rejects for oneself). But generalized community requires no concrete community to adopt a strong version of fallibilism as a condition of membership in generalized community, because fallibilism is a helpful but not a necessary feature of political and social tolerance. And surely not all concrete communities would be able to embrace a strong form of fallibilism without damaging the integrity of their identity. Such groups can still be accommodated by my approach.

Further, generalized community finds expression in concrete communities when they reject dogmatism and reflect on themselves in critical ways. Adherents of a concrete community adhere because they feel freely bound by that community, as a matter of freely embracing the community's thick identity. Adherence possesses a critical quality where mediated by generalized community: individual rights possessed through membership in generalized community also obtain in any concrete community.

Finally, individual rights that flow from membership in generalized community allow the individual a right of exit from any concrete community. A right of exit helps each member of a concrete community retain—through generalized community—the possibility of attempting to change his or her concrete community. A right of exit provides some leverage over, as well as protection for, members advocating change, hence a kind of pressure valve for internally conflicted communities.[27] Members can be members freely insofar as those who differ (including later generations) are always free to terminate membership. The concrete community has a right to "punish" a departing member (to excommunicate the apostate, for example) but only with respect to its internal rules and organization; it cannot bring generalized community's coercion to bear upon those who opt out.

Individual rights that flow from membership in generalized community do not themselves constitute a legitimate framework for a normatively heterogeneous society. As I argue particularly in chapter 7,
often enough a purely formal understanding of legal individualism in
fact perpetuates substantive inequality. A normatively thin approach
to individual rights constructs them not as possessions but as relationships between and among individuals. These relationships secure at
once the individual's private autonomy and his or her public autonomy,
his or her capacity to participate in political deliberation and contestation and decision making with other citizens. So conceived, individual
rights are an aspect of thin communitarianism. Chapter 4 develops this
theory of the individual as a theory of the moral agent, as a normative
personality. Under conditions of normative fragmentation, the moral
individual's social integration best occurs through thin forms of individual identity, thin forms of social solidarity, and thin forms of shared
cultural understandings.

SOLIDARITIES, UNDERSTANDINGS, IDENTITIES

4

This chapter develops, more fully than the preceding ones, a theory of the person, of the social subject, of the particular citizen, as entailed by my general theory of thick and thin forms of normativity. My concern is with the political subject, so I approach the subject in terms of his or her social relationships, in terms of his or her intersubjective behavior. The intersubjectively shared sphere of politics displays three mutually constitutive dimensions when viewed in the categories of Talcott Parsons (1964:6). With these categories he analyzes society as interlocking "systems": the social system, the personality system of the individual, and the cultural system instantiated in the individual's behavior.[1] Drawing on these categories (but in ways that go against the normatively thick Parsonian grain),[2] I shall develop a conception of normatively thin social integration. I do so by describing society, in terms of thin social solidarity; culture, in terms of thin, communally shared understandings; and personality, in terms of the individual's thin social identity.

Social integration concerns the continual coordination of the actions of individuals and groups, toward sustained though perhaps limited cooperation among the integrated. Society integrates the individual into the patterns of its institutions, including the legal, administrative, and economic spheres. With the development of modern liberal democracies, society's institutions become increasingly uncoupled from shared worldviews. Culture integrates the individual into the cognitive patterns of the various groups to which he or she belongs. To be integrated into cultural systems is to be integrated into patterns of shared understandings, such that the individual's beliefs are more or less consistent with those of relevant groups. Personality integrates the individual as an individual, as a unit in itself. To be an integrated personality is to be functionally adequate to the demands on one's behavior made by the social and cultural environments. With the development of modern societies, personalities are less and less swallowed up by cultural traditions and their "motives and ends are [no longer] accessible only under interpretations dependent upon traditions" (Habermas 1987:96)—as the individual gains more and more influence in interpreting his or her own needs, and in revising those interpretations in light of experience, changed circumstances, and new information.

Culture, society, and personality are held together through their carriers' normative behavior; these three elements are constitutive of normative action. Normative behavior is one kind of purposive activity, whose purposes are regulated by values. It can be thick, but it can also be thin.[3] In a normatively heterogeneous population, normatively thin forms of culture, society, and personality better serve social integration than thick forms. This claim resonates with the notion that social integration in modern, heterogeneous societies has a certain "negative" character. Some authors centrally concerned with the historical transition to modernity in the West—including Ferdinand Tönnies (1957), Emil Durkheim (1947), Georg Simmel (1950a, 1950b, 1950c, 1997), and Jürgen Habermas (1984, 1987)—examine modern societies as moral orders from which moral consensus is absent (and in this sense as orders with a "negative" character). Tönnies describes a historical movement in the modern West from holistic and integrated communities (which he calls *Gemeinschaften*) to societies (*Gesellschaften*) that are more like mechanical artifacts. Industrialization and urbanization entail the loss of a holistic system of meaning and the loss of morally consensual connections among people. They also entail the rise of autonomous, rational, individuals who, in the public sphere, are connected with each other only formally, often only fleetingly and "negatively" in the sense, again, of lacking moral consensus. Similarly Durkheim (1947) maps the historical movement from expiatory to restitutory law onto a larger social change from a strongly binding, deeply integrative moral system to a weakly binding, superficially integrative one. Restitutory law is part of a historical process in the course of which social life becomes divided and segmented through a comprehensive division of labor. The erosion of the penal code in favor of restitutory code of law marks the decline of what Durkheim calls a "common conscience," a kind of "social mind" or monolithically shared moral belief system. For both Tönnies and Durkheim, the loss of premodern community is a loss of common orientations, of a binding system of meaning or morality to guide individual behavior in everyday life. In this sense much of modern social life is "negative." They regard these circumstances as threatening to social stability and integration. But Simmel regards them as a peaceable arrangement marked by regularity and predictability (if also by fragility and precariousness), where individuals can nonetheless pursue their goals and seek remedies for injustices. I focus on several of Simmel's (1950b:396) claims. He argues that modern forms of social integration "develop their negative character as the groups, which are their instruments, increase in size. In mass actions, individual motives are frequently so different that their unification is the more easily possible, the more their content is merely negative." Given the ever increasing heterogeneity of individuals, this "negative" character remains as their chief common denominator.

What Simmel describes as social negativity I shall develop as thin normativity, specifically as thin forms of social solidarity, thin forms of shared cultural understandings, and thin forms of individual identity. But unlike Simmel (and Tönnies and Durkheim, for that matter), I do not construct normatively thick community as the traditional, often rural community swept away by the industrial revolution, widespread urbanization, and the rise to dominance of the scientific and technological worldview. In keeping with my usage in earlier chapters, I construct it in terms of associations, interest groups, and shared identities to which a person is committed in sufficient depth to affect his or her identity. Therefore I do not argue as Simmel, Tönnies, and Durkheim might have, had they employed my vocabulary: that in a modern society, the normatively thin personality can be no more than a "shell" when compared with the normatively thick personalities of yesteryear. Rather I argue that the normatively thin personality is a kind of "shell" for interactions in the overall or generalized society, while the personality is organized in depth only in one or the other thick community (or more likely in some combination of thick communities).

Society as Thin Social Solidarity

In complex modern societies, says Simmel (1950b:397), the "variety of persons, interests, events becomes too large to be regulated by a center; the center is left only with a prohibitive function, with the determination of what must not be done under any circumstances, with the restriction of freedom, rather than its direction." Norms that only prohibit some behavior but do not allow or even encourage others are minimal in their function. Thin normativity is a minimalist vision, to be sure, but I argue, quite beyond Simmel, that it is a vision allowing and even encouraging some types of behavior. It does not merely prohibit certain other types. While normatively thin social solidarity prohibits social intolerance (here it is negative or prohibitive), it also supports political and social recognition of differences in worldview, way of life, and cultural identity (here it is affirmative). A thin view is an inclusive one in which a member of a community may live or practice or perpetuate his or her personal thickness, but only in simultaneous support of communal thinness, in ways I describe in later pages. In this sense a normatively thin view opens up a kind of "public reason."[4]

Public reason has a normative content: a political commitment to general fairness. Validity here is rooted in the "publicness" of reason in the political sphere; it entails fairness by embracing as many participants as possible, rather than excluding as many as possible. Public reason "invites in" rather than "shuts out," in this way allowing for heterogeneity (and to allow for heterogeneity is the first step toward fostering tolerance of coexisting differences). This normatively thin understanding of "general fairness" makes participation possible without requiring participants to abandon some of the important and distinctive aspects of themselves. To be sure, general fairness excludes practices that violate the integrity of the normatively thin core of a liberal democratic society, such as racism, sexism, and actions violative of fundamental civil rights of children, spouses, and others. Participants whose identities are tied to such practices must abandon them as aspects of personal thickness incompatible with communal thinness—the support of which is a condition of participation in the public sphere.

Thin norms can allow or encourage certain kinds of behavior also in the sense of social solidarity based on a robust respect for individual autonomy. Simmel (1950b:397–398) identifies the autonomy that accrues to the individual in cosmopolitan societies, yet he does so only in a negative sense: the "larger the group is, usually the more prohibitive and restrictive the kinds of conduct which it must demand of its participants . . . to maintain itself: the positive ties, which connect individual with individual and give the life of the group its real content, must (after all) be given over to these individuals." But Simmel fails to see that, precisely under the conditions he specifies, citizens can be robustly autonomous if they can be self-determining in the sense of taking responsibility for their freely chosen ends. In this way they provide themselves the only standards against which citizens in modern societies can measure themselves—because external standards, such as traditions, religion, and metaphysics, have in modern societies become more or less privatized, valid in this or that thick "concrete community," but without purchase in the normatively thin "generalized community" of the constitutional order or the nation as a whole. The conditions Simmel specifies still allow for a distinctly positive norm where "autonomy" means that citizens can, as John Rawls (1993:32) says of individuals in liberal societies, "regard themselves as self-authenticating sources of valid claims, . . . entitled to make claims on their institutions so as to advance their conceptions of the good (provided these conceptions fall within the range permitted by the public conception of justice)"—provided, in my terms, that these conceptions are normatively thin. "Free" citizens are those who can "claim the right to view their persons as independent from and not identified with any particular . . . conception . . . of final ends. Given their moral power to form, revise, and rationally pursue a conception of the good, their public identity as free persons is not affected by changes over time in their determinate conception" of the good (Rawls 1993:30). Here individual autonomy refers to normative autonomy: where normativity is chosen, not imposed; where it is not beholden to a thick order of ends (where, for example, it requires no common hierarchy of particular ends) or, on the contrary, where the individual has a personally thick normativity but at the same time a normatively thin relationship to society overall (where autonomy is normatively thin with respect to demands from generalized community). Normative autonomy can mean, simultaneously, both thin autonomy (or the individual's autonomy to think and behave in normatively thin ways) and thick autonomy (or the autonomy to exercise thick normativity). For example, the social framework for individual choice may be thin (as a constitutional guarantee of freedom of belief in and practice of religion, as well as freedom from religion) and allow for normatively thick choices, such as conversion to this or that religious faith. Here the individual engages at once both a thin normativity (his or her relation to the liberal, democratic state) and a thick one (his or her personal choices in the public realm, or as public advocacy of a position that could not be a position taken by the normatively thin constitutional state).

Citizens even here may have final ends in common, which is why we properly speak of social solidarity, if only in a thin sense. Citizens may share the same normatively thin political conception of justice even as they differ in their respective, normatively thick worldviews or cultural communities.[5] They may share general political ends (belief in the constitutional order, for example) even as they differ in their thick commitments (disagreeing, for example, on this or that judicial interpretation of this or that constitutional clause). Citizens can have some final ends in common, and share at least some general political ends, if they share a notion of justice not based on any thick worldview.[6] In cases of conflict, thin rules or principles (normatively thin justice, for example) might trump normatively thick ways of life. Thus the thin principle of freedom of religious belief and practice—normatively thin in the sense that it neither prescribes nor prohibits any specific beliefs or practices—cannot extend to religiously mandated polygamy (which, as a specific practice of a particular worldview violative of general fairness, is normatively thick). And the thin principle of equality of men and women, for example, trumps the normatively thick practice of polygamy.

Thin norms can affirm or encourage specific behavior in a further sense, that of social solidarity achieved through procedural agreements that adjudicate among competing proposals of public policy. To determine criteria of choice for choosing among competing proposals, in a way most accommodating of the sensibilities of a liberal democratic society, is to employ normatively thin standards of choice. Proceduralism, as a thin ethic of consent, can generate answers that will affirm, encourage, or entail specific behavior, to which participants may freely consent because they will be able to regard those answers as legitimate (on a normatively thin calculus).

Tolerance, autonomy, and proceduralism constitute different forms of thin normativity; each contributes to a thin sort of social solidarity. Each can help check open conflict when social integration becomes difficult or when social breakdown or violent confrontation threatens. Each can help secure normatively thin agreement or cooperation when thick norms fail to bring about an adequate measure of mutual understanding among participants or when they fail to secure the coordination of everyday social behavior.

Solidarity through Negative Commonalities

Simmel (1950b:397) suggests that the "sharing of, at least, negative characteristics by many small groups may . . . prepare their unity" overall. Less and less personal connectedness among individuals—becoming more and more a citizenry of strangers—encourages the development of subcultures as it discourages shared society-wide understandings, and society-wide overarching agreement. Sociality here is marked by an indifference of many citizens to one another. But it might be marked equally well by mutual tolerance for some of their most significant differences. While everything other than a public order of thick moral consensus, sociality of this sort can nonetheless constitute some degree of social solidarity: the "negative character of the bond that unifies the large group is revealed, above all, in its norms. . . . [O]bligatory rules of *every* sort must be the simpler and the less voluminous . . . , the larger the sphere of their application. There are much fewer rules of international courtesy, for instance, than there are courtesy rules which have to be observed within every smaller circle; or, the larger the states of the German Reich, the briefer . . . are their constitutions. . . . [A]s the size of the group increases, the common features that fuse its members into a social unit become ever fewer. For this reason . . . a smaller minimum of norms can . . . hold together a large group more easily than a small one" (Simmel 1950b:397). As fewer and fewer norms hold together larger and larger populations, the scope for normative difference within society easily increases. Toleration of difference is a necessary (though not sufficient) condition of pluralism. In its allowance for difference, pluralism is normatively thin; that is, a capacity for pluralism is itself a kind of thinness (just as an incapacity for pluralism is a kind of thickness). A society that institutionalizes tolerance and encourages pluralism does not undermine its solidarity or unity, as long as "unity" can be far less than total or complete. Institutionalized tolerance and pluralism can constitute forms of social and political unity within difference—a kind of normatively thin solidarity. With the continuing expansion of global movements of people, ideas, and capital, traditional or mainstream norms are "deprimordialized" as cultures become less provincial and more cosmopolitan, as heterogeneity—even multiculturalism—replaces homogeneity as a criterion for political inclusion, as ethnicity becomes an identity to be embraced rather than a characteristic to be denied.[7]

This general replacement of thick norms by thin ones marks movement in a direction very much opposite to what Hegel thinks necessary for social solidarity among moral communities. Without socialization into some kind of thick, monolithic solidarity, "individual character would be a thin affair. Commitment to morality involves identifying with its demands so thoroughly that we resist taking seriously the possibility of giving them up. A life without them, we feel, would no longer be recognizable as our own" (Larmore 1987:100–101). For Hegel, it is "only as a participant in the public institutions of moral language that I exist as a bearer of moral rationality, and am subjected to the constraints imposed thereby" (Lovibond 1983:86). But his vision of thick normativity cannot capture the potential for solidarity where individuals and groups are more dependent than ever on the economic and other inputs of countless individuals, yet where individuals have less face-to-face interaction, and more personal autonomy from one another, than ever before. Simmel's (1950b:397) notion of social "negativity" captures a thin social solidarity where, in "spite of all positive differences," a "commonness of the merely negative" can make all members "conscious of belonging to a culture [or society] that transcend[s]" its individual members.

Solidarity as Formal and Impersonal

In normatively thick notions of modernity, like Hegel's, the "norms and ends expressed in the public life of a society are the most important ones by which its members define their identity as human beings. For then the institutionalized matrix in which they cannot help living is not felt to be foreign. . . . [B]ecause this substance is sustained by the activity of the citizens, they see it as their work" (Taylor 1975:383). By contrast, public encounters in modern societies are encounters increasingly between and among strangers, often among persons very different from one another, persons unlikely to define their identities largely in terms of public norms that connect individuals in some personal sense. But less personal connectedness need not undermine social integration and cooperation, where it can be a matter of thinly normative social integration. This was the argument of chapter 2. Thin is a sociality that generates benign, mutual disregard among members of a community or society in a sense captured, yet again, by Simmel's (1950b:400–401) notion of social "negativity":

> [T]heir observance is not characteristic of anybody, but their transgression certainly is: the most general norms of a group merely must not be transgressed, whereas (in the measure of their specialization) the par-

ticular norms, that hold smaller groups together, positively give their members character and distinction. On this situation rests the practical utility of social courtesy forms, which are so empty. Even from their most punctilious observance, we must not infer any positive existence of the esteem and devotion they emphasize; but their slightest violation is an unmistakable indication that these feelings do *not* exist. Greeting somebody in the street proves no esteem whatever, but failure to do so conclusively proves the opposite. The forms of courtesy fail as symbols of positive, inner attitudes, but they are most useful in documenting negative ones, since even the slightest omission can radically and definitely alter our relation to a person. And they both fail and succeed to the extent to which they are general and conventional, that is, characteristic of the large circle.

Here, too, Simmel fails to see that a sociality of benign, mutual disregard among members can nonetheless be quite positive in various ways. Under modern conditions of normative diversity and fragmentation, strangers can sustain institutional orders and systems of behavior without sharing many of the same norms or worldviews or behavioral expectations. Even as they pursue their own interests, they can contribute to the satisfaction of some needs and some interests of some of the other interactants, without knowing about them or, where they *do* know about them, without caring about them (or even needing to). Indeed such persons are "more likely to benefit from exchange the more their needs differ" (Hayek 1976:109). Under circumstances of normatively thin sociality, "we all in fact contribute not only to the satisfaction of needs of which we do not know, but sometimes even to the achievement of ends of which we would disapprove if we knew about them. We cannot help this because we do not know for what purposes the goods or services which we supply to others will be used by them" (Hayek 1976:110–111).

Adam Smith's (2000) model of how economic exchange is possible under such conditions is equally a model of how a normatively thin social order easily includes a spontaneous social order, guided in the way individual economic enterprises or agents continually and mutually adjust to one another's market-oriented behavior. In this sense, thinly normative is an order that reconciles different and sometimes competing interests, often in unanticipated micrological ways rather than, say, by centralized administration. F. A. Hayek (1976:110–111) describes thin sociality as more "means-connected" than "ends-connected," restricting coercion to the "observance of the negative rules of just conduct" and making possible the "integration into a peaceful order of individuals and groups which pursue different ends." He sketches a viable form of social solidarity, which, in its normative thinness, is much more formal, much less personal, than thicker forms.

Culture as Shared, Thin Understandings

With Clifford Geertz (1973:14) we might define "culture" as "interworked systems of construable signs," as socially institutionalized contexts of symbols in terms of which members coherently describe social events, behavior, institutions, and processes. Parsons (1964:327), too, speaks to this practical, behavior-guiding function of culture, where he defines culture as "patterned or ordered systems of symbols which are objects of the orientation of action." Whereas Geertz stresses how culture contributes to the individual's self-understanding (as well as to his or her understanding of others), Parsons emphasizes how culture constitutes a powerful means of regulating behavior. Each accents a different aspect of the same phenomenon; for both, culture connects ideas and behavior, symbols and action. As a system of cognitive symbols, culture is a system of beliefs. Cognitive systems motivate behavior in the social sphere. Members of the same culture know how to behave toward one another because they share elements of the same culture, because they perceive the same—or similar—patterns: beliefs motivate, and shared beliefs motivate all the more.[8] In a secular society, even citizens of religious faith do not expect public policy to be based on theology; here they have the same behavioral expectations as atheists.

Culture refers also to the reproduction, transmission, and renewal of shared knowledge within a society, in the form of worldviews, common beliefs, and mutual understanding. By communicating shared knowledge, culture reproduces it; in secular polities even parochial schools socialize their pupils to orient themselves in a secular society. In this sense communication is a cultural act: it is possible only through cultural media; it regulates by means of cultural elements; it makes possible the sharing of meanings, and it contributes to the stabilization of meanings. Without such stability individuals would lack the "complementarity of expectations" (Parsons 1964:327) among individuals, without which social integration would be impossible.

The Normativity of Culture

In cultural terms, normativity expresses shared meanings that render some interpretations plausible to this group or community yet implausible to that one. Thus racists will find legal prohibitions of "miscegenation" compatible with constitutional guarantees of legal equality among citizens, whereas antiracists will find them incompatible; or liberals are more likely than conservatives to find programs of affirmative action consistent with legal prohibitions of racial discrimination, whereas conservatives are more likely than liberals to find them incompatible. For this or that particular group, a horizon of plausible interpretations renders a situation "decidable" with specific, practical, and local reference to a given set of rules. For this or that particular group, a horizon of plausible interpretations frames situations requiring decision in ways that settled rules can be applied to decide them — much in the way an anthropologist attempts to "set local view in local contexts" or a jurist to "set instant cases in determinate frames" (Geertz 1983:215). Rendering a dispute or question "decidable" is a normative exercise, a means to answering the question: in this particular situation, what ought members of the collectivity believe, how ought they behave? In this sense culture is a major source for the individual's normative orientation, providing standards for behavior and belief. Norms motivate behavior; culture provides norms, selectively orienting the individual's behavior, selectively patterning social order. A culture that includes both racist and antiracist communities, or (to use a very different example) comprises political liberals and political conservatives alike, is possible because it somehow accommodates the chronic tension between such communities. Thus a political culture might provide competing communities freedom to believe and (within limits) to practice their respective norms, as long as each respects the right of the others to exercise the same freedom.

This normative aspect of behavior returns us to the distinction between thick and thin norms. Participants likely understand their everyday circumstances more in the flesh-and-blood terms of thick normativity than in the distanced, bloodless terms of thinness. Observers and participants alike can offer thin descriptions, just as the depiction a participating lawyer might give of a constitutional crisis would differ from the historian's. Most of what is available to a participant's perspective is also available to an observer's. In this sense Bernard Williams (1995:209) claims that the "unfortunate inhabitants of the previously communist world . . . were no doubt taking part in an ethical experiment, among other things, though the description of it and of its results would certainly differ between different points of view on it." Perhaps few of those participants would ever describe themselves as having taken part in an "ethical experiment," a perspective more easily attained by an emotionally detached, outside observer. And even participants who would not so describe themselves, but who nonetheless would recognize the description as apt, would be opening themselves to the plausibility (for some people) of a description they nonetheless could never adopt as their own. Accessibility by the outside observer—its "capturability" in terms of normatively thin structure—might end where the participant's "interiority" begins: within his or her subjective state of being, where outsiders at best can attain only partial access (and, from a Freudian standpoint, where even the participant often has less than complete access).

Thin Culture Whose Binding Norms Are Simple and Few

Let the term "ethics of principle" refer to a universal claim to validity (as everything other than merely local convention). Let the term "ethics of communal or intimate custom" refer to a relative validity, as in specifically Hopi ethics, in distinction to ethics as such. This distinction does not extend to one between judgmental and nonjudgmental standpoints: ethics of principle and ethics of custom are both judgmental. One no less than the other usually presumes both the superior validity and the prescriptiveness of the rules it announces, whether as rights or obligations, injunctions or prohibitions. Each society has one or more ethics of custom, binding only on those persons who accept them, as well as an ethics of principle, binding even on those persons who reject it.[9]

By this measure the participants' (normatively thick) perspective is more a matter of customary ethics; the outsiders' (normatively thin) perspective, more a matter of principled ethics. In addition to their custom-based viewpoint, of course, the participants may well assume a principled point of view. But then they would be distancing themselves from that particular community in the direction of the larger society (what in chapter 3 I describe as "generalized community"), which they might be disinclined to do, at least on a permanent basis (unless of course they are deeply disaffected from the relevant community). Correspondingly, the observers might well assume, in addition to their principled standpoint, a custom-based point of view—but then they would be transforming themselves from outsiders to insiders. "Going native" might well be a long-term goal of many immigrants (and a short-term goal of some cultural anthropologists), but for most observers it is no goal at all. Thus our best candidates for custom-based viewpoints are local; they orient the self-understandings of a given community. Often incommensurable with the self-understandings of other communities, they are a kind of "local knowledge" (Geertz 1983) not applicable or generalizable across historical and cultural differences.

In liberal cosmopolitan societies today, thick norms are less generalizable than thin ones. While prohibitions of murder, slavery, or theft are generalizable even though thick, specifically *religious* norms (for example) cannot be imposed on everyone in societies based on secular constitutionalism, political liberalism, and a market economy—such that specifically religious injunctions against murder, slavery, or theft are generalizable only if reformulated in secular terms. But thin normativity allows (sometimes even serves) the multiplicity of incommensurable ends within a heterogeneous population; this is *why* thin normativity is generalizable. Socially generalizable normativity is what Hegel (1996) captures in the term *Moralität*, a form of obligation to which the individual is subject, not in virtue of belonging to a particular community but simply in his or her capacity as a rational agent considered in the abstract. It corresponds to what I have called an "ethics of principle." *Moralität* is normatively thin, whereas thick is what Hegel calls *Sittlichkeit* (the particular ethics embedded in a specific ethos), what I've termed an "ethics of intimate or communal custom." In liberal, secular, democratic societies, *Moralität*, not *Sittlichkeit*, is generalizable.

Normative Minimalism in Shared Agreements

Modern societies must cope with chronic disagreement among competing groups over an array of normative issues. Disagreement is a continuous, even "normal," situation. Consider, for example, the intimate sphere of associational life, a sphere today increasingly diverse, perhaps more fragile, and certainly less fixed, in part because of increased legal, political, and economic equality of the sexes; changes in (as well as challenges to) gender roles; and increased social acceptability

(though hardly uncontested) of homosexuality and consensual sex between unmarried adults. These developments have occurred within,
not outside or in contravention of, a context of rules regulating interaction, such as legal provisions forbidding force, protecting privacy,
and recognizing the decisional autonomy and responsibility of adults.
This normatively thin context prescribes neither a single form of intimacy nor diverse forms of intimacy; like all social conventions, it is
open to interpretation and reinterpretation, challenge and revision.
Thus laws that refer to "marriage" may refer to a union between a
man and a woman, but in some liberal democratic cultures have been
construed to refer to a union between two men or two women; laws
that refer to "family" may refer to the nuclear family, but in some liberal democracies have come to refer to any number of alternative arrangements (such as single-parent households, grandparents raising
grandchildren, or adoptions by homosexual couples). Social rules are
deeply interpretive, that is, modifiable by interpretation, where a new
or revised interpretation may have distinct consequences for corresponding institutional arrangements (such as who qualifies for govern-
mentally subsidized housing for low-income "families" or who may
exercise legal, medical, and financial decisions on behalf of a severely
incapacitated "spouse"). Where social rules possess this fluid quality,
disagreements within the community or society are inevitable.

But in those limited cases where the organizing principle of social
integration can only be reciprocity rather than normative agreement,
there reciprocity might provide a thin alternative to disagreement. A
principle of reciprocity can reconcile the claims of different normative
ends by a process benefiting all participants, but only if "benefit" is
understood in normatively thin terms. Consider, for example, agreement "solely on the basis of a principle of reciprocity through which
the opportunities of any person are likely to be greater than they would
otherwise be" (Hayek 1976:113). Even here disagreement will occur, but
in a social and political context free of a compulsion to agree on thick
norms. Here normative dissent (or simply disagreement on normative
issues, or on the normative dimensions of an issue) need not endanger
social stability, and "approval and censure [need not] depend on the
concrete ends which particular actions serve" (Hayek 1976:111), within
certain limits (for example, as long as those ends are not illegal).

Of course, in all societies some measure of agreement is always necessary for social integration. Under modern circumstances of norma-

tive heterogeneity, agreement is possible even where it must be minimal. Contending groups can agree to be bound by the rule of law—and
can agree to the legitimacy of being so bound—even where one or more
of the groups regard the particular law in contention to be misguided
or even unconstitutional. Simmel (1950b:399–400) offers one form of
minimalism as a basis sufficient for mutual understanding, "without
which human society could not exist at all," and which "rests on a
small number of generally agreed-on norms, which we call the norms
of logic—although, of course, not everybody is conscious of them in
their abstractness. They constitute the minimum of what must be acknowledged by all who want, in any way, to communicate with one
another. On them rests the briefest agreement between strangers and
the common daily life of the closest persons." Thus "all who want . . . to
communicate with one another" must minimally agree to observe the
same rules of grammar, to employ words in the same or similar ways,
and so forth. But doing so implies nothing about the *content* of the communication. Beyond Simmel I would argue that minimalist agreement
can be adequate to the tasks of social integration in cosmopolitan societies where it provides a common normative core. As a set of shared
beliefs linking social institutions and the rules governing individual behavior, some kind of common core is fundamentally necessary to any
society—and all the more so to complex, heterogeneous ones, where
fewer rather than more beliefs are shared.

By contrast, a normatively thick core would link social institutions
directly to some conception of the overriding goals of human life,
where these goals define as well as justify social institutions. For example, the legal system of a theocratic state, such as Iran or the Vatican,
is concerned in part with the salvation of the citizen's soul. If the link
between social institutions and normative goals were weak or called
into question, shared beliefs might lose their force or coherence. Institutions might lose legitimacy as the populace became alienated from
them and, in its behavior, less and less guided by them. Thick core differs from thin in the kinds of shared meanings that constitute it. A
thicker core might be characterized by shared norms of family (defined
more narrowly than broadly), community (defined more homogene-
ously than diversely), and religion (fewer rather than more religions,
more mainstream rather than more marginal ones). Where the core
is thicker, socially integrated individuals share more homogeneous attitudes. A thick core can be "amplified" by traditional norms, say, by

theologically or metaphysically informed conceptions of justice such as Roman Catholic natural law[10] (perhaps emphasizing the individual's responsibility to the group), as distinct from secular or nonmetaphysical conceptions stressing individual rights and individual autonomy. A thick core is less receptive than a thin one to the demands of recognizing various social differences; it is less receptive to the "politics of recognition" and to group-differentiated claims to rights. A thick core cannot easily accommodate the increased differentiation of political, ethnic, religious, and other groups (and their legal and social recognition) so typical of modern societies. A thick core will find legal and social recognition of group-differentiated claims to certain rights inadequate to the task of creating social solidarity within the populace, building social trust, and institutionalizing norms generalizable to the entire society, thereby guiding the behavior of elites and ordinary people alike.

A thin core, by contrast, allows individuals greater flexibility in terms of their attachments to others and especially to institutions, because it binds the individual less tightly to any one community or institution. Where someone's ties are looser rather than tighter, his or her membership or participation does not depend on significant or continuous agreement with other members. Where disagreement does not entail exclusion from the group, the individual has greater freedom to disagree with others in the group. And yet disagreement between or among groups needn't preclude the circulation of individuals, ideas, interests, and goods among groups. Nor need cooperation depend on strong agreement; weaker forms of agreement often suffice, because the presence of significant disagreement is less fatal to cooperation where the ties that bind are configured more loosely than tightly. Where communication and exchange among groups or communities is more equal than unequal, different communities or groups may still feel bound by some thin solidarity among communities (for example, by the thin solidarity of mutual tolerance). After all, common bonds are always possible among individuals, groups, or communities where social solidarity does not require a common way of life or a collective normative consciousness. Common bonds are not necessarily less possible under circumstances of thin normativity; they are possible differently.[11]

When in these ways the social core is thin, member communities are not bounded as tightly as in thicker cores. The normative thickness

of this or that concrete community now becomes a thickness modified by ambient thinness: a normative thickness, but a "normatively
open" thickness. The flow of people, beliefs, information, labor, capital, and culture renders boundaries among groups and among institutions more permeable: "Social relationships can be established that
transcend the boundaries of specific organizations or communities,
and social norms facilitate such relationships. In a changing or uncertain social environment, porousness is an adaptive response that encourages looser and more functionally specific relationships" (Wuthnow 1999:28). Relationships among individuals, among communities,
and among institutions may be more temporary than before, perhaps
more brittle, but also more flexible because now requiring fewer forms
of face-to-face interaction (*among individuals:* think of shopping on
the World Wide Web, or neighborhoods composed of families who
are strangers to one another; *within communities:* consider organizations such as the National Rifle Association or the Sierra Club, whose
many members are dispersed across a large nation and who may meet
or know only a small percentage of their fellow members; *between
organizations:* think of videoconferencing and other forms of virtual
meetings). Social intercourse is atomized but also reconstituted over
long distances, on temporary bases, in flexible ways. In the economic
sphere, for example, smaller firms may be more flexible than larger
ones in adopting new technologies and in training and retraining employees with ever newer skills to match rapidly changing technological and economic environments.[12] The "normative porosity" of such
firms lies in their structural capacity (much greater than in the case
of more traditional firms, such as General Motors or the Boeing Company) to redefine themselves in multiple ways. Their porosity is their
openness to external influences and their structural capacity for self-
transformation in intelligent response to their changing environment.

Permeable boundaries, temporary relationships between people and
among institutions, and communities not bound together tightly, are
more likely to facilitate rather than discourage social diversity. Thin
principles can hold together a diverse society if they obtain for all,
in the sense of general fairness I introduced earlier: principles such
as equality for different ways of life (and opposition to a hierarchy
of acceptability of different ways of life), and principles such as the
right of each to find a presence in the wider society. In the presence of
such principles, porosity and diversity needn't spell social breakdown,

or moral decline, or the dissolution of modernity into postmodernity. They could spell—under normatively thin conditions—new forms of inclusiveness, new understandings of citizenship, and new ways of practicing democratic politics. Normative distinctions among communities can separate each community off from the other. But under thin conditions they needn't do so, because porous boundaries allow for interconnections configured more loosely than possible in a more normatively homogenous society. Increasingly porous communities and institutions may well entail greater individual freedom, greater freedom of choice among communities, greater freedom of movement between communities, more choice in normativities for oneself or one's family or other groups, and wider choices in forms of civic involvement.[13]

This is not to say that social connectedness and diversity are mutually exclusive; indeed, they may well coexist. To be sure, diversity and difference can pose significant problems for social integration where they discourage people from participating in (even caring about) civic issues, social responsibilities, national interests, or problems of the wider community (let alone of other communities). Diversity and difference can render agreement on public issues difficult if not impossible, or possible only in divisive ways, as in single-issue campaigns, or identity politics in the form of "us" against "them." Yet civil society is also possible under conditions of diversity and difference, as I argue throughout this book.

Personality as Thin Identity

Personality is a system of relations between a person and his or her social environment. These relations directly constitute the personality (Parsons 1964:17). In a normatively heterogeneous social environment, personalities are not integrated in the cultural system completely or identically. Nothing motivates all individuals toward complete conformity with cultural standards in the relevant social system because, says Simmel (1950b:399), the "more general the norm and the larger the group in which it prevails, the less does the *observance* of the norm characterize the individual and the less important is it for him— whereas its *violation*, on the whole, has consequences which are especially grave, which single out the individual from his group." Consider logic: it provides us "no positive possession at all: it is only a norm against which we must not sin—while we derive no distinction, no specific good or quality, from its observance" (Simmel 1950b:400), in the sense that it is a means to an end (such as successful communication) but hardly an end in itself (correct grammar is hardly the goal of linguistic communication, but a sine qua non of minimally successful communication nonetheless).

Integrated individuals are not completely conformist for other reasons as well. Social relations are not often structured as uniform rules, uniform for an entire group of individuals. Even when they are, they do not pattern "each of the different personalities in the same way" (Parsons 1964:17–18). Each person is integrated into a personality system in some important respects different from the personality systems of all other individuals. Consequently his or her relations with the social environment differ to some extent from those of other persons (shy people unsure of themselves will have a different relationship to public speaking than self-confident, gregarious people; shy people socialized to deny this aspect of themselves will have still another relationship to public speaking than shy people socialized to embrace their feelings). Even the most uniform structure of any given social role does not swallow up the individual's personality, because the roles the individual plays do not constitute the personality's characteristics. Each individual has a somewhat unique relationship to any given role; each performs the role in ways that may reflect some of his or her uniqueness. Hence at the level of personality, the individual's social integration can only be incomplete and partial. The "fundamental functional imperatives both of personalities and of social systems" do not lead to some "completely pattern-consistent cultural system" (Parsons 1964:16), to complete conformity of the individual with the standards of his or her social and cultural environment. Social integration is always something of a compromise between imperatives of the unique personality (itself formed by accepting some social and cultural imperatives) and imperatives of the society in which it moves.

The Social Constructedness of Thin Identity

Members of modern, cosmopolitan societies are unlikely to articulate their identities in essentialist or primordial fashion (they are unlikely to articulate them as simply given, as unchanging, as beyond challenge). The simultaneity in the same society of multiple ways of life, of diverse worldviews, generates simultaneity of different identities. Each individual is a composite bundle of identities. Some concern his or her social statuses and roles; some concern ways in which the individual both supports and is supported by other individuals. A housewife's identity may include that of spouse, daughter, sister, and mother; citizen, member of a parish, allegiance to a political party; an individual of distinct aesthetic tastes and erotic preferences; certain biographical experiences and ascriptive characteristics such as race, ethnicity, age, and sex. Her identity may be tied directly to her daily activities in the house, or she may identify herself precisely in rejection of those activities. She may identify both in terms of her heritage, or in terms of her acquired citizenship, or in terms of both—and so on.

Such differentiation of identities necessarily changes the ways in which modern societies construct identity. Understandings that are more essentialist—the notion that certain identities are fixed and immutable, such as cultural belonging, political privilege, but even the social meanings of ascribed characteristics like race or gender—give way to more constructivist understandings: the notion that identities are socially constructed and differently constructable according to different political, cultural, or economic commitments and circumstances. Identity so conceived is fluid, itself a negotiable and contestable variable in social conflicts and social change, open to redefinition by outside forces (think of the ways in which the identity of "housewife" has changed following the integration of women into the labor force, or in light of the women's movement in the 1920s or again in the 1960s). Under these conditions, identities personal, collective, cultural, and political may be discrete (though their unique combination in each person defines the personality, and interpenetrate one another to some extent; and where they don't, the person likely is conflicted or even pathological). But these identities are discrete only partially and temporarily, with none perpetually beyond challenge or influence. And the differences against which any identity articulates itself are themselves open to challenge and redescription.

The constructivist view is more sensitive to linkages between identity and contingent social forces (such as changes in the economy, politics, technology and science, changes through cultural movements, and changes in understandings of relevant histories). The constructivist view is more sensitive than essentialist claims to the political creation of new identities, and to the elision (sometimes dissolution) of established ones. It is sensitive to the creation of coherence out of the multiplicity of factors from which any given identity is constructed. Social constructivism is one more form of thin normativity. Under circumstances of normative pluralism and fragmentation, identity cannot depend on thick moral agreement, or on the thick authority of, say, age-old institutions (such as patriarchy) or sacred texts (like those of Confucianism or Judaism). To be sure, cosmopolitan societies still allow for identity to be foisted upon a group (where, for example, dominant groups have the power to define subordinate ones). But liberal democratic culture provides scope for individuals to influence their identity, to construct it (in part) in terms of their self-understanding (just as North American descendants of slaves ultimately rejected the deeply racist identity of "nigger" for the identity of "black"—which would seem no more or less racist than the "white" in terms of which the majority describes itself—or "African American," following the logic of "French Canadian" or "Japanese American"). Normatively thin identities may well be self-consciously chosen, whereas normatively thick ones generally are not. In this case the thin one is more intentional, less automatic, less a matter of "second nature."[14] Instead, identity is more an artifact, more an ongoing achievement of participants, than simply a given. "Thin" then refers to a more "political" conception of identity, "political" in the sense of social cooperation established only by an undertaking among the participants themselves, "in view of what they regard as their reciprocal advantage" (Rawls 1993:97). Groups in thin communities that cohere in terms of a distinct identity thereby achieve a certain sharedness (rather than having it forced upon them, as in the case of outcasts, slaves, or other socially marginalized groups). In the positive sense of the self-determination of groups under liberal democratic circumstances, "only by affirming a constructivist conception" can citizens "expect to find principles that all can accept" (ibid.) as a social core. A constructivist conception needn't violate the integrity of participants' respective thick commitments and viewpoints, as long as these are not imposed on the social core, and as long as one normatively thick community doesn't impose its commitments and beliefs on another. The various thick communities enjoy self-determination in a liberal democratic culture by affirming a constructed social core embodying principles all citizens can accept precisely because these principles are normatively thin. In this way citizens and communities of different normative convictions can nonetheless share a "political life on terms acceptable to others as free and equals" (Rawls 1993:98).

In this way political identities such as opposition to sexual or racial discrimination (identities organized around ideas of social equality) each orient the self-identifying individual's thought and behavior in many aspects of daily life. This orientation will be common to members of that particular group but likely not to other groups. Each of these identities contains within itself more or less organized ways of seeing and explaining the world. Feminism often uses notions of patriarchy as an explanatory logic for patterns of history and experience (as well as for patterns in current economic and social organization). Similarly, notions of racism provide a cognitively and behaviorally orienting explanatory logic for advancing certain civil rights legislation. The respective explanatory logics in each of these cases provides a basis for shared identity and common understandings. Even though constructed rather than given, these bases can be highly normative and socially integrative. The political activity of "consciousness raising" is an example of coupling an (affective) sharing of experience with a (discursive) interpretive schema, toward sustaining the identities and the normatively thick communities built around them—communities that integrate daily experience with moral values and deeper social meaning. These thick communities provide the social "glue" of shared morality, common experience, and joint purpose. Social integration at the level of these various thick communities differs from their normatively thin integration into a generalized community such as the constitutional order. While both levels of social integration orient members toward the political, in modern democracies the political is organized predominantly around a public sphere of disputation, contention, controversy, but sometimes also compromise, persuasive argument, even agreement. Insofar as thick communities have widely divergent, even competing interpretations of social structures, sources of oppression, interpretations of needs, and tactics of political engagement, an agonistic public sphere can be socially integrative only if organized along normatively thin ideas, ideals, and values valid for all of its constituent thick communities. Only then can the thin generalized community be legitimate in the eyes of each of the various thick communities.

In this sense legal individualism—understood in the normatively thin ways of chapter 3—provided the twentieth century's civil rights and women's movements an important point of agreement between these respective thick communities and the thin generalized community from which they sought legal and social recognition, social justice, and progressive political change. A normatively thin point of agreement can be valid for the worldviews and political orientation of these various social movements only if it is not totally alien to members of other communities within the same society. Here it provided a basis for at least some understanding, and for at least some support, of the groups' political claims. The thinness of the ideal of legal individualism made it potentially available to a wide variety of different thick communities that could still share this ideal. The communities' orienting logic (such as opposition to racial or sexual discrimination or oppression) is normatively thick in that it grounds the ideal in specific social sites and ties it to actual experience. But the normative thinness of the ideal of legal individualism, constructed in normatively thin ways, allows the ideal to connect with, and serve the goals of, these various thick logics.[15]

The mediation of various thick logics through thin norms stands at the heart of my efforts in part 1 of this book. Chapter 2 sought the mediation of individuals, thickly committed in this or that way, through a normatively thin form of social integration. Chapter 3 sought the mediation of communities defined in thick terms, through a generalized community conceived in thin terms. And this chapter argued for a normatively thin personality at the level of generalized community, but a personality organized in depth in one or more thick communities, able to live peaceably among yet more thick communities, able to cope with the various thick logics within society, culture, and personality. These chapters urge social integration that can accommodate normative difference by distinguishing thick and thin norms and then pursuing integration through thin norms as much as possible. Part 2 continues this analysis of social integration but focuses it more narrowly on several different concrete communities, each a forum for political judgment, each a venue for an agonistic public sphere. Chapter 5 extends the notion of thin normativity to political judgment in coping with indeterminate legal norms. Chapter 6 develops a thin approach to political judgment between competing systems of cultural values. Chapter 7 generates a thin critique of ideology, as a critique of thick judgment by thin.

PART II

Thick

Moralities,

Thin Politics

in Political

Judgment

POLITICAL JUDGMENT ABOUT INDETERMINATE LEGAL NORMS

5

Part 1 developed and defended the basic paradigm of this book: normatively thin approaches to problems of social integration and everyday politics generated by the moral diversity of late-modern societies. Each of the chapters of part 2 applies this model to a specific set of concrete problems: law (chapter 5), cultural values (chapter 6), and systematic forms of oppression (chapter 7). The three chapters all argue that persuasion and understanding within normatively fragmented societies, as well as across diverse communities, is possible on the basis of thin politics. This chapter in particular shows how thin politics, because it invokes only thin norms, can make agreement possible on contested meanings of indeterminate legal norms. Indeterminacy in the meaning and application of norms characterizes law as such, even if not all aspects of law in all instances. Among issues often indeterminate and therefore open to judicial manipulation are standing, standards of review and the demands of procedural due process. Proportionately few laws or other legal norms are deeply problematic because indeterminate, but those that *are* tend to be ones of significant social and political consequence, concerning fundamental normative issues affecting many people. In addition, some norms may be unproblematic simply because the political convictions they presuppose are so unchallenged as to be unrecognizable as such. Determinate laws or legal norms are usually those in which formal legal training can provide a unique solution to legal questions, where judges and others can interpret and apply norms unproblematically.

This chapter argues that a judge who interprets and applies indeterminate legal norms does not comply with them in the sense of preserving them intact; sometimes she or he "complies" with norms by manipulating them. Sometimes a judge has no alternative but to alter them because some norms often can be interpreted and applied in no other way. This is not to say we need to reject all norm-based explanations of how a normative order constrains or generates social behavior.

Rather, individuals in legal and other institutional settings often do not employ norms as practical guides to behavior simply by applying them in any straightforward or unproblematic way.

Some approaches in contemporary jurisprudence claim as much: that in important respects laws and other legal norms cannot be stable, consistent, or unchanging with regard to what particular norms mean and how they should be applied. H. L. A. Hart (1961:123), for example, asserts that "particular fact situations do not await us already marked off from each other, and labeled as instances of the general [norm], the application of which is in question; nor can the [norm] itself step forward to claim its own instances." Jurisprudence of this sort acknowledges that meaning and application are context-dependent. Context-dependent norms are socially constructed in a strong sense: in any given instance, meaning and application can only be ad hoc. Yet I shall argue that even a contextualizing jurisprudence fails to grasp how people actually use many legal norms in an indeterminate world. I shall then offer an alternative approach, a normatively thin approach, better suited to the task of analyzing supposedly norm-governed behavior particularly in legal contexts.

To construct this normatively thin approach I draw on a field as European as the social phenomenology of Edmund Husserl (1977) and as American as the founding generation of pragmatists (including George Herbert Mead, on whom I drew in chapter 3 and to whom I shall return in chapter 7). Both deemphasize behavior-influencing social structures external to the individual and focus instead on how the fragile interaction of individuals—observable and recurring behavior, voluntary but not necessarily conscious—contributes to the generation of social order (such as institutions, mundane practices, normative customs, and cultural expectations). The sociologist Harold Garfinkel coined the term (and the field) of ethnomethodology in the 1960s. It seeks the "methodology" or patterned action of mundane practices and routines of interacting individuals in their everyday behavior. It rejects the conviction of classical Weberian and Durkheimian theory, as well as more contemporary Parsonian theory, that patterned social behavior derives principally from individuals' internalizing preexisting or received norms.

To apply a norm we often must draw on knowledge or competence or interpretations not contained in the norm itself. In this sense norms do not specify behaviors, at least adequately for realizing the norm's goal. Such indeterminate norms cannot be norms in the strong sense of guiding determinate behavior. Hence while norm-guided behavior generates aspects of social order, we cannot explain that generation in normatively thick terms (as Weber, Durkheim, and Parsons contend) but rather in terms of whatever it is we draw on, in using a norm, that is beyond or outside that norm. I shall argue that using a norm by going beyond or outside it is not a nonnormative or antinormative approach but rather a normatively thin one. In Melvin Pollner's (1991:371) words, "[Norm] usage suggests complex, tacit processes in both everyday and scientific domains. More generally, it suggests a 'seen but unnoticed' (Garfinkel 1967) substructure of assumptions and practices implicit in the organization of social action." The generation and maintenance of social order is not available in purely psychological categories of internalization (any more than it can be found in purely mechanical categories of norm application free of all interpretive judgments). Individuals make sense of the world by generating and maintaining it *as* "sense-making," that is, as patterned, orderly, and familiar: they are "social phenomena" (Watson 1994:407). Therefore ethnomethodology is not hermeneutics or any other highly interpretive undertaking: "Enacted local practices are not texts which symbolize 'meanings' or events" (Garfinkel 1996:8).

We "stretch" a norm to fit the particular situation, or reconstruct relevant events of a situation to fit the norm's criteria, or reinterpret the situation to fit a norm, or ignore features and events of a situation that contradict a norm so as to sustain the norm's applicability (Rhoads 1991:192–193). Such behavior reflects a norm's "indexicality": the "rational properties of indexical expressions and other practical actions [are] contingent ongoing accomplishments or organized artful practices of everyday life" (Garfinkel 1967:11). Individuals treat new phenomena as "indexes" or markers for phenomena already recognized. Groups or communities of individuals render the unfamiliar familiar by relating what they newly encounter to what they already know. What they already know provides an index in terms of which they explain new objects or experiences to themselves and others. These accounts themselves constitute the context or setting or condition they purport to be describing, and, of course, they thereby describe the very context they are in fact constituting. The account itself constitutes the setting, that is, the individual subjectively reconstructs an objective condition: "accounts and the setting they describe mutually elaborate and modify each other in a back and forth process" (Watson 1994:413–414). We modify norms unconsciously to render them applicable to contingency and experience. We do so in the naive attitude that norms are guiding our behavior, when in fact our behavior is guiding our use of norms. In turn, those norms define that behavior, thus allowing us to maintain a naive attitude toward those norms, believing that we are simply applying them when in fact we are changing them. Changing norms so as to render them usable is a normatively thin method, an "ethnomethod" (Pollner 1991:371) in which we "disattend" the norm, that is, make it determinate rather than being defeated by its indeterminacy.

I shall extend an ethnomethodological perspective from its application so far—namely, only to particular instances of *some* kinds of legal behavior—to law as a conceptual whole, that is, to jurisprudence. I sketch ways in which an ethnomethodological approach is unique (above all in its normative thinness) and offers insights otherwise unavailable even to contextualizing jurisprudence.[1] This list is illustrative, not exhaustive.

As a foil, I shall first provide a sampling of claims from various types of "conventional jurisprudence." The term refers to a variety of competing approaches, all of which, in ways peculiar to each and in contrast to methods of common law, claim to preclude, escape, or overcome normative or epistemic indeterminacy, such as the following claims:

(1) *The meaning and application of legal norms can be noncontingent.* Natural law, for example, maintains that however mutable it may be, positive law, if sound, derives ultimately from eternal principles that are valid because reasonable, not because of the procedural correctness of their enactment (Finnis 1993:351).

(2) *A legal system can specify unambiguously the conditions under which a norm is a member of that system.* For example, Hart's (1961:100) "rule of recognition" provides "authoritative criteria for identifying primary rules of obligation" with respect to text, legislation, custom, and judicial precedent.

(3) *Legal norms may be applied in purely formal ways.* The American constitutional document itself contains few substantive values and leaves the embracing or rejecting of all other values largely to the political process. Its chief concern is "procedural fairness in the resolution of individual disputes" and ensuring, through procedure, "broad

participation in the processes and distributions of government" (Ely 1980:87).

(4) *The meaning of a legal norm can claim exclusive validity just as it can imply one and only one kind of behavior.* For example, lawyers consider all laws to be equally valid and equally binding (legal validity and legal obligation exist absolutely or not at all, certainly not in varying degrees), and legal obligations to neither overlap nor conflict with each other (Finnis 1993:309, 311).

(5) *Legal norms capture definite, finite, and in principle unambiguously identifiable meanings, namely, the putative self-understanding of the relevant legislators (or of the entire generation) at the time of legislation.* Justice Antonin Scalia's (1989:864) "originalism" claims to provide the legitimate criterion, quite beyond the particular personal values of the authoritative interpreters, by which to determine the proper meaning and application of legal norms.

(6) *(At least some) legal norms can be interpreted properly and adequately in ways that are entirely principled and not ad hoc.* Thus Justice Hugo Black interpreted the First Amendment clause prohibiting legislation abridging free expression to mean complete and absolute nonintervention by the government. Or Justice William Brennan thus claimed that the same amendment implicitly rejects obscenity on the grounds that obscenity lacks any redeeming social value.[2]

(7) *Legal norms can be animated by a certain moral evolutionism, from which they may draw their (correspondingly evolving) meaning.* Thus Chief Justice Earl Warren claimed that the Eighth Amendment derives its meaning "from the evolving standards of decency that mark the progress of a maturing society."[3]

(8) *A procedural approach to systems of legal norms can lead to impartial decisions in cases governed by those norms.* We can determine the constitutionality of the distribution of social goods on the basis not of actual results of the distribution but of its procedural correctness (Ely 1980:136).

(9) *Possible are systems of legal norms that contain only consistent premises, that is, for any norm and resulting conclusion, one cannot find a counternorm justifying a contrary conclusion.* Thus the rule of law exists only insofar as the legal system is free of norms that are incoherent or preclude compliance, and insofar as legal authorities apply the norms consistently and according to what John Finnis (1993:270–271) calls their "tenor."

Insights of a Normatively Thin Approach Unavailable to Conventional Jurisprudence

Competence, Not Correctness

Conventional jurisprudence distinguishes between the "correct" and "incorrect" application of norms, whereas an ethnomethodologically informed thin approach focuses on the "competent" use of norms. To distinguish between "correct" and "incorrect" is to presuppose a standard that holds across cases of correct norm application. But if norm application is ad hoc, as it must be when it is indeterminate, then each case of application must have its own, unique standard of correctness. A thin approach, by emphasizing competence instead of correctness in norm usage, doesn't need a standard that can't be defended anyway— namely, one that holds across different cases of norm application.

"Competence" refers to dexterity in action where norms cannot prescribe behavior. In a credentialing program for elementary school teaching, for example, Richard Hilbert (1981) found that the competence of the competent teacher presupposed knowledge quite beyond the teacher's job description and role prescription. To understand and employ these prescriptions competently entailed knowing that, and how, they were inadequate guides to practice, and how to modify and supplement them to render them adequate, even how to abandon their original meanings where competent practice demanded as much. Competent teaching differs from following norms: it involves the ability to "continually modify 'plans,'" to do so within "unknowable and . . . unpredictable situational contingencies," and to "convince relevant others that none of this is being done at random" (Hilbert 1981:216).

This notion of competence, rather than "correctness," finds support beyond ethnomethodology in Stanley Fish (1993), according to whom a legal professional arguing a case or drafting an opinion presupposes specific understandings of the relevant law and its terms and applications. Different professionals may begin from different presuppositions and therefore reach correspondingly different results—indeed, results that are "political" in the realistic sense that a choice had to be made under circumstances of disagreement, where even the criteria of choice were disputed. Such outcomes are normal, unavoidable, and professionally acceptable inasmuch as the parties involved share the overriding goal of determining the legally correct answer, whereby the "difference between reaching political conclusions and beginning with political intentions is that if you are doing the second, you are not really doing a job of legal work" (Fish 1993:738).

Don Zimmerman (1970:233) found that individuals use conceptions of a "normal" state of affairs to justify suspending a particular norm in a given instance, without thereby viewing themselves as violating the norm's intent. Individuals refer to norms not so much to verify compliance as to "create" it in any given instance. Like Hilbert's work, Zimmerman's suggests a way to replace the jurisprudential notion of correct norm usage with a concept of the competent use of a given norm or set of norms. Competent use is predicated on participants' grasp of what particular actions are necessary on a given occasion to provide for the regular reproduction of a "normal" state of affairs.

Known/Unknown, Not Legal/Illegal

To determine whether a particular law should be invoked, conventional jurisprudence distinguishes between "legal" and "illegal" activities to which the law might be applied. Niklas Luhmann (1989:140) speaks of "a binary code that contains a positive value (justice) and a negative value (injustice)." This distinction, a binary schematization of justice and injustice, while certainly valid, frames the issue in such a way as to miss an important phenomenon in the actual application of legal norms. Norm application functions unproblematically when both problem and solution are determinate. When however problem and solution are indeterminate, norm application itself can be a means to define both.

Aaron Cicourel (1995:107) observed procedures for coding certain kinds of police records. The procedures that guided the activity of coding presupposed what the police expected the outcome of the coding to be, that is, what they expected the recorded data to mean. Whenever the explicit procedures for coding could not answer questions that developed in the course of coding, the procedures allowed the coder to improvise decisions and thus generate the answers needed to complete the coding. The normatively thin approach is to distinguish between solutions to problems by known means and solutions to unknown problems by unknown means.

Such a perspective does not presuppose that norms and behavior are directly and causally linked. One alternative to the notion of causal linkage—an alternative unavailable to conventional jurisprudence—is the idea that norms and behavior are related mutually. Norm-governed behavior cannot be mapped one to one to the norms that ostensibly govern it, any more than conscious behavior can be mapped one to one with the actor's intentions. Norms, then, do not explain the norm user's behavior any more than behavior explains the actor's goals in using particular norms. Individuals "themselves typically use norms to explain and prescribe behavior with all the success they require" (Hilbert 1981:215). Because individuals do not need literal role prescriptions to act (or even to use norms), norms by themselves are inadequate to prescribe individuals' future behavior. By interpreting and applying a norm, we make it determinate, at least for that particular instance of interpretation and application. The act, manner, and method of applying a norm first define a problem as relevant to, and requiring, norm application. Likewise, application itself defines the solution as relevant to, and achievable by, norm application.

Norm-Autonomous Procedures, Not Norm-Needy Procedures

Ethnomethodological studies show how norms are not synonymous with the activity about which they instruct. For example, where a judge or a police officer or some other user of legal norms experiences difficulty in correlating a codified general norm with a specific instance of application, he or she cannot appeal to the legal code for clarification: like norms in general, a legal code is not self-interpreting. David Sudnow (1965) found that petty theft is neither situationally nor necessarily included in the typical burglary (burglars seldom take money or other goods from their victim's person). If we understand burglaries in terms of the penal code and then examine the public defender's records to see how burglaries are reduced in the guilty plea, we find no norm describing the reduction of statutorily defined burglaries to lesser crimes. The norm must be sought elsewhere, in the character of the non–statutorily defined class of burglaries. Sudnow (1965:260–261) found that features attributed to offenders and offenses often are unimportant for the way the statute defines the offense. Whether or not the premises were damaged is irrelevant for deciding which statute applies to any given case. While for robbery the presence or absence of a weapon determines the legal severity of the crime, the type of weapon used is immaterial. Also irrelevant is whether the burgled residence or business is located in a high-income or low-income part of town. Similarly, the defendant's race, social class, style of committing offenses, and (for most offenses) criminal history are irrelevant to the codified definition of the offense. But these features are immediately relevant to the public defender's determination of whether the information before him or her constitutes a case of "burglary," and they are crucial for arranging a guilty plea bargain. The public defender scrutinizes the case to determine its membership in a class of similar cases, while the penal code itself does not define the classes of types of offense, providing no adequate reference for deciding correspondences between the instant and the general case.

Often norms "paraphrase a procedure" (Hilbert 1981:215), if only roughly. From the perspective of conventional jurisprudence, a particular norm is "adequate" if the interested group or individual can follow the procedure paraphrased by the norm. By presupposing that a procedure can be accomplished only by following norms, jurisprudence is blind to a phenomenon that ethnomethodology can capture: that "correct" procedure is not always, maybe not even often, in need of clarification by norms. This normatively thin perspective is more sensitive than conventional jurisprudence to the fact that the role of norms in human behavior often turns on individuals' practical needs. Where an individual doesn't require clarification to accomplish a particular procedure, his or her activity is not really norm-governed in the jurisprudential sense of being guided and directed by norms, whether strongly or weakly. Alternatively, the individual discovers a given norm's "true" meaning and "proper" application in the course of employing the norm over a series of actual situations (Zimmerman 1970:232).

Creative (Non)compliance, Not Narrow Compliance

When someone invokes the law, conventional types of jurisprudence ask if he or she based the decision to invoke the law on reasons recognized by the law as valid. This framing loses sight of an important aspect of the actual application of norms. Because jurisprudence concerns itself here solely with the question of whether the law invoker complied with the law, it cannot recognize that invoking the law is one way to use the law as a resource, but not the only way. Sometimes not to invoke the law is another way—in some instances a more useful one—

to approach potentially legal issues. Because it doesn't focus narrowly on norm compliance, a thin approach is open to the fact that, in practice, compliance is not the sole way to utilize the law as a problem-solving resource.[4]

In a study of police officers who patrol skid rows, Egon Bittner (1967:709) found that officers necessarily exercise discretionary freedom in invoking the law. Conventional jurisprudents will ask whether a particular decision to invoke, or not to invoke, is in line with the law's intent. While legal doctrine recognizes notions of "prosecutorial discretion," "administrative discretion," and even "abuse of discretion," it confines discretionary freedom within what it takes to be the "spirit" of the law, a spirit that precludes, for example, violations of a defendant's or suspect's civil rights. A normatively thin approach resists this self-limiting concept of law. It does not demand solely decisions that can be based on reasons recognized (even if only in some ultimate or final sense) as valid by the law. From Bittner's (1967:711) standpoint, for the police officer to implement the law naively—to arrest someone because he or she committed some minor offense—may contain elements of injustice. Officers often deal with situations in which questions of culpability are profoundly ambiguous. If culpability is not the salient consideration leading to an arrest in cases where it is patently obvious, then, claims Bittner (1967:711), the officer may feel justified in making arrests lacking formal legal justification. Conversely, he or she may view arrests for minor offenses as poor workmanship if they were made solely because the offenses met specifications of the legal code. Any jurisprudence oriented strictly to norm compliance will hardly be open to such a standpoint and the phenomenon it analyzes.

Bittner (1967) also found that while the criteria specified by the law are met in the majority of cases of minor arrest, only rarely do police officers invoke a particular law simply because an action or situation satisfies its definition. Rather, compliance with the law is often merely the outward appearance of an intervention actually based on altogether different considerations. "Patrolmen do not really enforce the law, even when they do invoke it," but rather deploy it as one resource among others to "solve practical problems in keeping the peace" (Bittner 1967: 710). For example, an officer's decision not to arrest, when the circumstances meet the specifications for arrest, is likely not a decision not to enforce the law but rather a decision to enforce the law in an alternative manner.

Practical Methods, Not Abstract Principles

Some types of nonconventional jurisprudence are sensitive to the ways in which norm application is indeterminate.[5] Ethnomethodology certainly shares this sensitivity. But it offers a perspective that can go further and tease out the methods or ways in which indeterminate norms are actually applied, by uncovering one or the other calculus for the application of indeterminate norms. Cicourel (1995:47), for example, has observed how official communication by legal professionals such as police, courts, and probation officers complies with legal norms by heeding not the letter of the law, but "tacit knowledge or 'rules' not written or discussed explicitly in written and oral reports"—that is, by following lived norms or tried practices rather than abstract principles. While some types of nonconventional jurisprudence recognize the existence of ad hoc applications, from ethnomethodological studies we learn how to identify actual methods of "ad hocness."

Bittner (1967:700), for example, discovered the indeterminate phenomenon of police in the role of "peace officers," when police operate under some other consideration and largely with no structured and continuous outside constraint, in activities that encompass all occupational routines not directly related to making arrests. Under such circumstances, norm users cannot adhere to high standards of justification. Instead, appliers of indeterminate norms assess their applications against the background of a system of ad hoc decision making, a system encompassing various social institutions such as the courts, correctional facilities, the welfare establishment, and medical services. And Sudnow (1965:262) found that public defenders and district attorneys tend to develop sets of unstated recipes for reducing original charges to lesser offenses. The reduced offense often bears no obvious relation to the originally charged offense, yet legal professionals consider the reduction from one to the other "reasonable."

Situations Applied to Norms, Not Norms to Situations

Jurisprudence emphasizes ways in which norms are applied to situations, while an ethnomethodologically informed thin approach reveals ways in which not norms are applied to situations, but situations to norms. In the latter case norms are themselves resources to determine how a context should be approached. For example, police can go about their work investigating or otherwise dealing with a case only after they have "mapped" the relevant events, behavior, and objects onto given legal norms, categories, and definitions (Cicourel 1995:113). To warrant intervening in a situation, they must first construe it in terms of warrant-granting legal norms.

A normatively thin approach agrees with conventional jurisprudence that norms determine behavior. But only a thin perspective recognizes how norms are dependent on the context of their application, and how norms are related internally or constitutively, not merely externally or neutrally, to the behavior they determine.[6] A thin approach draws on an ethnomethodology that can recognize that in performing a role, norm users do not passively follow norms and roles but actively manipulate them, even instrumentalize them, toward achieving their goals. Norms then are a "*lived* feature of the settings" in which they function (Maynard and Clayman 1991:391).

Even as dependent, contextual, and endogenous thin norms can accomplish the tasks conventional jurisprudence assigns only to thick norms, understood as independent, acontextual, and exogenous principles. For example, norm users do not need some principled, underlying moral orientation to life—they do not need a thick normativity —to find in norms a "method of *moral* persuasion and justification" (Wieder 1974:175).[7] Norms can be both endogenous and part of an individual's way of life:[8] to obey a norm is then to participate in a way of life, in its patterns and constraints. If individuals do not share thick norms in the sense of objective, transcendental principles, then perhaps what they share is a normatively thin way of life, in patterned behavior that can generate, sustain or change conventional meanings within what Fish (1989:153) calls "interpretive communities" that provide members with access to public meanings and delimit, to those meanings, members' understandings.

Continuities in belief patterns are ways of life, and in everyday life we establish continuities as we pragmatically[9] seek alliances among groups with divergent viewpoints, and as we pragmatically fashion agreements that may be temporary and fragile. Even a population deeply divided by differences over a broad range of issues nonetheless pursues necessarily transient and provisional understandings. Thin norms are then instruments rather than prescriptions: as lived norms, they help groups or communities to achieve ends quite independent of the norms, rather than constricting behavior and making it dependent on the norms.

Features of a Normatively Thin Account of Legal Indeterminacy

The various ways in which thin jurisprudence differs from conventional jurisprudence share several features: indeterminacy in legal norms is often not a problem where norm usage is self-generatingly orderly, pragmatist, and locally based.

Norm Usage Is Self-Generatingly Orderly

We have seen that a thin approach shares the insights of some types of jurisprudence into the fundamental ambiguity of law and into the constant need to interpret law in its course. Yet in distinction to even the latter types of nonconventional jurisprudence, ethnomethodological studies show that behavior often is not ordered or patterned by individuals' following norms or abstract prescriptions. Norms do not organize behavior at all times; sometimes the order displayed by behavior is itself self-generating. Another name for self-generating order is "autopoiesis," an order created by the production and reproduction of its own elements.[10] In ethnomethodological terms, the "organization of everyday interaction is due to participants' own contingently embodied activities and actions as those arise in and as the concrete plenitude of lived experience" (Maynard 1996:2). Among everyday interactions are the use of a wide variety of norms, and legal norms in particular. An ethnomethodologically informed thin approach does not deny the presence and effect of structures—technological, cultural, economic, historical, political, and so forth—on agency or "free will." Rather, it recognizes structure as an "achieved phenomenon of order" (Garfinkel 1996:6)—structure not only as a conditioner of agency but also as a product of agency. For example, a legal system reproduces itself self-referentially—that is, through the will and consciousness of the participants—and thereby generates its own limits: the will and consciousness of actors is then bounded by the system thus created. Self-generation is also self-limitation—neither arbitrariness nor entropy nor chaos, but predictability, order, and self-containment. By reproducing itself in this autopoietic fashion, the legal system realizes its unity and coherence.[11]

Garfinkel (1968) hypothesizes an autopoietic order embedded in concrete activities, accessible to social science but not through empirical generalization or through the formal specification of variable elements and their analytic relations. Even so, "'raw' experience is anything but chaotic." Rather, the "concrete activities of which it is composed are coeval with an intelligible organization that [individuals] 'already' provide"—an organization therefore available to the social scientist (Maynard and Clayman 1991:387). Individuals themselves create the context in which they recognize themselves and their environment. According to Lawrence Wieder (1974:29), we may view any social setting as self-organizing with respect to the intelligible character of its own appearances, as either representations or evidence of social order. A context itself organizes its activities to make its properties —as an organized environment for behavior—detectable, reportable, even analyzable. A setting's "accountability" may be "accomplished" simply through the participants' use of the idea of norm-governed conduct in talking among themselves about their affairs. Indeed, language use itself "renders" human affairs orderly by serving as "embedded instruction" for seeing those affairs as orderly. Wieder (1974) found that by "telling the convict code," that is, by articulating a set of general, indefinite maxims governing behavior in a halfway house, residents made their affairs appear orderly to any outsider who heard their talk and "employed it as embedded instruction" for seeing those affairs. Residents also used the code as a framework of description and injunction in making sense of their own organizational setting. The code produced and sustained the very institutional reality it commented on and regulated.

Norm Usage Is Pragmatist

Indeterminacy is not often a problem in the ordinary functioning of a legal system for the same reason it is not often a problem in the nonlegal aspects of everyday life of individuals, groups, even whole societies.[12] The constituents of patterns are routinely and repeatedly tested, pragmatically, through experience. Every time an idea or practice enables a person to make sense of a situation or to accomplish a goal, its claim to validity is reinforced. Such pragmatist verification has a confirmatory bias: individuals develop new theories often only to the extent needed to incorporate new experience under a familiar category. Individuals often will make extensive elaborations before relinquishing their initial understanding and approach in instances where these ill fit new experience or additional information.

Social and legal change sometimes occurs when the patterns (or portions thereof) cease to accomplish practical tasks or to generate psychologically satisfying understandings. Change may be driven by developments in or alterations of the relative usability of patterns as much as by the introduction of new or modified worldviews. The interpretation of legal texts, notably statutory and constitutional ones, is itself pragmatist to the extent that the possible or probable consequences of any interpretation guides interpretive activity. In 1954, for example, the Supreme Court in *Bolling v. Sharpe*[13] held that racial segregation of public schools in the District of Columbia was unconstitutional. In *Brown v. Board of Education*,[14] decided the same day, the Court reached the same conclusion with respect to the states. The Court based its *Brown* decision on the Fourteenth Amendment's guarantee of equal protection, that is, on a guarantee of equality of citizenship precluding a racially segregated public education that conferred second-class citizenship on the black minority.[15] Because the Fourteenth Amendment applies to the states but not to the federal government—hence not to the federal entity of the District of Columbia—the Court, desirous to obtain the same result in the national capital as in the rest of the country, found a guaranty of equal protection in the Fifth Amendment, which does apply to federal entities. Yet that amendment has no equal protection clause, and the Court found a guaranty of equal protection in the amendment's due process clause. In a conventional sense the Court's reasoning was specious: the due process clause cannot imply, as can an equal protection clause, a prohibition of racial segregation. Any conventional jurisprudence would have to accept segregated schools in the District for lack of any constitutional basis for rejecting them—and would thereby undermine the moral authority and political efficacy of *Brown*. From a pragmatist perspective the Court's reasoning was quite plausible, however: the Court must have recognized an "intolerable anomaly, in the political rather than a conventionally 'legal' sense, in allowing the public schools of the nation's capital to remain segregated when the Supreme Court, sitting in that capital, had just outlawed segregation by states" (Posner 1990:145). As in this example, interpretation is pragmatist when the legislative or legal text is used instrumentally as a resource in fashioning that result. The relevant consequences can include systemic ones, such as debasing the currency of statutory language by straying too far from current usage. Pragmatist behavior is guided by consequences, and consequences may include long run, systemic, stabilizing, pattern-maintaining consequences.

Neither the world nor norms themselves tell us what meanings and applications of a given norm are legitimate; however, this does not imply either that a choice among possible meanings or applications is arbitrary or that the choice expresses something "deep within us." We change from one interpretation or application to another for pragmatist, contingent reasons. Our criteria for defining or redefining a norm, or for deciding how to apply a norm, surely involve some notion of consistency; yet consistency alone can hardly explain our choices fully or adequately. Rather, our criteria for choice involve the pragmatist consideration of adequacy. And we can define the term "adequate" only contingently, in an ad hoc manner; in different cases, moreover, we will define it differently.

The pragmatist creation of a new or changed meaning or application is not a discovery about how old meanings or applications fit together. Thus the creation of meaning or the proper application of a norm is not an inferential process, starting with or from premises formulated in earlier interpretations or applications. Such creations are not discoveries of a reality behind appearances. To create a new meaning of a norm (or to change an existing meaning) is like inventing a new tool to replace an old one. It works better but not more truthfully or justly.

Here we see how, building on ethnomethodology, a normatively thin jurisprudence differs from conventional jurisprudence's strictly cognitive approach to indeterminacy and the problem of order. It approaches reason as practical and observable worldly conduct, as a pragmatically oriented account of the creation of knowledge. Jurisprudentially, the individual's actions are patterned because individuals share internalized frames of reference and value systems that enable individuals to define situations in similar or even identical ways. Such jurisprudence regards "procedures" as solitary resources that individuals mutually impose on each other. An ethnomethodologically informed jurisprudence, by contrast, regards "procedures" as resources that groups of persons, such as community, employ in concert (Maynard and Clayman 1991:388).

Norm Usage Is Locally Based

Ethnomethodology allows us to see how groups and individuals discover, locally, the scope and applicability of a norm.[16] Ethnomethodology analyzes a context's features as the accomplishment of members' practices for making these features observable (Zimmerman and Pollner 1970:95). A context's features are unique to the particular setting in which they are assembled and hence cannot be generalized to other settings. Jurisprudence refers to general, and generalizable, norms, while ethnomethodology refers to local norms, which may be plural, applicable to different cases yet not necessarily consistent with each other (Elster 1992). The validity of local norms is nongeneralizable, hence their application is best left to the participants themselves (Dews 1986). Although they afford a partial, nonprivileged account of particular areas of life (Boyle 1985), they can nonetheless provide for a nonreductionist understanding of one system of cultural values by another (an understanding of religious faith by secular social science, as I urge in chapter 6), as well as for the critique of ideology, of claims to universal validity for the interests of only one social sector (as I show in chapter 7).

According to Garfinkel (1967:vii–viii), people construct definitions and interpretations of legal norms in particular situations; they do not carry them over from the past. Definitions and interpretations of legal norms are ongoing constructions or "situated accomplishments," what Garfinkel calls "accounts," the "everyday activities as members' methods for making those same activities visibly-rational-and-reportable-for-all-practical-purposes, i.e. 'accountable.' " The meaning, for example of a legal norm, is made rather than found. Richard Rorty's (1989:5) similarly pragmatic assertion about truth holds equally well for norms understood in a normatively thin way and finds support in ethnomethodological studies that truth is a predicate of propositions—in other words, of human language. It is not a quality of the external world, which does not describe itself as true or false, but which humans, in language, may so describe. "Truth," then, is not ahistorical, eternal, unique, absolute, noncontingent, unchanging, or free of context and perspective. It is made rather than found, which is not to say there is no truth but rather to describe a particular conception of truth (one not inconsistent with this sentence, yet one that cannot guarantee its validity).

Whenever a legal norm is applied, it must be applied within a specific social situation—it must be "localized" to be useful—because no social situation is independent of the individuals within it. The very invocation of a norm alters the situation because individuals, norms, and situations ceaselessly inform and mutually elaborate one another. Norms, like individuals and situations, do not even appear except in a mesh of practical circumstances. The individual, norms, and the present definition of the situation—all intertwined—constitute the situation; no one of these elements can be abstracted out and treated as cause or effect. Every legal norm is used and usable only within a web of practical circumstances that "fill in" the incompleteness of a norm, particularizing what Garfinkel (1968:220) calls the empty but promissory "et cetera aspect" of norms: practices whereby persons make what they are doing *happen* as norm-analyzable conduct. Differences among situations falling under the jurisdiction of norms reduce the fit between norms and their contexts of application: exceptions arise that limit the generality of norms. To the extent a norm is overwhelmed by idiosyncrasies, situational constructions of meaning rush in to fill the gap between norms and contexts. Only in extreme cases would this process lead to a complete denial of the existence of norms, where norms would dissolve in the complete uniqueness of the particular situation.

Because people's body of social knowledge and practical interests is ever shifting, they never judge a situation once and for all. Every judgment is only situationally absolute, based on the realization that later determinations may change the certainty of the here and now (Mehan and Wood 1975:75). Legal norms have local meanings and local applications; correspondingly, social order is largely the result of ad hoc, local constructions. Yet the absence of some logically closed, self-contained normative order, grounded in a small number of ultimate values, need not entail the limited impact of norms. Unlike conventional jurisprudence, ethnomethodological studies suggest that the impact of norms is independent of underlying principles or transcendent meanings. Norms do not inhabit some high ground overlooking the terrain of human action; they are constituents of this terrain, local not universal.

Ethnomethodological research shows that people decide, locally, issues of "neutrality and commitment; the fact/value distinction; the is/ought dichotomy; the issue of relativism and objectivity, universalizability and specificity."[17] This notion of localism comports with Garfinkel's (1967) claim that the world does not lend itself to being generalized in the sense of universal structures of experience. Perhaps humans need to believe that even locally produced norms are repeatable, accountable, and generalizable. If this belief is an illusion, then it may be a necessary one, for we often seem unable to live without turning specific situations into instances of general norms and roles, even though the latter exist only in our systems of accounts. Perhaps for this reason, among others, jurisprudence tends to view norms as functioning in a principled and universalist fashion. For the same reason, an ethnomethodologically informed thin jurisprudence is better able than a conventional one to identify the pragmatist, localist functioning of legal norms.

Limits of the Model: Thin Normativity in Distinction to Nonnormativity

Nonetheless, ethnomethodology needs to appreciate why any jurisprudence places so much emphasis on normativity. Despite the many differences between conventional and thin jurisprudence, both are oriented on such concepts as the rule of law; both view norms as an important, sometimes the most powerful, means toward securing social goals such as an administration of governmental power that preserves the institutional balance of power, the individual's realization of legal rights, the fair and equitable functioning of bureaucracies, and the provision of legal equality among legal equals (chapter 7 will return us to the topic of legal equality and, beyond that, to the related topic of legal autonomy).

From the standpoint of any jurisprudence, some ethnomethodological studies uncover distinct civil-libertarian dilemmas in the ways some legal norms are routinely used. Striking examples of such quandaries emerge in Bittner's (1967:702) work, describing how "police tend to impose more stringent criteria of law enforcement on certain segments of the community than on others." He found that police working a skid row beat perceived socially marginalized groups or social pariahs, who do not lead "normal" lives, as creating special problems requiring special procedures. For example, the officer, familiar with habitués of his beat, has observed how person X, when in the company of persons Y and Z, often gets into trouble with the law. Knowing that Y and Z are passing through the area on a particular day, the officer arrests X simply to remove him from the streets while Y and Z are in the area. While the officer may urge that "arresting a person on skid-row on some minor charge may save him and others a lot of trouble, but it does not work any real hardship on the arrested person," Bittner (1967:713) clearly recognizes the ethical and legal problems he has uncovered ethnomethodologically. After all, the officer's action has no statutory basis and violates constitutionally guaranteed civil rights. The officer distributes the "burden" of violated rights—even if toward reducing the potential for a disturbance of the peace—unfairly on only one or some of the potential candidates, in a manner that is ad hoc and arbitrary. Cicourel (1995:123) similarly found that legal "requirements often lead to a kind of window dressing necessary to making the sometimes nasty business of police work compatible with demands for legal safeguards." Window dressing is the presumption of innocence; common sense and long experience "allow" the police to accomplish the task of law enforcement by distinguishing, on an ad hoc basis, between persons assumed innocent and those assumed guilty. The police view legal norms as irrelevant when they are pursuing someone they assume to be guilty or at least suspect. This perspective raises the multiply problematic claim that, in the short run, due process and civil rights do not further daily law enforcement but actually impede it; but that in the long run, the accused will receive both due process and civil rights if he or she is in fact innocent.

For methodological reasons, ethnomethodological studies do not address normatively problematic observations like the violation of civil rights, precisely questions that jurisprudence—whether thick or thin—attempts to confront through distinctly normative conceptions of law. The observer's attitude to observations of normative dilemmas is central to any jurisprudence yet beyond the scope of ethnomethodology, which describes but doesn't explain, asks how but not why, observes social behavior or legal outcomes yet has no opinion on their moral acceptability. Nor will ethnomethodology characterize the individuals observed as "deficient, pathological or irrational (or superior, normal, or rational)—such attributions are themselves endogenous constructions" and "thus a topic of study rather than a resource for an analytic critique" (Pollner 1991:371). Whereas ethnomethodology, like pragmatism, has no inherent normative or political valence, all types of jurisprudence are normatively committed (and committed in as many different ways as there are types of jurisprudence). While most ethno-methodological research (but not all)[18] professes indifference toward the nature and status of the knowledge, behavior, or norms examined or uncovered, all jurisprudence rejects any conception of law devoid of all normative justification. A normatively thick jurisprudence rejects any conception of law devoid of some external (especially moral) justi-fication, whereas normatively thin jurisprudence, informed by ethno-methodology, argues for internal forms of justification. But even as it is informed by ethnomethodology, a normatively thin jurisprudence differs from it on the issue of normative neutrality: a thin jurispru-dence, like any jurisprudence, is normatively committed, even if com-mitted in ways very different from its normatively thick alternatives. Correspondingly, even as it is informed by pragmatism (as I showed in previous pages), a normatively thin approach differs from pragmatism again on the issue of normative neutrality. If pragmatism is a "future-oriented instrumentalism that tries to deploy thought as a weapon to enable more effective action" (West 1989:5), it can be put to ends of any normative stripe. Ethnomethodology lacks pragmatism's instrumen-tal utility yet shares its normative agnosticism, a feature that neither enhances nor detracts from its explanatory potential.

To the extent modern law is no longer in the business of norming the individual citizen's conscience but distinguishes between itself and morality and assigns to morality all questions of conscience, the law is not a carrier of conscience but—where it makes demands on con-science—sometimes even its enemy. The question of whether, from a normative standpoint, this disjunction of law and morality is desirable or not (and for what reasons and by what criteria) remains to jurispru-dence, including thin jurisprudence. On the one hand, the normative indifference of ethnomethodology makes it better attuned than any form of jurisprudence to grasping modern law in its anormative as-pects. By the same token ethnomethodology cannot well grasp modern law in its irreducible normative aspects. There a thin jurisprudence, better than conventional or normatively thick jurisprudence, can grasp the ways in which judges and others actually deal with indeterminate legal norms. In this sense thin jurisprudence is informed by ethno-methodology yet cannot be reduced to it.

Descriptively, a normatively thin jurisprudence observes thin norms in action and explains how judges and others can deal with the challenge of indeterminacy. Prescriptively, a thin jurisprudence offers possibilities for constructing agreement in the face of contested interpretations of the meaning and proper application of otherwise indeterminate laws. Where it functions prescriptively, it functions as a form of normatively thin political judgment. The following chapter examines a different but related form of political judgment; it examines a different but related way in which thin norms make understanding possible even under conditions of normative difference, divergence, and fragmentation. Whereas this chapter looked at creating understanding "internally," *within* the normative commitments of a legal system, the next one looks at creating understanding "externally," *across* competing normative commitments. In particular it examines the normative commitment in competing systems of thick norms, namely, competing systems of cultural values.

POLITICAL JUDGMENT
ABOUT COMPETING CULTURAL
VALUES

6

Indeterminate legal norms, on the one hand, and competition between different systems of cultural values, on the other, can equally be socially destabilizing. Presumably a democratic order does not require the complete equality of all its members (if it did, no polity today would qualify as a democracy and likely none could aspire to become one). But if it requires some degree of equality among at least some of its citizens, then indeterminate norms of legal equality would threaten its viability unless and until those norms were rendered determinate. Similarly, perhaps no culture, and certainly no culture in late modernity, enjoys complete coherence. But if a culture requires at least some degree of compatibility among its various components, then stability and coherence become impossible where various of its values stand to one another in mutual incomprehension and overt hostility. In this sense this chapter continues the general concern of the preceding one: how to create conditions of social stability in the face of any number of destabilizing factors; how to achieve democracy in the face of divisive worldviews; how to create political and cultural coherence amid far-reaching difference and chronic disagreement.

Systems of cultural values embrace a variety of complex patterns of social meanings expressed in symbols of various kinds. Religious faith is one kind of value system; the secular study of religion, in the sense of detached or objectivating study, is another. The Christian cross to the believer may symbolize something about the ultimate meaning of life and perhaps as well something about right conduct appropriate to that meaning. A sociological treatment of this symbol, for example with respect to its function in social integration, may invoke such symbols of the trade as the academic degrees and affiliations of the author, signaling reasons to give credence to the author's claims quite apart from the merits of the claims themselves. Differences among value systems indicate the likelihood that the problems involved in understanding one value system will be different from those involved in understanding another. Located in the individual's subjective consciousness, the meaning of any religious symbol is difficult to elicit, sometimes even for the person holding it. Subjective meanings cannot be observed and are contingent on the context of their occurrence (Wuthnow 1988:475). And some symbols involved in the practice of science may yield to the analysis of philosophers of science or sociologists of science but may be opaque to the scientists themselves. Observers of science, for their part, generate claims about the practice of science some of which the scientists themselves may reject. Thomas Kuhn (1970:46) might surprise some scientists when, as an observer, he writes: "Scientists work from models acquired through education and through subsequent exposure to the literature often without quite knowing or needing to know what characteristics have given these models the status of community paradigms. And because they do so, they need no full set of rules. The coherence displayed by the research tradition in which they participate may not imply even the existence of an underlying body of rules and assumptions that additional historical or philosophical investigation might uncover."[1]

Value systems also compete where the "logic" of the observing system (a sociology of religion, for example) differs from the "logic" of the system under observation (such as religious faith). Reduction occurs where one value system tries to understand a different one in terms only of the former's "logic," for example where an external, objectivating analysis of religious ritual "measures" that ritual against the highly rational, self-reflective axioms of scholarship. A scientific worldview attempts to be clear and self-conscious about its presuppositions, whereas aspects of any number of ways of everyday life are uncertain and fuzzy because they are situational, partial, and opaque. Think of common practices such as parenting (for example, how to teach children self-defense); determining at least some of one's political preferences on specific issues at specific times (some citizens may experience tension between their usual preferences and changes in some of those preferences when their country is engaged in a popular war); defining at least some of one's cultural preferences (for example, chamber music rather than opera). To bring a scientific value system to bear on some unclear and uncertain aspect of life would strip the latter of everything defining it in its distinctiveness, for example (in the case of some value systems, including some religious ones) the "uncertainty and 'fuzziness' resulting from the fact that they have as their principle not a set of conscious, constant rules, but practical schemes, opaque to their possessors, varying according to the logic of the situation, [and] the almost invariably partial viewpoint which it imposes" (Bourdieu 1990:12).

Each value system displays a peculiar set of thick norms defining its identity and guiding the individual's behavior in ways appropriate to that system (as in the concrete communities I discussed in chapter 3). Thick norms of religious belief likely include otherworldly definitions of reality as well as prescriptions for a highly articulated conception of moral behavior, prescriptions directed above all at behavior toward the community of co-religionists. Thick norms of the secular, scholarly study of religious faith, on the other hand, include this-worldly definitions of reality and rational, discursive standards of validity, directed mostly to a small community of narrowly specialized scholars. Each system tends to insulate itself within its own community, maintaining boundaries potentially always under challenge from without (and of course sometimes from within, for example when some people within want to assimilate some people from without). In terms of this boundary-maintaining function of specific value systems, while "evidence clearly documents the irreligiosity of scientists themselves, it shows that this irreligiosity is far more pronounced among the least scientific disciplines—the social sciences and humanities—than it is among the natural sciences. . . . [S]cientists in the social and humanistic disciplines may adopt an irreligious stance chiefly as one of the boundary-posturing mechanisms they use to distance themselves from the general public and, thereby, to maintain the precarious reality of the theorizing they do" (Wuthnow 1989:157). In other words, scholars in the social sciences and humanities "rely frequently on values, attitudes, and life-styles to maintain the reality of science by setting up *external boundaries* between themselves and the general public or those who represent the realm of everyday reality" (ibid., 153), taking the posture of irreligiosity as a way of legitimating their normative commitments as scholars. These scholars "carve out a space in which to work by dissociating themselves from the powerful claims religion has been able to make throughout history, and which it still appears to command over the everyday life of American society" (ibid., 157).

As distinct ways of looking at the world, the respective systems of science and religion inevitably compete with respect to various claims, such as the nature of reality, or the appropriate criteria of truth, or the validity of propositions about the meaning of human experience, or the proper norms of behavior in everyday life. Probably neither system can observe the other without making at least some claims about the other that the other will reject. Even if both systems subscribe to the same method of understanding a different system, each might well reject the other's self-understanding. And they might well reject each other's self-understanding precisely because they agree, for example, that observation is not sufficient if the ends of an action are too different from the observer's own for the observer to "understand its motive without any imaginative effort" (Alexander 1983:31) or that "just as no empirical argument can be made without presuppositions, no theoretical argument can be conducted without first 'translating' competing positions into a theoretical language whose presuppositions are complementary with one's own" (Alexander 1982:113). If "complementary" is understood in a strong sense, then a value system that adopted the prescription of the preceding sentence would "understand" the competing system only by reducing it to the observing value system. By reduction one does not understand the other system so much as obscure it; or, if by reduction one understands something, even something basic, one does so only at the cost of not understanding the rest. Reduction is a significant barrier to understanding between competing systems of value;[2] it collapses one set of thick norms into another.[3] I shall argue that "translating" one set of thick norms into another set of thick norms defeats cross-system understanding; I shall also argue that understanding requires translating thick norms into thin ones.

When one system of cultural values reduces another to its own thick norms, the one negates the other as a way of life different from its own. If, for example, a "common feature of all scientific theory is the logicality of the relations between its propositions" (Parsons 1937:754), then science assumes a normatively thick relationship to religion where it insists that it can understand only those religious beliefs that relate their propositions with the same logicality that science does. The validity of any such requirement cannot "be demonstrated by any knowledge without returning us once again back on itself" (Savage 1981:90). In that case, justification is wholly internal and precludes understanding across different value systems.

With any value system, the outside observer may have difficulty understanding the participant, and the participant may well disagree with the observer's claims about the participant's activity in that sphere.[4] One system of values likely understands itself differently than an outsider would, especially an outsider invested in a different value system. And yet in the public sphere, adherents of the two different systems may need to interact, even cooperate—just as different faiths might cooperate, despite their differences, in the defense of legal guarantees for religious belief and practice; or the religionist and the nonreligionist might cooperate as citizens of the same polity; and, of course, someone who studies religion from an objectivating, dispassionate stance and who also happens to be a person of faith relates in him- or herself two competing value systems, and must do so successfully to avoid schizophrenia. In that case some kind of mutual understanding between adherents of the two different systems is desirable, perhaps even necessary. The alternative I develop allows competing sets of thick norms to relate on a normatively thin basis, facilitating understanding across competing value commitments.

Thin normativity rejects purely immanent justification of any system's cultural values. It rejects, in other words, a normatively thick justification of thick cultural values, in favor of a normatively thin justification of thick cultural values. This approach is nonreductive (as I show in the first part of this chapter) but also rationally critical (as I show in the concluding part) because it requires external or detached justification (or justification at the level of what, in chapter 3, I introduced as generalized community). A normatively thin approach can render public forms of competing value systems capable of working in generalized community.

I examine forms of both reductionism and nonreductionism in the efforts of Karl Marx, Émile Durkheim, Max Weber, and Talcott Parsons to understand the phenomenon of religious faith. My goal is the identification of multiple ways for competing value systems to relate to each other on a normatively thin basis. Through this examination I shall generate three proposals for avoiding reductionism in the relationship among competing systems and then two further proposals for configuring a normatively thin relationship among competing value systems. In other words, I shall develop five proposals for structuring cross-system relationships in normatively thin ways.

Reductionism and Nonreductionism in Classical Approaches

The historical antecedents of the late nineteenth- and early twentieth-century sociology of religion, in the work of Marx, Weber, and Durkheim, lie in the European Enlightenment. The Enlightenment was an attitude of thorough-going rationalism that systematically brought into question many previously accepted beliefs and norms, even the most fundamental, ranging from the nature of the physical universe and the place of humans within it, to the grounds of political obligation and the possible forms of legal justice. It regarded rational standards as the ultimate instrument for comprehending reality, natural or social. To be accessible to rational analysis was to be transparent to highly rational value systems such as science and other forms of scholarship, easily excluding nonrational dimensions of human experience and existence and often reducing nonrational value systems to rational ones. This is precisely the program of the seventeenth-century Englishman John Toland in his book with its programmatic title, *Christianity not Mysterious* (1984). Christianity, according to Toland, must be completely freed of obscurity because its content is, in fact, merely the content of reason. Therefore supernatural revelation, dogmas, and their human administrators (above all priests and church officials) have no rationally justifiable purpose. This general approach also appears in the late eighteenth-, early nineteenth-century French thesis of "priestly deception," notably in the work of Antoine Destutt de Tracy (1817).[5] Like Toland, Destutt de Tracy argues that religion has always existed solely because certain groups have an ulterior, namely economic, interest in its maintenance. Similarly the eighteenth- and early nineteenth-century German Enlightenment[6] claims that revelation provides nothing that human reason, left to its own resources, cannot itself arrive at.[7]

As social scientists, Marx, Durkheim, Weber—and later, the American Talcott Parsons[8]—immediately share one important legacy of the Enlightenment: an external standpoint from which religion appears as a social construction entailing certain relations of authority. Religion then appears as a phenomenon of the finite world and, like all things finite, open to causal analysis and explanation. But an external standpoint becomes reductionist when it posits the "true" world of the scientific observer over against the "false" world of the religionist.

Here the thick norms of scientific rationality relate to those of religion in a normatively thick way. A thick relationship could well run in the opposite direction, for no less reductionist is an internal standpoint that posits the "true" world of the religionist — "true" because based on faith in an ultimate, extraphenomenal source of truth and reality — over against the "false" world of the secular scholar — "false" because lacking ultimate or transcendental validity. Valid knowledge then takes the form of claims of faith not open to falsification by the various means of science. A normatively thick value system can relate thickly to any other, similarly thick system.

Some elements in Durkheim's thought are clearly nonreductionist, including those that show how a value system operating with religious symbols is irreducible to the value system of the scientific observer. For Durkheim, "neither ritual practices, magical or religious, nor the beliefs about supernatural forces and entities integrated with them can be treated simply as a primitive and inadequate form of rational technique or scientific knowledge; they are qualitatively distinct and have quite different functional significance in the system of action."[9] Yet another element in Durkheim's theory is reductionist, specifically his "formulas for the translation of religious symbols into their real meanings" (Bellah 1970:249). For Durkheim (1973b) the reality behind the symbol is society itself, as well as the morality that "expresses" society. While Durkheim rejects Marx's claim that religion is an illusion, like Marx he undercuts the perspective of religious value systems, implicitly denying the validity of the perspective religious people have on their own faith. On this account only the Durkheimian observers, and never the faithful themselves, can know what religion's "real" base is.

Weber treats religion as a constitutive part of culture, not as an illusion. He does not reduce ideas to interests (for example, he doesn't reduce a certain economic spirit or mentality to forms of economic organization) but instead looks for "elective affinities" between them. When he states that "not ideas, but material and ideal interests, directly govern men's conduct," he emphasizes that "very frequently the 'world images' that have been created by 'ideas' have, like switchmen, determined the tracks along which action has been pushed by the dynamic of interests. 'From what' and 'for what' one wishes to be 'redeemed' and, let us not forget, 'could be' redeemed, depended upon one's image of the world" (1958b:280). This approach is also nonreductive where it explores rationalism as a world of antitheses, where it characterizes the relation between religious ideas and profane interests not as one of reconciliation but as the endurance of paradoxes. Science and religion then emerge as different realities separated by an unbridgeable chasm; a comparison of the two generates paradoxes that can only be borne, never resolved. Unlike Marx and Durkheim, Weber claims no key to a reality behind a façade of religious symbolization. Weber treats religions as "systems of meaning to be understood in their own terms from the point of view of those who believe in them, even though in the observer they strike no personal response" (Bellah 1970:250). Weber's theory of meaning distinguishes the cognitive patterns of religion from those of science and precludes the reduction of religious ideas to those of science or vice versa.[10] His concept of *Wissen* or knowledge applies not only to empirical objects but also to the grounds of meaning, to what Weber calls "religious ideas." *Wissen* is not a form of ideology: "both empirical science and the grounding of meaning are alike in referring to matters of what 'is,' of what 'exists' " (Parsons 1967c:146).

Rationality and Nonrationality

One value system relates to another in a normatively thick way when it can relate to the other in terms only of its own rationality. Weber (1949:72) again offers an alternative, arguing that the "finite human mind" struggles to "reflect about the way in which life confronts us in immediate concrete situations, presenting an infinite multiplicity of successively and coexistently emerging and disappearing events, both 'within' and 'outside' ourselves." The human mind can never grasp this "uniqueness of the reality in which we move."[11] The conviction that the rational mind is frail explains Weber's (1993:1) ambiguous judgment about the rationality of religion. From one perspective, religion appears rational: "religiously or magically motivated behavior is relatively rational behavior, especially in its earliest manifestations." Because religion "follows rules of experience, though it is not necessarily action in accordance with a means-end schema" (Weber 1993:1), religious behavior or thinking "must not be set apart from the range of everyday purposive conduct, particularly since even the ends of the religious and magical actions are predominantly economic" (ibid.). From another perspective, however, religion appears quite irrational: the "religious experience as such is of course irrational. . . . In its highest, mystical form it is . . . distinguished by its absolute incommunicability. . . . Every religious experience loses some of its content in the attempt of rational formulation, [and] the further the conceptual formulation goes, the more so. . . . But that irrational element . . . does not prevent its being of the greatest practical importance" (Weber 1958a:232–233). Unlike Marx, Weber (ibid.:193–194) does not reduce the irrationality of religion to the rationality of science but renders religious faith *and* secular scholarship alike relative and perspectival: "A thing is never irrational in itself, but only from a particular rational point of view. For the unbeliever every religious way of life is irrational, for the hedonist every ascetic standard."[12]

Durkheim arrives at the same conclusion from a rather different route, claiming that the "binding power of intellectual rationalism as a general value is not itself based on rational justification. The universal binding quality of scientific knowledge is based . . . on the fact that rationality itself is a common value in a universal community. In this respect, science as a social institution has the same non-rational basis as every other institution" (Münch 1988:46). The bond between citizens and normative ideals expressed in some symbols, such as the constitution,[13] may itself be irrational. Individuals feel commitment to values not only on the basis of rationality but also on the basis of emotional affect. Thus commitment to "democracy" can be rational (as a commitment on the basis of a rational justification of democracy, such as a belief in universally valid basic rights for citizens). But it can also be affectual (as in a "love" of democracy), given diffuse emotional bonds the citizen may associate with democratic ideals. And a commitment to science can be rational (as a commitment to a way of knowing, based on rigorous methods, empirical evidence, logical deduction, and fallibilism) but also affectual (as in a "love" of a particular subject matter).

Parsons, too, distinguishes between the "rational" and the "non-rational" in his approach to religion. For him the rational refers to positive knowledge, whether or not scientifically formulated. The non-rational refers to ignorance and error, "failure to conform with logico-empirical standards," but also (with reference to religion) to "theories which surpass experience" (Parsons 1954:200). Parsons (ibid.) is no reductionist where he is agnostic on what he terms the "question of the more ultimate nature of noncognitive factors." Nor is he reductionist by distinguishing between "constitutive," "expressive," and "moral" symbols, all of which help make sense of reality, yet none of which are cognitive in the sense of scientific propositions. While "constitutive," "expressive," and "moral" symbols are integrated with one another to some extent, no one of them occupies a privileged position, and none is deducible from systems of cognitive symbols. Thus by itself science can never accomplish the entire task of making sense of the world because "part of the reality that man needs to make sense of is nonempirical, simply unavailable to any of the resources of science" (Bellah 1970:242). Nonreductionist is Parsons's (1954:200) claim that moral and social norms are crucial to the individual's "adjustment to the total situation," for which "rational knowledge and technique [cannot] . . . provide adequate mechanisms." But Parsons also believes that attempts to find meaning are nonrational, residual to rational-empirical knowledge; the significance of the religious quest for meaning lies in its purely psychological and adjustive role in human life. From the standpoint of the person of faith, a functionalist argument of this sort can only be reductionist.

Symbols

For Durkheim (1963:114) "everything . . . social consists of representations, and therefore is a result of representations." Social life, "in all its aspects and in every period of its history, is made possible only by a vast symbolism" (Durkheim 1965:264). He associates symbols with an attitude of respect for sacred things, in particular an attitude identical with respect for moral authority. For Durkheim (according to Parsons 1954:206), religious ritual is a "mechanism for expressing and reinforcing the sentiments most essential to the institutional integration of the society."[14] On the one hand, he reductionistically urges that the true referent of religious symbols is society itself. On the other hand, he regards religious symbols not merely as an intellectual representation of society but as a prime constituent of social life: "for the emblem is not merely a convenient process for clarifying the sentiment society has of itself: it also serves to create this sentiment; it is one of its constituent elements" (Durkheim 1965:262). Religious symbols then appear "neither merely emotional nor as a residual category of what science has not yet solved" (Bellah 1973:li) but rather as "real." Weber and Durkheim approach religion nonreductionistically as a (collective and individual) realm of signs and symbols in its own right. Like Marx, Durkheim and Weber recognize the projective character of religious symbolism; unlike Marx, they maintain that the relationship of sign and signified can be approached without reducing religious symbols to ideological projections. For Durkheim and Weber the religious realm expresses genuine human experience, the experience of absolute dependence upon an indefinable "absolute other," or what Durkheim terms the "sacred."

Against Durkheim, Parsons (1954:206) holds that such symbols have no intrinsic qualities of sacredness (noting that "almost everything from the sublime to the ridiculous has in some society been treated as sacred"). He views them as empty vessels for the symbols' referents, and he connects them with culture, not society: "A social system is . . . organized about the *interaction* of a plurality of human individuals. . . . A cultural system . . . is organized about patterns of the *meaning* of objects and the 'expression' of these meanings through symbols and signs. . . . [T]he 'structure of culture' consists in patterns of meaning as such" (Parsons 1967c:141). Parsons avoids reductionism in his claim that the true referent lies in a nonempirical realm, beyond the scope of scientific investigation. On the other hand, he shares Weber's conviction that an unavoidable and unbridgeable gap exists between religious behavior's meaning for the social scientist and its meaning for the believer. Both Weber and Parsons posit absolute, intrinsic limits to what the secular analyst and the person of religious faith can share with each other. From the standpoint of believers, no purely scientific representation can grasp their faith and its experience adequately; for social scientists, the intrinsic claims of religion cannot be represented as direct first-order statements to their own public (Wilson 1982:17–18). Yet unlike Parsons, Weber does not privilege the rational dimension of human existence and experience over nonrational ones. To be sure, Parsons (1967b:87) is quite sensitive to the sometimes nonrational springs of rational action, even in science: the "scientist himself, as a total human being, must find his commitment to his science meaningful in terms of *his* values—it must be his calling."[15] Social science, like any other rational discipline, is grounded in culture, as an "enterprise of the human investigator in his quest for interpretation of the meanings of the human condition that are relevant to him" (Parsons 1967b:97). In some cases rationality may be motivated by irrational or nonrational preferences, for example where a "love" of science springs at least in part from an emotional attachment to the activity or methods or goals of science.

Values

One value system relates to another in a normatively thick way where it makes *inclusive* normative claims about values, that is, where it can approach the normative assertions of another value system in terms only of its own. This thick approach can be reductionistic, for example in competing efforts to define reality (a topic I developed in chapter 2). Pierre Bourdieu (1990:141) captures, at least implicitly, the tension inevitable between the value system of social science and the respective value systems of the various spheres of society it analyzes: the "object of social science is a reality that encompasses all the individual and collective struggles aimed at conserving or transforming reality, in particular those that seek to impose the legitimate definition of reality, whose specifically symbolic efficacy can help to conserve or subvert the established order, that is to say, reality." Here Bourdieu articulates the inclusive normative claims of social science, of which he is highly critical. Uncritical of such claims is Marx, who makes his own inclusive claims by presupposing the validity of one and only one set of epistemic values, one and only one set of cognitive norms, notably the singular value of what he takes to be "scientific" truth. He privileges science, viewing it as the only viable avenue to grasping social reality (and beyond that, shaping and reshaping social reality). His methodology then regards any alternative to "scientific" truth as fraud to be exposed; because only scientific consciousness is "true," religion can only be an ideology, and his approach to religion inevitably is a critique of ideology, seeking to unmask a false consciousness in the name of a true one. When a scientific study of religion identifies the projective and hence illusory character of religious symbolism, it seeks to reduce that symbolism to "reality." Through labor performed on nature, humans overcome the nonidentity of nature with humanity; labor and exchange realize the "essential" identity of human subject and non-human object, in an epistemological—and ultimately political—sense of reconciling the difference between them but also, by extension, between and among political and economic subjects. On this approach the norms of science and the norms of history are one: to realize (for the scholar, intellectually, and for *homo faber*, practically, the unitary or monistic character of reality). The norms of the religious domain cannot accord with those of science and history, because religion expresses a person's nonidentity with him- or herself and with nature, as well as a person's alienation from society. In words that could just as well have been written by Marx, Feuerbach (1957:29–30) states: "Man—this is the mystery of religion—projects his being into objectivity, and then again makes himself an object to this projected image of himself thus converted into a subject; he thinks of himself, is an object to himself, but as the object of an object, of another being than himself." People objectify their being and then make themselves an object of this objectified being; they think themselves, are objects to themselves, but as the object of an object, as the object of another being. The notion here of a nonalienated society presupposes the absence of a need for religion, or perhaps a complete reconciliation of human and environment, including the individual's environment of other humans. In some texts Marx posits this possibility,[16] in other texts he would seem to deny it.[17] In the latter instances nature is never fully dissolved into identity with the person through labor; a residuum of nonidentity remains. That residuum need not be interpreted religiously; it might (as Weber could argue) be borne as an irresolvable nonidentity. And yet any such residuum suggests the possibility of either the eternal need for religion or perhaps of a longing for complete identity (with God, or the supernatural, or some other source of ultimate meaning) that might be offered solely by religion.[18] This possibility appears only where Marx's normative claims about values are less than inclusive.

For his part Parsons (1967c:143–146) defines values as "conceptions of the desirable," as culturally prescribed definitions of commitments that affect behavior. Values are institutionalized in and through culture; conversely, cultural and social systems interpenetrate by means of values. Parsons makes no inclusive normative claim about values. He considers them always problematic with respect to their legitimation and argues that societies respond by institutionalizing patterns of meaning in terms of which their values "make sense." Thus both large-scale collectivities such as nations and small-scale collectivities such as business firms make demands on their members in terms of obligations and commitments. Members feel these obligations and commitments to be binding only if they "make sense." Parsons would agree with Durkheim's (1961:120) claim that "to act morally, it is not enough . . . to respect discipline and to be committed to a group. Beyond this [we need] . . . as clear and complete an awareness as possible of the reasons for our conduct. . . . [T]he rule prescribing such behavior must be freely desired, that is to say, freely accepted." Indeed, values are fully institutionalized only when members regard as legitimate the goals and functions of their collectivity and internalize this belief in ways that motivate their commitments.[19] Because "internalized values and norms . . . are involved in the motivation to conformity," says Parsons (1967a:28), "certain crucial components of that motivation . . . are not fully or directly attributable to 'reason,'" at least in the sense that an internalized bias, of which the person is unaware, may nonetheless steer the person's behavior in certain ways.

Weber and Durkheim make no inclusive normative claims; for both men the value of empirical truth does not exclude other values, nor does it exclude values of other kinds of truth. Neither privileges science as a way of knowing. For Weber, effective communication in symbolic terms always involves the sharing of values. Social science for Weber must have its own value system, but one that articulates with two other value systems: that of the culture in which the scientist participates and that of the social institutions or behaviors or beliefs under study.[20] Science is characterized by values that claim to be universally valid, "universal" in the sense of being independent of any particular culture; Weber is no radical relativist.[21] For Weber, the "object is both 'out there' and part of the observer himself, i.e., is internalized" (Parsons 1967c:150). Weber posits nothing less that a "fundamental unity of human culture and of the conditions of human orientation to the world" (ibid.), a position consistent with a notion of universal criteria of empirical validity. Variability exists within this framework,[22] but not randomly so because neither human values nor the human situation vary randomly—but often within definable dimensions over limited ranges. Science is one element of a cultural system governed by general norms, namely objectivity both in the verification of statements of empirical fact, and in logical inference and analysis. The values of science can become autonomous relative to the larger, surrounding culture, and relative to the scientist's other value commitments. A social science of religion can be autonomous because the values of secular scholarship can be differentiated from the diffuser values of the culture in which it is embedded and because the process of scientific investigation can be controlled through a general theory of the *logical* type now established in the natural sciences.[23]

In this sense the values of social science—including conceptual clarity, consistency, and the generalizable validity of its propositions, on the one hand, and empirical accuracy and verifiability, on the other —can, for the secular scholar, take priority over his or her subjective understandings and particular motivations. Weber advocates value freedom not as abstention from all value commitments but rather as the "freedom to pursue the values of science within the relevant limits, without their being overridden by values either contradictory to or irrelevant to those of scientific investigation. [It] involves the renunciation of any claims that the scientist qua scientist speaks for a value position, on a broader basis of social or cultural significance than that of his science" (Parsons 1967b:86). Yet scientific values for Weber are not completely independent of the values of the particular cultures in which science is practiced at any given time. No matter how fully empirical propositions are validated, "their inclusion in a body of knowledge about society is never completely independent of the value perspective from which those particular questions were asked [and] to which these propositions constitute answers" (Parsons 1967c:149). To some extent social science is necessarily integrated with the values of the society and culture in which it is practiced. It must be integrated in the sense that "truth" for human beings can be elaborated and possessed only within an ongoing social tradition, and in the sense that people cannot evaluate a statement if they remove it from any presupposed type of discourse and suspend all presuppositions of the background knowledge appropriate to this type.[24] As such, social science can provide answers not to *all* possible significant problems of societies but only to those that have meaning within a given integrate of society and social science.

Proposals for a Nonreductive Yet Critical Relationship between Competing Value Systems

Examination of these contending positions within the scientific study of religion suggests five ways of taking a thin approach to understanding religious faith. A normatively thin relationship between competing value systems is possible where reductionism can be avoided. It can be avoided at the levels of what I shall describe as "ontology," rationality, values, "solidarity across difference," and autonomy. I shall conclude with one more proposal, for securing the *critical* potential of a thin, nonreductive relationship.

First, at the level of "ontology" (in the sense of "How many legitimate spheres of value are there?"): Marx employs a notion of science *qua* critique because his notion of science does not allow for the coexistence of competing systems of value. It allows only the value system of science and thus reduces any competing system to that of the scientific observer. By contrast, Weber, Durkheim, and Parsons assume to varying degrees a dualistic ontology that need not reduce the participant's religious domain to the observer's scientific domain. But the differences are equally salient. For Durkheim the dualism of sacred and profane is not absolute; each sphere, though equally real, might be regarded as a different expression of one reality. Weber regards the dualism of ideas and interests as an unbridgeable chasm between two realities.

On the other hand, Durkheim's method leads to a search for universal characteristics of religious phenomena. His approach seeks to identify, in a given society, social structures and functions supposedly found in any society. Not so Weber. Because his method posits the impossibility of any kind of reconciliation between internal and external conditions, it contents itself with identifying paradoxes and antitheses between them. For his part, Parsons, like Weber, views the dualism of science and religion as unbridgeable. But unlike Weber, he tends to reduce the cognitive and normative integrity of religion to psychological needs.

The varying degrees of nonreductionism in the work of Weber, Durkheim, and Parsons allow for competing value systems, for more than one "true" or "valid" value system. In this sense, and toward a normatively thin relationship between competing cultural systems, I propose that reductionism be avoided at the level of ontology by allowing for more than one "world" or sphere of valid values. Thus sociological claims and counterclaims about religion can be evaluated only if the sociologist assumes the reality of religion beyond all discourse about religion, as the external or independent referent of discourse. Georg Simmel (1997:129–130) offers one example of a normatively thin relationship between religious faith and secular intellectuality:

> Religious belief, because its origin and purpose are to be found in morality and not in intellectuality, is completely withdrawn from the intellectual demands of truth. . . . Anguish, doubt, isolation, and even an overflowing sense of life that passes the limits of the finite can lead to a belief in God. But belief itself still is not defined in this way, be-

cause even here it still could be a purely theoretical supposition, even though the same supposition born of emotional needs would result in emotional satisfactions. The intimate essence of religious belief . . . can be expressed in this way only: it designates a state of the human soul, an *actuality* and not a simple reflection of an actuality, like all that is theoretical. Intellectuality itself doubtless also designates a certain mode of existence for the soul. But in relation to the role that it plays in the whole of our existence, the mental process itself and the existential form that is expressed by it are effaced entirely in the presence of its content.

Second, at the level of rationality (in the sense of "Does understanding presuppose that the observer and observed share the same rationality?"): to varying degrees Weber, Marx, Durkheim, and Parsons share an external, objectifying standpoint that regards religion as a phenomenon of the finite world and therefore open to causal analysis. Marx absolutizes this standpoint: for him scientific reason is the sole point of reference, one that cannot tolerate the ambiguities and paradoxes of a dualistic model that recognizes nonrational dimensions of human experience and existence. Marx must regard as ideological any standpoint other than science. To some extent Parsons shares this Promethean urge to Enlightenment rationality. While he views what he takes to be the nonrational sphere of religion to provide an indispensable function in the individual's social and psychological adjustment to the world, he cannot recognize the claims to truth made by religion. Marx posits one "world" and one truth, while Parsons posits two "worlds" and one truth.

Durkheim and Weber provide an alternative, by allowing for depths of reality beyond rational conceptualization. Their approaches contain central terms that, as Robert Bellah (1970:240) says, do not so much explain something as point to nonrational, noncognitive factors of central importance to the understanding of human action. Durkheim (1965:479) appreciates depths of reality beyond rational conceptualization, as well as the importance of nonrational dimensions of human existence: "Thus religions, even the most rational and laicized cannot and never will be able to dispense with a particular form of speculation which . . . cannot be really scientific." Yet Durkheim's approach also shares certain characteristics of Marx's. Whereas Weber views reason and religion as sometimes complementary, he excludes the possibility of their reconciliation. Durkheim, on the other hand, expects traditional religious beliefs to be transformed into a new cult of humanity. On the latter view, individualism in its true form—the religion of humanity, the cult of the dignity of the individual—is the true moral basis of modern society (Durkheim 1973a, 1973b; Wallwork 1972:150), just as the cult of the individual is the highest moral ideal of society.[25]

And yet Durkheim, like Marx, brings religion and science together. Where Marx does this by *reducing* religion to reason (in the sense that reason is "true" and religion "false"), Durkheim collapses religion and reason, equally, into one (in the sense that both are "true" where religion becomes a new cult of human rationality). On this point Durkheim is something of a reductionist after all, if in a different sense than Marx. Both adopt a normatively thick approach of one value system toward another—in Bourdieu's (1990:39) words, "sliding from the model of reality to the reality of the model," confusing a particular approach or interpretation of reality with reality itself, confusing a construct that reduces the complexity of a phenomenon (that it may be grasped) with reality as it exists independently of human efforts and means to understand it. Against this background I propose (toward normatively thin political judgment among competing value systems) that reductionism be avoided at the level of rationality and that it *can* be avoided even by an external, objectifying standpoint, by allowing an abiding autonomy to some spheres or some forms of nonrationality.

Third, at the level of values (in the sense of "Does understanding require that observed and observer have the same values?"): Marx's method acknowledges solely scientific values (as does Parsons's), just as it thematizes religion in terms of religion's nonreligious sources and in terms of the individual's nonreligious needs. Marx's "monist" approach (the notion that there is but one reality, namely, the object of scientific research) views truth and value as one. Weber and Durkheim reject this stance; their respective methods do not exclude values other than those of science. The "ontological dualism" of both men entails, in their minds, value pluralism: the norms and truths of religion are recognized as norms and truths in their own right, approachable outside an anthropocentric frame of reference. At times Durkheim argues that moral and other social facts are sui generis and not reducible to any other kind of reality.[26] Weber regards factual and evaluative questions as irreducible to each other and therefore life as unavoidably marked by problems of value. Parsons makes much the same point where he argues that all action involves tension between subjective norms and objective conditions. Durkheim's approach displays affinities with Marx's. Like Marx, Durkheim regards the problem of value as solvable—Marx through science, Durkheim through a science of morality. But unlike Marx, Durkheim is highly ambivalent about this implied homogeneity of factual and evaluative questions. Weber and Parsons by contrast agree in what they regard as the irresolvable nature of problems of value. In this connection, my third proposal (for a thin relationship between competing systems) is that reductionism be avoided at the level of values: by not collapsing evaluative questions into factual ones, that is, by allowing at least some socially legitimate values to be autonomous of truth.

Fourth, at the level of "solidarity across differences": a normatively thin relationship between competing value systems might follow in a given case if it could be shown that one value system shared both distance and proximity with another, a "kind of solidarity beyond cultural differences" (Bourdieu 1990:15). The relationship would not abolish the distance between competing value systems by "bringing the outsider fictitiously closer to an imaginary native, as is generally attempted; [rather,] it is by distancing, through objectification, the native who is in every outside observer[,] that the native is brought closer to the outsider" (Bourdieu 1990:20). We observe both proximity and distance between competing value systems in Parsons's argument that reality resides in both religious symbol *and* human subject and that each sphere of value is in some ways dependent on the other, competing one: the "canons of empirical science apply primarily to symbols that attempt to express the nature of objects, but there are nonobjective symbols that express the feelings, values, and hopes of subjects, or that organize and regulate the flow of interaction between subjects and objects, or that attempt to sum up the whole subject-object complex or even point to the context or ground of that whole. These symbols, too, express reality and are not reducible to empirical propositions."[27] Indeed, the "ultimate nature of reality" is not subject to empirical specification, though any cultural system must have some way of symbolizing it.

Durkheim captures the copresence of distance and proximity between competing value systems where, as a scientific analyst of religion, he recognizes nonrational aspects of reality, claiming that science itself has a nonrational foundation, that rational inquiry "rests on a necessary substratum of sentiments and representations that have neither the form nor the function of scientific hypotheses" (Bellah 1970:251). Not only science but "most moral and social institutions are due, not to reasoning or calculation, but to obscure causes, to subconscious sentiments, to motives without relation to the effects which they produce and which they cannot consequently explain" (Durkheim 1887:45). Durkheim (1982:167) argues that "men never do perceive the true motives which cause them to act. . . . This is therefore even more true when we act under the influence of social causes which we fail to perceive even more because they are more remote and more complex." Hence "social life must be explained not by the conception of it formed by those who participate in it, but by the profound causes which escape their consciousness" (Durkheim 1982:167). Durkheim shows that the respective value systems of science and religion, while very different, are inescapably embedded in the limitations of the human beings who pursue them, in the limitations of human finitude, including inherent and unalterable limitations to understanding.

Weber, too, identifies the copresence of distance and proximity between competing value systems. While he distinguishes between reason and religion, he also sees them as sometimes complementary, not always antagonistic. Thus the rationalism of world mastery originates at least in part from a religiously motivated orientation to the world. Rationalism of this sort brings about in certain groups a constancy in their inner relationship to the ultimate religious values and interpretations of life.[28] Like Durkheim, Weber identifies extrarational guides to behavior, specifically the extrarational need for "meaning"—a need also experienced in rational scientific behavior. Among the goals and values orienting scientific behavior may be the individual scientist's need for "meaning," a need in addition to and distinct from what might be the rational needs for science (such as the "need" to know, and to know in as rigorous or rationally robust a sense as possible). The quest for "meaning" may be irrational but nonetheless compatible with the quest for rational understanding.

At still another site Durkheim and Weber identify distance between, yet proximity of, competing systems of value: in the relationship between rationality (as a value system) and affect-based meaning (as another value system). Durkheim considers sentiments and emotional reactions essential to the functioning of a social system, as phenomena "necessarily integrated with cognitive patterns" (Parsons 1954:209); without these phenomena the coordination of action would be impossible. What Durkheim calls "collective representations" are based on the sentiment of respect; rational thought is possible only through the discipline that respect imposes (Bellah 1970:251). For Weber (1949:57) the "fate of an epoch which has eaten of the tree of knowledge is that it must know that we cannot learn the *meaning* of the world from the results of its analysis, be it ever so perfect; it must rather be in a position to create this meaning itself." Human action, says Weber, tends to integrate the "religious" level of problems (problems of meaning) and the "secular" level of problems (problems of empirical causation). Action integrates them in the sense that neither nonrational needs (such as emotional ones) nor rational needs are sufficient to determine human behavior by themselves: the "influence of religious doctrine is not exerted through the actor's coming to a conviction and then acting upon it in a rational sense" (Parsons 1954:209). "Even a natural scientist selects those aspects of the external world for study that have an inner meaning to him, that reflect some often hidden inner conflict" (Bellah 1970:254). "[C]hoice is, like all social action, also guided by moral commitments and moral preferences," attempting "not just to disclose reality but also to preserve and extend the relevance of a particular interpretation of it" (Alexander 1982:124).

Fifth, at the level of autonomy (that is, autonomy of competing value systems from one another): Weber (1958b:269–270) suggests how to structure, in normatively thin ways, the relationship between competing value systems where he identifies the autonomy of religion vis-à-vis secular scholarship. He does so where he captures the distinctiveness of religion in its peculiarly nonsocial sources (for example, transcendental or otherworldly ones), and in its origins in peculiarly nonsocial needs (in the sense, for example, of a need for otherworldly salvation or redemption). Religion is never a "simple function of the social location of that stratum which [appears] as its distinctive carrier; [religion] is neither its 'ideology' nor a 'reflection' of its material or ideal interest constellation" (ibid.).

Durkheim posits this kind of autonomy where he treats the human agent's *and* society's ideas as if they had a life of their own, as if they were agents within the agent and independent of the agent.[29] For Durkheim (1974:31) "collective representations" are able to "attract and repel each other and to form amongst themselves various syntheses, which are determined by their natural affinities. . . . They are immediately caused by other collective representations and not by this or that characteristic of the social structure." For Durkheim (1947:388) the *conscience collective* "more and more comes to consist of very general and very indeterminate ways of thinking and feeling, which leave an open place for a growing multitude of individual differences." Durkheim rejects Marx's notion that religion is the outcome of social structure with his counterargument that religion creates itself, that it has a will of its own.

Parsons views religion in its functional relationship to society. The distinctiveness of religion, from this vantage, lies precisely in its social sources, and in its origin in social needs. Here religion is not autonomous; viewed separately from these sources and needs, religion has no distinctiveness. Hence a social science of religion then cannot recognize as valid the norms religion claims for itself.[30] On the other hand, Parsons (1937:421, 428) locates autonomy between competing value systems where he asserts that religious symbols refer to a nonempirical realm beyond empirical sociology, to "aspects of 'reality' . . . outside the range of scientific investigation and analysis." Parsons (ibid., 425) believes that his own argument vindicates the "general views of partisans of religion." And he argues that the interest of religion is unlike the scientific interest in cognitive truth, that religious commitment is not a commitment to truth in the sense that science is. While religious ideas may display cognitive elements, in general humans "do not . . . 'believe' their religious ideas in quite the same sense that they believe the sun rises every morning" (ibid.). The cognitive patterns of religion, then, are distinct from those of social science: "Where there is an explicit symbolic interpretation of his actions on the part of the actor, it need not agree with that which would be imputed by the observer" (ibid., 420).[31]

I turn now to a final proposal for constructing a thin relationship between competing systems of cultural values. My first three proposals advocate various forms of nonreductionism. Nonreductionism allows for competing value systems, for more than one "true" or "valid" value system. By itself, however, nonreductionism provides no guidance for how competing value systems might seek to understand each other critically. To understand religion, secular scholarship need not reduce religion to science; but it also cannot be content to understand religion by analyzing its meanings and consequences solely in light of religion's own traditions, values, practices, and beliefs (nor should people of religious faith refrain from evaluating secular scholarship by their own lights). Critical evaluation is always possible even of a competing system of values. Anthony Giddens (1994:251) distinguishes "between *respect for the authenticity of belief*, as a necessary condition of any hermeneutic encounter between language-games; and the *critical evaluation of the justification of belief*." Here understanding concerns winning access to "foreign" or "alien" systems of cultural values. Part of the attempt involves understanding the other as the other understands itself. Giddens (1994:251) calls such understanding "mutual knowledge," that which is shared by observer and observed when understanding comes about. But such understanding does not require that the observer share the observed's estimation of the validity of his or her value system or belief claims. To respect the authenticity of the value system in question, to respect the fact that those who adhere to it, do so sincerely, in good faith, is not necessarily for the observer to embrace that system or its beliefs. On the one hand, understanding can bracket questions of the validity of what is understood. On the other hand, it can evaluate the observed system's claims to validity from its own standpoint. Giddens (1994:251–252) argues that the "language of schizophrenics is meaningful, so long as we see that some of the notions that are taken for granted by the majority of the population are questioned or expressed in quite different form by schizophrenic individuals. The development of dialogue with schizophrenic persons, as a hermeneutic endeavor, is only possible if we accept that their utterances and behavior may be treated 'methodologically' as authentic. To treat such utterances and behavior as authentic means to hold in abeyance their possible validity or falsity." But it is not to preclude, as a step subsequent to understanding, the critical evaluation by standards other than the schizophrenic's self-understanding.

Beyond the understanding of one value system by another, each system may consider the factual status of the claims of the other. "Mutual knowledge" does not require the suspension of critical evaluation: "Mutual knowledge is the necessary medium of identifying what is going on when a sorcerer places a malicious spell upon an individual in order to procure that person's death. But this is no logical bar at all to critical inquiry into the empirical grounding that can be marshaled to support the validity of the belief-claims held in relation to this practice, or into their possible ideological ramifications" (Giddens

1994:252). Thus "accurate characterizations of the beliefs and practices connected with Zande sorcery are 'rational'—insofar as that term
means . . . that there exist internally coherent frames which both a
sociological observer and the Azande draw upon in generating descriptions of witchcraft. [But it is not true that] . . . this acknowledgment of
the 'rationality' or authenticity of Zande witchcraft and oracular divi-
nation precludes critical evaluation of the beliefs and the activities thus
characterized or identified" (Giddens 1994:252). The same approach
holds for the outside observer: in the face of questions, objections, or
other evaluation about the accuracy, validity, or appropriateness of the
observer's claims, the observer is constrained to justify those claims.
Of course, if the challenge comes from another observer, the challenge
may be based on the same system of cultural values. But even within
scholarship, many positions distinguish themselves from one another
by adherence to very different presuppositions, and persons holding
one position may well seek to justify that position in terms of an outside critic's standards and presuppositions.

In this spirit I propose that any given system seek to evaluate the
validity of the claims of any other system *in nonimmanent (or external
or detached) terms.* This idea is of a piece with the recommendation in
chapter 3 that each concrete community be constrained to justify itself
in terms of generalized community. My first four proposals seek a normatively thin understanding among competing value systems, where
understanding is not corrigible to the observer. My final proposal seeks
to include, as one element in this relationship, a critical perspective of
one system toward another, rendering the observed system corrigible
by the lights of the observer.

This final proposal also goes toward a normatively thin conception
of understanding that encourages observer and observed alike to entertain alternative claims, by competing value systems, that might cast
doubt on any given system's validity or coherence or desirability. To
be appropriately critical the outside observer, whether social scientist,
social critic, or a competing system of values, must continuously overcome some all-too-human inertia. The observer does so by the ener-
getic and taxing effort to continually entertain alternative criteria of
truth (likely a difficult effort that demands the best of the observer,
but one familiar to anyone who has ever attempted to "keep an open
mind"; and sociologists of religion might regard their stance as scholars to akin to being "protonovitiates" of whatever faith they study,

not sacrificing the integrity of their scholarly identities but remaining always open to exploring ways in which the religionist's experiences and beliefs might be no less "authentic" than the sociologist's). If the claims of any given value system were "true" or socially valid in the sense of merely having to justify themselves only to themselves, that system might well have no compelling reason to understand competing systems. In the context of secular scholarship on religious faith, to entertain alternative criteria of truth is to reject empiricism. To argue that there is one inclusive reality, that there is only one type of rationality for asking questions of truth or meaning, that there is solely one set of norms for both science and religion, is to argue that religious beliefs and actions can be exhaustively understood as products of their social environment. This is an empiricist stance. The more social science approaches religion as a purely social phenomenon, the more empiricist its claims. But to reject empiricism is not necessarily to embrace a strong form of relativism (for example, the idea that some parts of what might be called the "discourse" or "logic" of religion cannot possibly be translated into the "discourse" or "logic" of social science). The respective value systems of secular science and religious faith may overlap in part, but only in part. Even if, as value systems, they are entirely distinct from each other, "translation" of one into the other would still be possible, and possible without reducing religion to one more social phenomenon (in the sense that social science is such a phenomenon). To the significant extent that religious and scientific value systems are distinct from each other, social science should refrain from limiting its scope only to (ultimately) empirically testable truth claims about social phenomena. In terms more general: each value system must entertain criteria of truth distinct from its own, employing a weak form of relativism; sensitivity to different criteria of truth or validity implies some form of relativism.[32]

Contingent and relative is the validity of any given value system, necessarily situated and oriented on its own standards. But standards of validity must exceed any particular value system if that system is to be valid in more than a merely parochial sense. A value system's claims to validity must be able to span the tension between the more limited conditions of any given value system, and the less limited conditions of a standpoint *beyond* any particular value system. A value system can span this tension without breaking on it if it can resist appeal to universal criteria. A value system's claims to validity that are less than universal can nonetheless escape parochialism. It must overshoot itself, as it must overshoot any particular value system without positing some universal one. Secular scholarship fails to do so where it asserts the *universal* superiority of scientific knowledge over the many forms of nonscientific knowledge; religious faith fails to overshoot itself, as only one particular value system among others, where it refuses all appeals of its critical observer to common sense. In Bourdieu's (1990:28) imaginative terms, the "most formidable barrier to the construction of an adequate science of practice . . . lies in the fact that the solidarity that binds scientists to their science (and to the social privilege which makes it possible and which it justifies or procures) predisposes them to profess the superiority of their knowledge, often won through enormous efforts, against common sense, and even to find in that superiority a justification for their privilege, rather than to produce a scientific knowledge of the practical mode of knowledge[,] and of the limits that scientific knowledge owes to the fact that it is based on a privilege."

External justification of any given value system is provided only at the normatively thin level of what Jean Cohen and Andrew Arato (1992:24) call "cultural or political modernity (based on the principles of critical reflection, discursive conflict resolution, equality, autonomy, participation, and justice)." In this way a normatively thin approach can reject a purely immanent justification of cultural values—it can oppose a normatively *thick* justification of thick cultural values—for a normatively *thin* justification of thick cultural values. And it can do so in ways that do not misconstrue the thick norms of the value system in question (in this sense my first four proposals attempt to confront the epistemological difficulties of understanding the other as the other understands itself). This final proposal offers a reflexive, nonauthoritarian approach to the critical function of observing and understanding other systems of cultural values: evaluating them not on their own terrain but outside it. Sociologist and religionist alike can appreciate that no system of cultural values can ground or defend every last one of its presuppositions, and each might then be willing to acknowledge that his or her own system is problematic just as competing systems are problematic, even if to different extents and in different ways. Both can appreciate how, in any system of cultural values, various presuppositions are made toward maintaining or achieving that system's internal coherence, and each might then be willing to entertain the "reasonableness" or "logic" of a system adopting this or that presupposition toward filling out its overall vision or approach. To do so would require neither sociologist nor religionist to sacrifice the integrity of his or her system of values. And it might render the observer more open to understanding the participant's beliefs and behaviors in some of the ways the participant understands them.

A value system that relates to other value systems in terms only of its own thick normativity is (in the language of chapter 3) like a concrete community that refuses to relate to other concrete communities (each with its own thick normativity) in the normatively thin manner of generalized community. Fundamentalism of this sort makes itself vulnerable to misunderstanding, nonunderstanding but also, at the extreme, to the intervention of thin norms, as when a particular value system violates constitutionally guaranteed rights of one of its adherents: there the state properly enforces those rights even against those communities that refuse or deny them. But the nonfundamentalist observer who takes a normatively thin approach becomes aware of how the object of observation understands him- or herself, but equally aware of how the observing subject understands him- or herself. A thin approach requires the observer to call into question not only the presuppositions of the value system he or she observes but also those inherent in his or her own position as the observer "who, seeking to interpret practices, tends to bring into the object the principles of his relation to the object, as is shown for example by the privileged status he gives to communicative and epistemic functions, which inclines him to reduce exchanges to pure symbolic exchanges" (Bourdieu 1990:27). A normatively thin approach is nonfundamentalist.

From the moment immanent understandings are not accepted as "adequate" explanations ("adequate" at the normatively thin level of generalized community) but are placed into question or viewed with a feeling of distance, the questioner exceeds a merely immanent perspective and analysis. The act of discursive contestation itself minimally implies procedures of argumentation and standards of adjudication that can be valid far beyond merely immanent understandings.[33] Understanding among competing value systems is possible if noninternal criteria can be discovered or constructed with which to understand, even if those criteria are ad hoc. Only then is understanding possible not merely within any one value system but across different ones.

Chapter 7 extends the thrust of this one—creating forms of understanding across different and often competing standpoints—to the intersections of sexual discrimination with race, marriage and divorce, social class, or status as immigrant. This chapter criticized the simple reduction of one value system to a competing one; the next chapter critiques sectional interests that masquerade as universal ones. The present chapter advocated noninternal criteria by which to construct understanding across different value systems; the following one identifies principles of critique that hold across the various partial and limited perspectives that the critic must temporarily assume if she or he is to avoid privileging one at the expense of others.

POLITICAL JUDGMENT

AS IDEOLOGY CRITIQUE

7

Normatively thin political judgment is possible in the treatment of indeterminate legal norms (chapter 5) and in the treatment of competing systems of cultural values (chapter 6). How is it possible as ideology critique? How can a normatively thin standpoint critically evaluate normatively thick standpoints, when "evaluate" means distinguishing between "valid" standpoints and ones not valid because "ideological"? This chapter answers these questions in terms of ideology as a form of distorted communication.[1] Distortion is more than merely misunderstanding or understanding based on inadequate information; it is the *active* manipulation of information, its instrumentalization, toward achieving some goal far afield from "truth telling." It is characterized by complexity, as a web of beliefs intricately woven together; by institutionalization, as the integration of those beliefs into public knowledge, and by the reproduction of that web through the regular channels of communication. The standard by which critique identifies ideology can only be some conception of truth, and "ideological" is the degree of deviation from that standard, which is at once critique's normative foundation. This foundation is also its political goal: beyond the elimination of deviation, or its limitation as much as possible, lies the critic's preferred state of affairs. Karl Marx grounds his critique in a conception of nonalienated labor, free and creative activity that allows actors to realize their multifaceted potential as unique human beings. With this standard Marx identifies deformations and perversions of the laboring capacity, perverted to self-degrading and self-enslaving activity (and which renders agents incapable of grasping their situation). Jürgen Habermas rejects Marx's notion of nonalienated, instrumental practice for one of nonalienated communicative practice, among citizens in the public sphere engaged in communal self-determination free of force, compulsion, and distortion. Habermas (1973) conceptualizes the work of overcoming barriers to achieving public agreement by transposing, to the level of society in general, the model of psychoanalysis that Sigmund Freud articulates at the level of individuals. Freud's model overcomes barriers to distorted communication by identifying the pathology of the individual's self, the hidden springs of troubled and opaquely understood behavior, the ideologically camouflaged source of distorted communication. Habermas (1984:21) adopts and extends the argument: through *therapeutic* critique, a "form of argumentation that serves to clarify systematic self-deception," whole communities can work their way from distorted to undistorted communication, "removing restrictions on communication" (Habermas 1970:118), eliminating ideologies blocking the way of rational communication and political practice in a public sphere equally accessible to all citizens.

As in Marx, so also for Habermas: the foundation of critique is equally its political goal. Rationality for Habermas is both the means of criticizing a rigid and repressive normative system and the goal of social norms transparent to individuals and freely embraced by them on the basis of their discursively understood merits.[2] Habermas (1975:107–108) locates the logic of this everyday practice in something quite beyond mundane practice, in "discourse," a counterfactual form of communication "removed from contexts of experience and action and whose structure assures us: that the bracketed validity claims of assertions, recommendations, or warnings are the exclusive object of discussion; that participants, themes, and contributions are not restricted except with reference to the goal of testing the validity claims in question; that no force except that of the better argument is exercised; and that all motives except that of the cooperative search for truth are excluded." This critique of "epistemological bondage" bases itself on the standard and possibility of "epistemological freedom," freedom from the hidden interests that drive ideology. The critique of ideology, says Marx (1972), must be more than the critique of consciousness by consciousness; it must pierce systematic distortion to uncover the real basis for actors' behavior, its material basis in ideologically obscured interests. Not the ideas themselves but the interests behind the ideas generate ideology.

I shall adopt this view in the following sense. Ideological is any claim that asserts universal validity when it merely reflects the interests and experiences of only one sector or group (predictably a socially dominant one) in the sense of Marx and Engel's (1930:50) dictum, "The ruling ideas of each age have ever been the ideas of its ruling class."[3] Sectional interests masquerading as universal interests perpetrate an ideological perspective, which critique can expose if it can reveal alternative ways of looking at the world (such as those of the socially subordinate). For example, legislation, or public policy, or industrial relations constructed solely or mainly from the perspective of men, or derived mainly from their experience, or articulated mainly in terms of specifically men's needs (think of medicine developed mainly by reference to the male body alone) can be relativized in its claims to validity in the face of women's perspectives. Critique brings to the surface of social consciousness the hitherto submerged or unacknowledged perspective of subordinated groups by "framing" its inquiries in various ways: which of various perspectives is the participant assuming? Which is the critic or observer assuming? To what extent is the perspective of participant or observer laced with hidden interests? Which embodiments, social locations, or economic circumstances (from race, ethnicity, and age to sex, socioeconomic class, and sexual orientation) define the perspective in question? As an exercise in framing, thin critique is a kind of "perspectivalism," an antihegemonic perspectivalism that privileges pluralism and in that sense is normatively thin.[4] While the partial or particular perspectives unearthed by thin critique are less than universally valid, they are valuable if authentic expressions of this or that socially situated group. Perspectivalism encourages sensitivity to forms of sensibility different from the observer's— in Clifford Geertz's (1983:181–182) words, welding the "processes of self-knowledge, self-perception, self-understanding to those of other-knowledge, other-perception, other-understanding," helping "both to free us from misleading representations of our own way of rendering matters" and to "force into our reluctant consciousness discordant views of how this is to be done." The object that critique targets is socially constructed, and critique cannot be some sort of "social mechanics, a physics of judgment" but rather (as an intersubjective creation) a kind of "cultural hermeneutics, a semantics of action" (ibid., 182).[5]

In regard to the contemporary social situation of women, thin critique begins with questions of how best to frame difference. Which differences are relevant? Which intersections of which differences are relevant? For example, as the standard by which to determine deviations signaling discrimination, disadvantage, or other inequality, should critique assume one model of employment—the one to which most men are subject, namely full-time employment—or engage alternative models as well, such as part-time employment, or wages for homemakers, or wages for indigent homemakers with dependent children? Should deviation ever be defined in terms other than those of a male standard? Should women seek assimilation to standards now applied to men, or should they insist on the relevant differences of women from men? For Deborah Rhode (1989:97–98) the "question should not be simply whether women are, or are not, 'like men' with respect to a given occupation. Of greater significance is whether that occupation can be redefined to accommodate biological differences and whether gender as a social construct can be redefined to make those differences less occupationally relevant." By contrast, the rules for eligibility in social assistance programs in the United States are written in sexually neutral language yet reflect the pattern of male employment, "rewarding continuous attachment to the labor force, long years of service, and high wages," thereby disadvantaging "women whose shorter and more irregular work histories make it more difficult for them to obtain full benefits" (Quadagno 1990:14). In this way the rules replicate the inequities of the market.[6]

Among the most socially significant differences framed by perspectivalism is the intersection of sex and race. Both are immutable characteristics, highly visible, historically consequential as criteria for the distribution of public burdens and public goods (for example, in the United States the franchise originally extended only to white males). Both have served as badges of inferiority: women, on this perspective, are suited for childrearing and housecleaning, not for prosecuting wars or conducting commerce (even as motherhood for women is regarded less socially significant than military service for men); blacks are suited for sports or entertainment but not for high politics or the learned professions. Both characteristics have defined legalized disadvantages (exclusion from voting, serving on juries, owning property, following certain professions such as the law). In other respects political and legal culture in the United States has treated sex and race differently: the fact that only women can become pregnant and bear children distinguishes them from men in ways multiply relevant to public policy (maternity leave, abortion, the provision of child care), unlike chromatic differences among citizens' skins. Unlike African Americans, white women were never legal chattel, and the sexes, unlike the races, have never been segregated residentially (even if segregated in other ways, for example in schools and workplaces).

Thin Critique in Distinction to Hegemonic Critique

If perspectivalism is to be a viable form of knowledge, it must be more than simply relativism. And it cannot be viable if it is some form of cognitive parochialism.[7] Critique becomes impossible where all perspectives are equally valid, one canceling out another. All critique, including the normatively thin form I propose, must invoke standards. Later in this chapter I shall develop equality and autonomy as the standards of normatively thin ideology critique. But I first turn to the issue of how thin critique can avoid being itself a form of ideology. I argue that it can do so by avoiding a "hegemonic" approach. Hegemonic, for example, are feminisms that take to be universally valid, or applicable without further distinction among its objects or addressees, the partial perspectives of white, middle-class North American or Western European women. A hegemonic approach absolutizes the particular social situation of some women and thereby denies or ignores differently situated women. Thin critique rejects the notion that there is *a* woman's standpoint as such; hegemonic, for example, is that analysis of inequality that assumes that all women are white: "Nancy Chodorow's (1978) work on sex role socialization and Carol Gilligan's (1982) study of the moral development of women both rely heavily on white, middle-class samples," promoting the "notion of a generic woman who is white and middle class" (Collins 2000:6). Where race and sex both structure the individual's experience of inequality, hegemonic critique assumes, for example, not only that all women are white but that all relevant people of color are male. It misses the fact that, in the workplace distribution of authority and wages, black women tend to be disadvantaged with respect to both black men (male trumps female) and white women (white trumps black).[8] Hegemonic critique also misses the fact that white male often trumps white female "more" than black male trumps black female: "Familial patriarchy, which is based on the privileging of the white father as modeled in the traditional white heterosexual family, has different resonance for white women than for women of color. Male privilege is racialized: white men are more privileged than are black men, especially outside the family" (Eisenstein 1994:201). It misses the fact that, in the marketplace, race trumps sex: "Gender places most women within the sexual ghetto of the labor force, and

race further orders that ghetto," placing women of color dispropor-
tionately "within racial ghettoes within sexual ghettoes" (ibid., 202).
And it misses the fact that, in the market economy, race trumps sex,
the more so when actors are of the advantaged race, less so when they
are of a disadvantaged one: "Patriarchy does not allow black men the
same control over their lives as it does white men. It . . . positions black
men against black women. The privileging of black men is deformed by
racism. The market is racially structured via grossly unequal employment opportunities; it traditionally privileges white men as 'providers'
for white women" (ibid., 203–204).[9]

Hegemonic critique loses sight of the fact that, in the gendered organization of work, in the allocation of positions, and in the setting of
wages, male often trumps female: "Hierarchy is reinforced through the
obscuring of certain skills and competencies in many female-defined
jobs. The invisibility of some skills in typical women's work is actively created in a number of ways, while in contrast, the visibility of
other skills, traditionally identified with masculinity, is also actively
produced. The definition, control, and transformation of skill are central to work and class; their allocation and recognition on the basis
of gender indicates a profound connection between gender and class"
(Acker 1989:222). A hegemonic approach also misses the complex ways
in which sex and class are intertwined: "Writers on patriarchy have
sometimes asserted that the primary cause of women's oppression is
the interests of men in maintaining the subordination of women. Critics point out that such theories assume inaccurately that all men, as
men, have similar interests, but that reality is more complicated," with
the "interests of managers and male workers . . . [sometimes] at odds"
and male-dominated unions disinclined to "undercut the interests of
male members," thus sometimes "supporting women's interests and
sometimes opposing them" (ibid., 206–207). And hegemonic critique
is unable to capture the fact that, in the workplace, some middle-
class women can trump sex bias, but often low-class women cannot:
some middle-class and college-educated women may "escape the grind
of routinized office," whereas "countless others (often working-class
women and women of color) [are left] to entry-level jobs that are more
boring and de-humanizing than ever" (Strom 1992:406).[10]

Unlike hegemonic approaches, thin critique neither privileges one
vector of oppression over another nor excludes one at the expense of
another. Precisely its pluralist approach positions it to see, for example,

parallels between the respective ideologies of sexism and racism. Both impose a very rigid template on very diverse individuals, leaching out most differences among them. Both are forms of social integration that devalue, diminish, and deform the socialized. Both rob society of the potential contributions of their respective victims. Prejudice on the basis of putative "natural" differences (between men and women, or between whites and people of color) parallels a putatively "natural" division of labor and social status that slates men and white women for better life chances, women and people of color for lesser ones, and white women for better life chances than black women.

Thin critique opposes the assimilation of women to men's current status, practices, and expectations in public and private spheres, because assimilation reduces difference to identity by claiming in effect that solely men's status, practices, and expectations are valid or appropriate or desirable for women. Thin critique also opposes any return to traditional understandings of a woman's role where "gender inequality stem[s] less from denial of opportunities available to men than from devaluation of functions and qualities associated with women" (Rhode 1989:306). Sexual equality cannot simply be mandated by legislative fiat imposing formal equality, and thin critique rejects purely formal understandings of legal rights that in fact perpetuate factual inequality. But it does not reject law *tout court* as a means to the social equality of men and women. Beyond conventional understandings of rights, the law can help identify and eliminate some sexual stereotypes. It can distinguish between those instances where sexual difference is relevant to achieving a policy or program and those where it is not. The first category might include middle- and high-school classes in mathematics available only to female students (in an effort to counter the well-documented sex-specific slide in performance at the point of adolescence) but perhaps also nursing schools for men only (as one means to combat institutionalized sexual bias against male nurses).[11] In the second category, where sexual difference is irrelevant to the goals of a program or legislation, the state should not presuppose that all women are dependent on their spouse's income for purposes of awarding workman's compensation benefits to a surviving spouse or social security death benefits to a surviving spouse or parent. In the same vein the state should not always require men, but never women, to pay alimony upon divorce.[12]

If the relevant differences are cultural, socially constructed, and contingent (such as definitions of the family, or gender, or occupational limitations that supposedly follow from one's sex), then legal treatment runs the danger of essentializing what is only contingent, normalizing what is merely one option among others, or privileging one tradition and marginalizing another. In the legal sphere, writes Deborah Rhode (1989:82),

> traditional approaches have failed to generate coherent or convincing definitions of difference. All too often, modern equal-protection law has treated as inherent and essential differences that are cultural and contingent. Sex-related characteristics have been both over- and undervalued. In some cases, such as those involving occupational restrictions, courts have allowed biology to dictate destiny. In other contexts, such as pregnancy discrimination, they have ignored woman's special reproductive needs. The focus on whether challenged classifications track some existing differences between the sexes has obscured the disadvantages that follow from such differences. . . . We must insist not just on equal treatment but on woman's treatment as equal.

In Martha Minow's (1990:309) words, "Interpreting rights as features of relationships, contingent upon negotiation within a community committed to this mode of solving problems, pins law not on some force beyond human control but on human responsibility for the patterns of relationships promoted or hindered by this process. In this way the notion of rights as tools in continuing communal discourse helps to locate responsibility in human beings for legal action and inaction."

But normatively thin ideology critique is more than simply nonhegemonic. I turn now to limning its contours at the twin levels at which it engages ideology: at the macro level of structure and then at the more micro level of agency.

Thin Critique at the Level of Structure

This chapter adopts one of the several definitions of ideology critique that Marx (1972) offers in *The German Ideology:* the critique not of consciousness but of hidden interests. It rejects the notion of ideology as primarily a matter of ideas, as argued for example by Antonio Gramsci yet not by Georg Lukács, both of whom draw heavily if creatively on Marx. Lukács (1976:51) analyzes "class consciousness" as the particular belief systems shared by members of the same socioeconomic stratum; he links the "objective economic totality, the imputed class consciousness and the real, psychological thoughts of men about their lives." Here "class consciousness implies a class-conditioned *unconsciousness* of one's own socio-historical and economic condition, where the " 'falseness,' the illusion implicit in this situation, is in no sense arbitrary" but "simply the intellectual reflex of the objective economic structure" (ibid., 52).[13] Gramsci, by contrast, employs a conception of ideology as consciousness critiquing consciousness. For him ideas, not structural factors like economic exploitation and material deprivation, spawn mass political movements for revolutionary reform. The masses themselves are incapable of developing the kinds of ideas that might seize the masses and spawn political revolt; solely an intellectual social elite can forge the abstract and symbolic tools of mass action and social revolution. On this conception the masses remain merely carriers of ideas they can never really understand, the external subjects of a paternalistic elite that alone can help them help themselves.[14] Thin critique, by contrast, is not only a critique of interests quite beyond consciousness; it directly rejects elitism for the participation of all affected persons, in the public deliberation of such issues as how best to define the relevant respects in which men and women are equal and unequal.

Unlike the critique of consciousness by consciousness, thin critique identifies sexual inequality as ideological at a structural level, in the ways sexism distorts the socially productive activities of women, rendering their contributions in the economic sphere all but invisible; romanticizing their contributions as mothers and child rearers; undervaluing their contributions to the household economy of cooking, cleaning, shopping, and other housework; and orienting them to socially vital yet relatively low-status, low-paying roles such as day care providers and elementary-school teachers. Thin critique identifies ideology-spawning social structure in three forms among others: (1) in social expectations internalized by the individual in the course of socialization, (2) in the patriarchal family, and (3) in certain social institutions, such as male-oriented models of employee representation.

(1) Chapter 3 worked out a conception of "generalized community" and "concrete communities," drawing on George Herbert Mead's notion of intersubjectivity generated through role-taking, where the individual learns to approach others, and eventually him- or herself, through the "generalized other." Mead (1967:154) defines the general-

ized other as the "organized community or social group which gives to the individual his unity of self," namely, as the "attitude of the whole community."[15] One must be a "member of a community to be a self. Such responses . . . give him . . . his principles, the acknowledged attitudes of all members of the community toward what are the values of that community. He is putting himself in the place of the generalized other, which represents the organized responses of all the members of the group. It is that which guides conduct controlled by principles" (ibid., 162). The generalized other is a mental construct, an amalgam of behavioral characteristics that capture the actual behaviors of "concrete others," actual human beings who together constitute the individual's social environment and structure many of his or her experiences. This model presupposes the relative equality of the participants, and chapter 3 proposed a model for the legal and social equality of different concrete communities. By contrast, this chapter shows how thin critique can identify where that kind of equality is not given, where, for example, women learn through socialization to see themselves as innately inferior to men. The sexually differentiated structure of socialization generates ideology where it socializes women to take not the role of the "generalized other" but the role of the male other; to see themselves not the way men see themselves but as many men see women: as inferior to men. An ideological socialization teaches women to take the stereotypical male view of the female self, thereby patterning everyday microstructural interaction along the lines of microlevel structural bias. Central to any process of socialization is the individual's internalization of dominant social norms. Mead analyzes internalization as the individual's learning to assume the role of the generalized other. To learn to deal with the wide range of behavior any given person displays, the individual adopts one general set of social expectations, the expectations he or she has of the generalized other. To learn to deal with a vast plurality of behaviors, the individual adopts a singular set of expectations, supposedly one coherent, cohesive expression of socialized behavior, the generalized other. Hegemonic critique misses the fact that, in a society of sex-based inequality, the generalized other as the expression of dominant norms expresses sexist norms, and women who learn to take the role of the generalized other damage themselves in their own eyes as inferior to men. In this context of a critique of ideology (in distinction to the context of chapter 3), thin critique rejects the model of a politically equal, generalized other as incapable of grasping the phenomenon and experience of sexism. The generalized other is the generalized other of socially dominant groups. Characterized hegemonically—in the singular—it can only deform the self-understanding of those individuals whose interests are not furthered by society's dominant norms. To be a self is not the same for the socially inferior and the socially superior.

(2) Social interaction is facilitated by collaboration and the cooperative construction of meaning, but these practices do not require the participants' equality. Wherever inequality is a feature of the macro structure, there it likely patterns the micro structure as well. Sexual inequality at the macro level—patterns such as the institutionally biased distribution of power, knowledge, prestige, and wealth—influence microlevel interactions, such as relations between men and women in the workplace, at home, and in school; in courtship and marriage; in the spheres of politics, economics, and culture; in forms of address, discourse, body language, even eye contact. The family is a macrolevel institution of particular relevance here, as one inflected with microlevel interactions. Miriam Johnson analyzes the family as a unit of social production, for functional reasons essential to society no less than the economy, the legal system, or culture; and like each of them, the family makes its specialized functional contributions, too: it reproduces society biologically and culturally. For some of its adult members it has become something of a sphere of emotional interiority, even of respite from some of the many demands and experiences of public or social life. It reproduces many of the values of society and is one element securing the social cohesion of disparate individuals. For the largest part of Western history and culture, the familial structure has been the woman's principal social environment, and to this day she functions as the primary laborer in the domestic sphere, often as the family's emotional and relational virtuoso, as society's primary purveyor of "expressiveness," in Johnson's (1988:53) sense: the "male role is anchored in the predominantly instrumental occupational sphere, and the female role . . . in the more expressive kinship sphere," such that husbands "tend to be the primary breadwinners" and wives "continue to be primarily responsible for 'taking care of the relationship,' " in a culture and economy that places a premium on the instrumental behavior of the male provider role, rewarding it with power while systematically devaluing the expressive, care-taking role performed predominantly by women.[16]

Within the family, the expressive orientation emotionally centers the children and emotionally renews the adults. Beyond the family, especially in male-dominated occupations, women often are handicapped or criticized for this expressive orientation, even as women in the workforce are encouraged to enter types of employment regarded as more expressive. Further, they are disadvantaged and undervalued in a sexually hierarchized system centered in an unequal marriage relationship that "juvenilizes" them. And yet childbearing and child rearing are not the springs of women's secondary status but rather the male-dominated context of those activities, such that "women are strong as mothers but made weak by being wives" (Johnson 1988:269). On Johnson's (ibid., 13) analysis, "women's mothering provides a basis for women's solidarity and power, but women's being 'wives' in the 'modern family' separates women from one another in the pursuit of husbands and isolates women from one another in nuclear families."

To be sure, for many middle-class white women marriage today is losing some of its centrality as more and more women realize forms of individualism formally the preserve of white middle-class men. Thin critique goes beyond Johnson's analysis of patriarchal structure to show that race and ethnicity are significant factors in families beyond the white middle-class, exposing, for example, the "rhetoric of family crises as immigrant lifestyles and family forms are measured against a mythical family ideal. Inevitably, some interpretations of diversity will revert to cultural explanations that deflect attention from the social opportunities associated with race. Even though pleas for 'culturally sensitive' approaches to non-white families are well-meaning, they can unwittingly keep 'the family' ensnared in a white middle-class ideal. . . . Immigration will undoubtedly introduce alternative family forms; they will be best understood by treating race as a fundamental structure that situates families differently and thereby produces diversity" (Zinn 1994:305). Normatively thin is the critique that allows for diversity; hegemonic, critique that insists on, or that can perceive only, homogeneity.

(3) Once viewed by many feminists as masculinist and antagonistic to the interests of women, unions today appear more interested in a stronger relationship with female workers. And yet women tend to "occupy jobs that are quite different from those held by labor's traditional constituency, the blue-collar hard hat. The new majority tends to be found in service jobs, in decentralized workplaces with under

fifty employees, and in jobs with less of a permanent, continuous attachment to a single employer" (Cobble 1993:4). Many unions "remain wedded to an industrial model of employee representation," an increasingly outdated model oriented on the needs of "blue-collar male workers toiling in large industrial worksites" (ibid.). Thin critique rejects the reduction of a wide range of different experiences to a singular homogeneous experience, for example patterning employee representation on models that no longer correspond to many employees. One alternative to a reductionist model is a plurality of varied models; one alternative to unionism conceived monolithically is unionism conceived and configured multiply. A female workforce (for example, in service industries) cannot be well represented by a union patterned on the interests of male industrial workers. Thin critique in this sense is antireductionist; it identifies forms of ideology quite lost on hegemonic critique.

Thin Critique at the Level of Agency

Ideology at the level of agency takes the form of deep repression, internalized by individuals and rendering them agents of their own domination, *carriers* of repressive social structure, unable to grasp the dominated status and their roles in perpetuating it. Thin critique does not construct the agent monolithically, as a generic category; different forms of oppression are not all equal. Sites of domination at the level of agency range from ascriptive characteristics to social status, from the consequences of unequal distribution of legal rights or social wealth, to the implications of social stratification, to the intersection in one person's life of multiple vectors of oppression. Consider hierarchy among women in the office: "Women in office work, whatever their class or race, face common problems: sex discrimination, gender stereotyping, sexual harassment, homophobia, lack of day-care, and a long work day that robs parents of important time with their children. But differences among women in salary and power mean that women clerks and their women bosses have vastly different resources for solving these problems" (Strom 1992:406–407). And "white women and women of color who work outside the home may also have similar experiences in seeking to control their fertility and sexuality in order to survive outside the traditional boundaries of the patriarchal family," and some women's "experiences within the private realm—marital rape, battering, incest, unequal distribution of domestic labor—. . . cut across racial lines" (Eisenstein 1994:202).

Thin critique uncovers racial difference among women in connection with the racially coded differentials in the social position of their men. Unlike many women of color, bourgeois white women can easily disregard the many ways in which they differ from poor white women and women of color and insist on common bonds among all women. But their common sex hardly unites women, for example because notions of equality tend to be configured in terms of the advantaged group's model of relations between the sexes. Here the "call to be 'treated like a man' is based on extending to men of color the full 'rights' of manhood in the United States, including those of gender privilege. Because the relations of oppression often involve 'feminization' of men," "stripping them of the privileges of masculinity, women of color are caught between the need to assert their equality and the desire to restore the prerogatives of masculinity denied to their men. For women, then, the struggle for racial . . . equality may involve according the protections, as well as the limitations, of private patriarchy" (Mullings 1994:281). Thin critique at the level of agency does not homogenize women, for some of whom the struggle for equality is conceivable not individualistically but only in the context of overcoming multiple forms of oppression of men and women alike. For example, some Mexican immigrant women, concerned to maintain ethnic solidarity, have claimed that "Mexican women 'did not want to be liberated.' When Chicanas did begin organizing autonomously, male comrades accused them of selling out to white, middle-class feminists," even as Chicana activists "focused on changing the position and status of women within their own communities," using "women's organizations to improve their options for joining men in a common struggle for community empowerment" (Gabaccia 1994:90–91). Thin critique exposes other differences between native-born feminists and immigrant women. Whereas native-born feminists often focus on affirmative action, pay equity, equal access to jobs and professions, and abortion rights, immigrant women have focused on "unwieldy immigration bureaucracies, low wages in industry and service jobs, poor schools, discrimination, street violence, and crime" (Gabaccia 1994:90). It is this sensitivity to difference, and the resistance to the homogenization of different kinds of ideology, and different kinds of experiences with ideology, that marks thin critique.

Equality as a Goal of Thin Critique

By opposing thin critique to hegemonic critique, I have already invoked the former's normative foundation—the thin principles of equality and autonomy—that ensures that thin critique's perspectivalism does not become parochial or hopelessly relativistic. As in Marxist or Habermasian critique, the normative foundation of critique is also its political goal. In this sense of political goals that are more than relative, thin critique asserts that equality and autonomy are in the objective interest of persons subject to the bondage of ideology; that they are in the objective interest of the citizens of a self-determining legal community. Citizens have an objective interest in equality and autonomy precisely *as* members of such a community. The identification of these interests, and of the means to realizing them, is as open to objective determination as is any other object of social science or social theory, and in this sense thin critique is not more problematic, epistemologically, than any other means of social and political analysis.

Thin critique insists that equals are equals without specifying exactly what is equal; a normatively thin approach specifies relationships without dictating content or by dictating only normatively thin content. Equality depends on a mix of both behavior and things, of both being in a certain way and of having in a certain way. The behavioral component concerns participation in the public sphere, such as the elimination of legal and other barriers to the holding of public office. It entails not only a positive "freedom to" but also a negative "freedom from." In the context of sex-based inequality, for example, this means freedom from violence (hence support for battered women and their children but also regulation of cultural phenomena such as depictions of women in advertising and other media that may create a climate for violence against women) and freedom from coercion (hence support for reproductive choice, including access to family planning as well as abortion rights). The possessive or material component includes an economic base sufficient for the citizen's existence that can sustain his or her participation in communal self-determination (hence also prerequisites for such participation, including adequate child care and work schedules that allow some flexibility in disposition over the employee's time).

This section develops a notion of thin critique that pursues two kinds of sexual equality at once: as "women equal to men" and as "equal free-dom of individual choice." The final section develops thin critique in terms of autonomy.

Women Equal to Men

The goal of "women equal to men" calls for including women where they are now excluded, or included but discriminated against. It also calls for including men in tasks, responsibilities, and activities cul-turally delegated mostly or exclusively to women, such as parenting and housework. It calls for equality for women in the spheres of eco-nomics, politics, and education; for equal access, equal opportunities, and equal pay for equal work; for equality in socialization, in school, at home. And it calls for the equality of women also in mass culture, toward social roles not defined rigidly or stereotypically, for example, by associating technical or mechanical skills with men and selfless commitment to repetitive chores with women.

From the standpoint of thin critique, a central aspect of the differ-ential treatment of men and women concerns the reproduction of a male-centered public sphere and a female-centered private one. The private sphere may have the advantage, vis-à-vis the public one, of emotional openness, but it is also the preserve of socially unrewarded, financially underremunerated work, often in addition to responsibility for the emotional nurturance of other members of the family, isolation in the home, burdened with the responsibilities of household and child rearing, perhaps with little or no support from a spouse. For many people some of the most significant rewards of life are to be found not in the private sphere but in the public one: social recognition, cultural prestige, political power, individual development, confirmation of self-worth.[17]

This aspect of sexual inequality is compounded where those women in a position to chose a life outside the house, in the workplace, then face sex-based inequities in housework and child rearing: "Most women work one shift at the office or factory and a 'second shift' at home" (Hochschild 1989:4). "Even when couples share more equi-tably in the work at home, women do two-thirds of the *daily* jobs at home, like cooking and cleaning up—jobs that fix them into a rigid routine" (ibid., 8). Work typically done by men—house and car main-tenance and household finances—need not be done every day, at a fixed time, but can be planned around the man's schedule. Not so cooking dinner or tending children, typically done by women. "Employed mothers of young children . . . meet their responsibilities to job and children chiefly by taking time out of their own sleep and passive leisure" (Goldscheider and Waite 1991:111). And even if the "husbands' *share* of housework increase[s] when wives work," women "continue to be responsible for most household tasks" (ibid.) regardless of whether they are employed beyond the home. Indeed, "traditional sex-role orientations are *anti-family*" in the sense that they "encourage men to put career success ahead of everything else and reinforce the idea that 'women's work'—*in other words, family work*—is inappropriate and even demeaning for men to do" (ibid., 41).[18]

Sexual inequality marks the workplace as well, because of the concentration of women in lower-paying jobs; because women are still discouraged from entering certain predominantly male professions, from physics to auto mechanics; because women work fewer hours on average, and are less likely than men to be unionized; because women tend to be paid less for the same work done by a man; because work done by women tends to be underpaid relative to the level of skill required; because work done by women tends to be culturally devalued.[19] In this context the sexual equality sought by thin critique is sex neutrality: different kinds of employment available to people regardless of their sex, where criteria for evaluating the relative cultural value of any given kind of employment do not include the sex of those persons who traditionally have filled it. The object of critique is a sexual division of labor that bars women from traditionally male jobs and systematically undervalues jobs traditionally done by women.

Equal Freedom of Individual Choice

An additional approach to equality (compatible with the previous one) is the idea of equal freedom of individual choice. It construes the individual as an agent of choice ideally in an environment of equal opportunity. Thin critique identifies the violation of this form of equality in marriage as in divorce. Whereas divorce law in the past "assumed that all married women were first and foremost housewives and mothers," no-fault divorce "assumes that all married women are employable and equally capable of self-sufficiency after divorce" (Weitzman 1985:373). But by "interrupting employment for child-rearing, taking part-time or less skilled work to accommodate family demands, or failing to seek advanced education in the interests of the family, individual women re-

duce their human capital" (Morgan 1991:10). Women with more education and women who work outside the home during marriage are
better placed at divorce than homemakers, who among women are the
most dependent on their husband's human capital.

A related object of thin critique is the violation of equal freedom of individual choice in the workplace treatment of pregnancy
and motherhood. On the one hand, female-specific statutes facilitate
women's combining employment and childbearing by providing job-
protected leave to workers temporarily incapacitated by pregnancy.
But they are "strategically risky, as are mother-only parenting leave
statutes" (Vogel 1993:156). On the other hand, sex-neutral statutes provide leave for fathers and mothers alike, yet "does nothing for the
worker temporarily unable to work because of pregnancy-related disability" (ibid.).

Thin critique identifies the denial of equal freedom of individual
choice by inequalities in access to health care, contraception, prenatal
care, abortion, and education about sex and sexually transmitted dis-
eases. Some women are subjected to such inequalities on the basis of
their socioeconomic status, race, or ethnicity, immigrant status, age,
or educational level. Zillah Eisenstein (1994:220) points out the "denial of access to abortion directly contributes to increased maternal
mortality rates, which are nearly four times higher for black women
than for white women in the Untied States." On the other hand, "for
many black women, who are more at risk for breast and cervical cancer,
hypertension, diabetes, lupus, and other problems, abortion appears
as only one among many health needs" (ibid.). From the standpoint
of thin critique, hegemonic is a feminism that focuses on abortion
rights to the exclusion of needs no less pressing for (typically nonwhite,
non-middle-class) women, including the need to prevent teenage pregnancy, other needs for sex education and access to contraception, and
as a means of preventing the spread of AIDS.

Autonomy as a Goal of Thin Critique

Reflection on the goal of equality leads to the further goal of autonomy,
just as reflection on a formal right leads to substantive conditions necessary if the individual is to be in a position to exercise that right:
autonomy as a precondition for real equality. Individual rights distributed equally by the legislature may not be possessed equally, for ex-

ample by citizens lacking the kind of autonomy that derives from a minimally adequate economic base or education sufficient to allow a person to pursue career interests. In this sense a poll tax or a literacy requirement, as a condition for exercising one's equal right to vote, perpetuates factual inequality. Autonomy in an economic or educational sense means not being vulnerable to such inequality in the first place.

The twin institutions of marriage and divorce can undermine the autonomy of women: given inequities in the distribution of family labor and inequities in opportunities and wage levels in the labor market, "marriage becomes the only means of ensuring income security for themselves and their children. Marriage thus becomes a necessity for the majority of women to guarantee their economic well-being," rendering it a "coercive institution for women, required if they are to minimize the risks of becoming poor" (Morgan 1991:12). And just as some women lack autonomy in marriage, some also lack autonomy after marriage ends, all the more so as no-fault divorce laws render marital commitments more optional and time-limited: "While they free men from the responsibilities they retained under the old system, they 'free' women primarily from the security that system provided" (Weitzman 1985:370), an autonomy-robbing dependence on the economic security provided at least by middle-class husbands. No-fault divorce laws may decrease the woman's share in community property and in amount of alimony, while freeing many men from the financial obligations of marriage and family and, in that sense, even providing some wealthier men an incentive to divorce. And "women of color and those from disadvantaged backgrounds experience higher risks of poverty even during marriage, and are much more likely to find themselves poor once marriage ends" (Morgan 1991:12).

Thin critique under these circumstances identifies both prospects and problems in the response of the welfare state. Where it compensates society's weaker members for inequalities deriving from the economy or marketplace, it helps realize the promise of formal legal equality. The primary form of equality in the treatment of women and men is legal equality, the idea that men and women should equally be addressees of the legislature, that they should possess the same legislated rights, that the judiciary should recognize those rights for the sexes equally. Further, where the welfare state compensates society's socially and culturally disenfranchised members for inequalities deriving from a maldistribution of power (a maldistribution not only of economic capital but also, for example, of social and cultural capital),[20] it facilitates the equal use of equally distributed legal rights. Yet the hard-fought achievement of equality through the welfare state can transform itself into one more form of inequality, ironically as an unintended consequence of fighting inequality. Formal legal equality between men and women means that women should be legally able to obtain a divorce to an extent no less than men. Once achieved, however, women may find that, because wives on average earn less than husbands and are more likely to receive custody of children, the personal wealth of the woman usually decreases with divorce, whereas that of the man increases. An equal right to divorce may have the unintended consequence of transferring to the woman the larger part of the divorce's material burdens. Or the goal may be provisions for the woman when pregnant or for maternity leave but with the unintended consequence that women become more vulnerable than men to losing their job. Or the goal may be protection of women in the workplace but with the unintended consequence that the protection is accompanied by restricting women's competitiveness to jobs less rewarding, or less well paid, or of lower status. In many cases the realization of formal equality has material prerequisites, such as wealth or education. Yet compensation by the welfare state for the maldistribution of these material prerequisites may have the unintended consequence of actually *restricting* the welfare recipient's freedom, for example where

> statutory regulations on work and family life *force* employees or family members to conform their behavior to a 'normal' work relation or a standard pattern of socialization; when the recipients of other compensations *pay* for these with dependence on normalizing intrusions by employment offices, welfare agencies, and housing authorities, or when they must accept court decisions that directly intervene in their lives; or when collective legal protection, the right to unionize, and so on, provide an effective representation of interests only at the cost of the freedom to decide by organization members, who are condemned to *passive followership* and conformity. Each of these critical cases concerns the same phenomenon: satisfying the material preconditions for an equal opportunity to exercise individual liberties alters living situations and power positions in such a way that the compensation for disadvantages is associated with forms of tutelage that convert the intended *authorization* for the use of freedom into a *custodial supervision* (Habermas 1996:416).

Autonomy is denied women where their political self-determination is foreclosed either because various inequalities render formal legal rights useless or because the welfare-state's compensations for those inequalities rob the recipients of some measure of freedom and choice: "Patriarchal control, although still located with the husband if he is present, can also be exerted through the state welfare system. The social welfare network is redefined as family structures change" (Eisenstein 1994:202).

Thin critique here identifies social arrangements—institutional, economic, and cultural—that effectively deny or deprive some citizens the means to exercise autonomy in senses both public and private: the private autonomy of individuals who, as the addressees of the relevant social arrangements, receive equal treatment. The goal is also the public autonomy of citizens who, as the makers of these arrangements, must themselves decide how best to structure them toward the goal of individual autonomy, how best to define equality as well as autonomy. Only the participants themselves, in debate and discussion (best guided by rational, discursive justification of claims) can determine which respects are relevant when treating equals equally in all relevant respects. The interpretive work cannot be left to academic or cultural "experts" or to the avant-garde, nor can it be delegated to legislators or judges. The social constructedness of sexual identity and relations between the sexes allows significant room for interpretation, bounded only to an extent by biological differences and conditioned, but only to an extent, by particular historical concretions. The attribution of rights and the interpretation of needs are no less social constructions. But complete interpretive freedom is not given: the definitions at stake are among the most fundamental, the most sensitive, and the most consequential of how any society or culture sees itself.

From the standpoint of thin critique, the determination of the relevant respects in which equals are to be treated equally must be oriented to securing equal rights for equally entitled individuals without detracting from the individuals' political autonomy. Legislation and policy intended to provide the individual greater autonomy in his or her private sphere must be configured to enhance or deepen the individual's political autonomy at the same time, so that citizens do not become "privatized" consumers of rights in a society of private niches but rather simultaneously secure rights in ways that raise their consciousness through participation in the political process. Given thin critique's goal of autonomy, rights are best conceived as relationships between and among human beings, not as possessions in the ways physical objects can be possessed. Rights "exist" in a meaningful sense only where they are exercised in relations between and among people. Indeed, rights specify those relations and the actions only possible within it. The goal of thin critique is not simply that private parties receive their "fair share" of whatever public good is at stake but the equal participation of all affected persons in communal self-determination; not simply the establishment of individual rights, but the fulfillment of individual needs. The goal is autonomy rather than, say, comfort or prosperity. The welfare state's distribution of benefits is not the goal of justice, but the means to autonomy. From the standpoint of thin critique, then, welfare benefits that privilege an intact family with an employed male over single women[21] only further diminishes her autonomy: benefits "tied to the primary breadwinner's wages and to family size . . . reduce the importance of the wife's economic contribution to the household and subsidize[s] childbearing, thereby encouraging her to leave the labor force" (Quadagno 1990:19) and stay at home caring for children, denying any measure of autonomy to either mothers on welfare or mothers in working-poor households.

This chapter completes my exploration of thin normativity in three concrete areas of social life in liberal modern societies. Thin norms, I argued in part 1, make possible social integration within any given concrete communities (which may be diverse within themselves), as well as across concrete communities very different from one another. I argued in part 2 that thin norms can help make indeterminate legal norms determinate in ways that facilitate agreement in the face of contested interpretations; that thin norms allow competing systems of cultural values to understand each other in nonreductionist ways; and that ideology critique, conducted through thin norms, allows the multiplicity of partial perspectives within distressed, marginalized, or oppressed groups to emerge in ways that do not privilege one over the other or cancel one another out.

CODA

I began this book with the argument that social integration in complex modern societies depends in part on tolerating, rather than eliding, many of the normative differences within the populace. I shall conclude it by arguing that neither the phenomena this book describes, nor my proposals for how best to deal with those phenomena, constitute or reflect a crisis of moral decline. Social integration can accommodate normative difference by pursuing integration through thin not thick norms. These norms provide a better basis for a common core of social and political beliefs (chapter 1); secure within a diverse community greater degrees of popular agreement on communal issues and even encourage civic participation (chapter 2); facilitate political cooperation among diverse communities in democratic constitutional states (chapter 3); and structure individual identity in ways that encourage the development of a personality structure well integrated in a morally diverse society (chapter 4). Because it invokes only thin norms, my theory offers realistic possibilities for constructing political agreement under social and cultural conditions that discourage agreement: conditions such as, first, contested interpretations of the meaning and proper application of indeterminate legal norms (chapter 5); second, the normative commitments of competing cultural values (chapter 6); third, ideological obstacles which invite a critique that, I argue, may proceed by invoking thin rather than thick norms to capture discrimination in its complexity, as the intersection of multiple vectors of oppression, rather than merely to reproduce it by approaching it in undifferentiated ways (chapter 7). These chapters aim to show the capacity of thin normativity to cope with various characteristics of contemporary, liberal, cosmopolitan societies. By way of suggesting that the power of my thesis is not exhausted in the spheres and examples analyzed in the preceding chapters, I shall briefly discuss three further, topical phenomena: differentiation within various social structures, greater diversity within the population, and increasingly less connectedness among the citizenry. In each case I would argue that neither the phenomena nor the response I have developed in this book are aspects of what some conservative critics (I identify two among others) describe as "moral decline."

Differentiation within Social Structures

The ongoing differentiation of social structures entails the increasing "porosity" of social institutions. These institutions are porous in the sense of letting more people (and more kinds of people) than historically ever before into other societies, into old and new communities, and into relationships social, economic, and cultural. Where institutions are highly porous, socially successful immigration, for example, need not entail that immigrants adopt all or even most of the host country's beliefs and mores. Conversely, some of the differences immigrants bring with them find space sufficient for their perpetuation within the porosity of existing institutions. Some of those differences change the host community, and when they do so, diversity increases not only from without communities and their institutions but also from within. And where the relationship among levels of social structure becomes more porous, looser and more impersonal forms of association are displaced from the national level to that of communities and groups.

In these terms the central normative issues posed by, say, immigration or multiculturalism—who should be allowed entrance, in the first case, or which cultural values deserve society-wide recognition, in the second—concern structural change, not moral decline. A social structure of increasing porosity confronts neither normlessness nor normative anarchy in contemporary liberal societies but the coexistence of competing, even mutually exclusive norms, such as both religious belief and atheism, or "homosexual lifestyles" and the "heterosexual lifestyles" that reject them, or corporate culture and environmentalism, so often at loggerheads. An increasingly porous social structure allows many interactions among individuals to be more impersonal and more segmented than in an early modernity characterized by more direct contacts and by contacts sustained over longer periods of time.

To be sure, the distinction with respect to an increasingly porous social structure, between early modernity and contemporary late modernity, is not a dichotomy between "modern" atomistic fragmentation and "traditional" social wholes, all of whose parts were animated by a single shared identity sustained through the deep similarities among all of its inhabitants, in a social structure largely impermeable to unwanted, or uninvited, or unplanned outside influences. Early mod-

ern societies were not undifferentiated monoliths free of conflict and
tension. The argument, rather, is that the greater porosity of complex, modern, liberal societies renders social integration (analyzed in
part 1) and forms of political judgment (developed in part 2) more
likely and more successful, the less thick its normative commitments.
Again: thicker kinds of social integration and political judgment have
less promise in late modernity than they did in more traditional societies.

But thin socialization and thin judgment do not, as Jose Casanova
(1994:229) fears, "reduce the common good to the aggregated sum
of individual choices" or contradict his assertion that "morality can
only exist as an intersubjective normative structure and that individual
choices only attain a 'moral' dimension when they are guided or informed by intersubjective, interpersonal norms," or impede or even
preclude modern societies' "task of reconstructing reflexively and collectively their own normative foundations." Thin socialization and
thin judgment do not, as Stephen Carter (1993:36–37) warns, discourage mediation "between the citizen and the apparatus of government"
and preclude the "independent moral voice." Contrary to Carter's
(ibid.) claims, precisely normative thinness, not thickness, "split[s] the
allegiance of citizens and press[es] on their members points of view
that are often radically different from the preferences of the state."

To be sure, increased porosity may well bring about changes, some
of which will be complex, open-ended, multitracked, and equivocal or
ambivalent, hardly driving society in one clear direction rather than
another. While increasing porosity requires thinner forms of social
integration and political judgment, some of those forms will challenge
established identities and norms; some will generate tension or confusion about which norms are best, which needs are appropriate, which
differences are worthy of social recognition, and which parts of one's
culture are best maintained and might best be changed or even jetti-
soned.

But structural change and institutional porosity of this sort is not a
form of moral decline. Consider: particular assumptions about what
sex is often prescribe corresponding behavioral norms. The valoriza-
tion of any particular sexual behavior easily devalorizes others: if one
is normal, the other is pathological; if one is moral, the other is immoral—even if the activity is legal, even if it involves only consenting
adults, even if not "harmful" to participants. Any particular assump-

tion generates disagreement: whether an act is acceptable only if tied to "love" as defined by a particular culture, such that "if we assume that the meaning and purpose of sex is to express and consolidate 'love,' only those sex acts and social interactions are legitimate that exhibit the qualities of love" (Seidman 1999:185); whether sexual behavior is acceptable only if tied to a narrow definition of family, such as close biological relationships, or a man and a woman joined in marriage; whether society should embrace a diverse array of sexual practices (nonromantic and nonmarital ones, for example) and kinds of families (including persons neither married nor biologically connected). Social disagreement lies behind these challenges to the social privileging of "heterosexuality, marriage, two-parent families, romanticized sexuality, monogamy, and the privatization of sexuality. Such sexualities and intimacies receive social benefits, juridical-administrative recognition, symbolic esteem, social legitimacy, and a normalized, morally valued social status. Much of sexual politics involves struggles to alter and maintain this sexual hierarchy through battles around rights, resources, and representations" (ibid., 167). Here disagreement concerns the very nature of sexuality and sexual behavior, whether human sexuality is fixed by nature (merely finding various cultural expressions of the same basic universal nature) or constructed (in every historical period and culture) by social, political, economic, religious, and other forces; whether particular sexual desires and practices have a fixed normative status, an intrinsic moral meaning, a necessary social role—or whether their meaning and normative status depend on their particular context, perhaps one in part generated by the participants themselves (even if bounded by formal legal constraints such as requirements about mutual consent and minimum age). Sexual identities are complex and significant (yet often enough not too complex to fit into such traditional binary identities of male/female sex, masculine/feminine gender, heterosexual/homosexual desire). The questions societies face include: which identities should in some sense be allowed socially, should be legitimate, should receive social and legal recognition—and which not—and by what criteria? Should groups even be defined by sexual identity (homosexuals, bisexuals, transsexuals), and should they on that basis either receive legal, cultural, and other institutional recognition as a group, or on that basis be denied?

Clearly sex has multiple meanings, multiple acceptable and unacceptable forms of expression, and multiple social roles. The array of meanings and roles is bounded, if not always clearly or definitively. To fix these boundaries in a way most accommodating of the sensibilities of a liberal democratic society is to employ normatively thin standards. The thinness of proceduralism, for example, provides negative freedoms for the socially and culturally disfavored side of the equation (thus protecting homosexuals from discrimination in housing, employment, or education). It also provides positive freedoms to a range of different sexual beliefs and practices, by being tolerant of them, perhaps even nonjudgmental toward them. In other ways as well, a thin approach offers practical guidance and delimits moral boundaries, for example through thin standards of consent, reciprocity, and responsibility. Thin morality is not morality in decline.

Greater Diversity within the Population

Normative fragmentation and structural porosity need not spell social fragmentation where they still allow connectedness among the persons involved. Fragmentation and porosity pose significant problems for social integration only where they discourage people from participating in (or even caring about) civic issues, social responsibilities, national interests, or problems of the wider community, or of other communities. They pose problems only where they render agreement on public issues impossible, or possible only in divisive ways, as in single-issue campaigns or identity politics in the form of "us" against "them." Further, moral diversity and porous social structures by no means necessarily generate equality among the differences; they may well perpetuate old inequalities or even generate new ones. A plurality of cultural groups can itself be a predicate of intergroup conflict. Inequality occurs, for example, where cultural differences in consumption patterns serve not just as a means for groups to articulate their respective identities but also as symbols segregating one group from another. The increasing porosity of social institutions may render some people more indifferent to one another as they become less and less connected to one another in meaningful ways.

My theory, conscious of these various problems, constructs a form of *communitarianism* within normative fragmentation. It offers a normatively thin communitarianism that both encourages participation and facilitates agreement. It can accommodate additional kinds of social integration as well, for example, reciprocity rather than normative agreement. Reciprocity can reconcile the claims of different normative ends by a process benefiting all persons if "benefit" is understood in terms of a normatively thin core. This might be agreement "solely on the basis of a principle of reciprocity through which the opportunities of any person are likely to be greater than they would otherwise be" (Hayek 1976:113). Even here disagreement would occur, but while it would make for a social and political life not untroubled, at least social and political life could be free of a compulsion to agree on thick norms. At least dissent wouldn't endanger social stability. At least "approval and censure" would not "depend on the concrete ends which particular actions serve" (ibid., 111).[1] In this context the market provides a compelling example. By normatively thin means, it can integrate persons cooperating in ways that sustain differing individual interests and the institutions that mediate them. Thus the "same currency, the same consumer product can have at the same moment universal and local meaning. Indeed, in recent years, we've seen mass markets themselves reaching out to specialized markets with ethnic focus, connecting the group with the central circuit of production. Unexpectedly, capitalized modern markets may increase ethnic options and therefore diversity. Critics have thought otherwise because they have conflated mass production with uniformity and differentiation with segregation" (Zelizer 1999:205). Actions at a local level (consumer purchases, for example) may allow some people to realize personal visions or preferences, even as those same actions help sustain a network of interaction, like that between consumers and producers. While the market homogenizes to an extent (one can only purchase what producers make available), it also allows some consumers to differentiate themselves from one another, to some extent, especially where consumption possesses particular meaning for the consumer. Thus cuisine and eating rituals can reinforce ethnic identities or articulate political standpoints or express lifestyles. In this sense economic activity at the local level can be fragmenting or "particularizing," even as economic activity is also potentially "universalizing," for example where using currency or a banking system places the actor within a potentially universal web of relations.

Of course, fragmentation is hardly confined to the economic sphere. It represents a response to increasing diversity and complexity at the level of social institutions, from the economy and law to politics and culture. It allows individuals to check or prevent increasing complexity at the macro level of society from "infecting" the micro level of individuals' everyday life. As societies grow in size and become more diverse, subcultures increase in number. Subcultures constitute a particularization of the individual's experience in the face of increasing density and diversity in the social environment. The individual's own social network need not grow as complex as the overall institutional networks in which he or she is embedded.

The use of a universal medium—for example, money in economic spheres or language in almost all spheres—allows one to individuate oneself. In the case of natural language, one can capture one's innermost thoughts in a language that is no more or less one's own than it is that of any other competent user; the linguistic medium of the speaker's particularity is a social institution that preexists him or her. But one's passive assimilation of language does not preclude or restrict one from using and manipulating it actively. Indeed each and every time they use language, speakers unintentionally and unconsciously reproduce it; even the most casual conversation contributes to the language's reproduction as a whole. The shared or universal aspects of any given language needn't vitiate the individuality or authenticity of what the particular user expresses or experiences. Indeed, "every instance of the use of language is a potential modification of that language at the same time as it acts to reproduce it" (Giddens 1994:220). By differentiating him- or herself from all other persons through a medium shared by many other distinct individuals, the individual needn't "fragment" the community of competent language users. No moral decline here.

Increasingly Less Personal Connectedness among the Citizenry

On the other hand, less personal connectedness among citizens results from thinly normative social integration, from socialization more institutional than personal, from a social structure increasingly porous. At the level of social agents, less and less personal connectedness among the citizenry issues into a mosaic of subcultures. An impersonal sociality can be both indifference of many citizens to one another and mutual tolerance for many of their significant differences. Such a public order is not moral consensus—but it is not moral breakdown, either. Nor is there moral decline at the level of functional social systems, where modern society loosens the structural complementarities of systems and their environments (that is, other systems) and decouples some systems from others. Decoupling readily entails less connectedness. In earlier societies the family, for example, would socialize the individual for roles both in and beyond the family, whereas late-modern societies increasingly leave socialization to a variety of educational institutions, long ago differentiated from the family and much less personal than the family. In these ways, among others, fragmentation and porosity do not undermine the socialization of individuals and groups, even as they entail socialization more institutional than personal. Consider, for example, the integration of individuals within a particular political and legal culture. Citizens may disagree on the desirability, wisdom, or usefulness of specific laws but nonetheless agree that all persons should be bound by the law, hence also that all persons should be bound by legal means when attempting to change or nullify what to some appear as noxious laws. Patriotism centered around belief in a constitutional order, rather than in alleged national characteristics of blood, soil, religion, or culture, offers another example. The abstract principles of a constitutional order (what I developed as generalized community) do not dictate a single way of institutionalizing those principles, or a single cultural order. They can support different ways of life, multiple worldviews, and a range of personal and collective identities. Again, normative fragmentation in late modernity is not moral decline; it is moral adaptation to social heterogeneity, moral flexibility, and moral tolerance for difference. It is thin politics rather than thick moralities, but thin politics accommodative of thick moralities.

NOTES

Introduction

1 *Coping in Politics with Indeterminate Norms: A Theory of Enlightened Localism* (Gregg 2003) examines indeterminacy as the lack of clear, distinct, and rationally persuasive knowledge of what a normative rule means and how groups and individuals should apply it. Where norms are indeterminate, no theory, rule, or principle constrains us (whether citizen or judge, social critic or policy maker) to interpret or apply the norm in a particular way. Consequently, a normative question or problem could have many different answers or solutions, all of them valid. *Coping in Politics with Indeterminate Norms* responds to this problem by answering two questions. First, how are social equity and legal justice possible where aspects of the social, political, and legal order appear to be arbitrary, inconsistent, and subjective? Second, how should a society deal with indeterminacy? A theory of enlightened localism can answer these questions in central domains of normative behavior, from social critique, to public policy, to law and morality. By combining elements of proceduralism with elements of pragmatism, it can explain why indeterminacy in social norms is not always a problem in the day-to-day functioning, or even legitimation, of modern polities. And it can show that normative determinacy is not necessary to justice in political, legal, moral, and cultural contexts of social integration.

2 These authors, including the feminists, are sociologists or sociological theorists (except for Hegel, but even he is the most empirically sensitive member of the German Idealists). In respect of this literature, my work differs markedly from other current work on issues of cultural and normative diversity, including Carens (2000), Mason (2000), Reich (2002), Spinner-Halev (2000), and Williams (1998). As an attempt at political theory with sociological ambitions, my work seeks normative theory that offers points of departure for empirically oriented investigations.

3 The amendment reads in part: "nor shall any State deprive any person of life, liberty, or property, without due process of law; nor deny to any person within its jurisdiction the equal protection of the laws."

4 Indeed Rawls (1993:51) distinguishes "rational" agents from "reasonable" ones and assigns an other-regarding outlook only to the latter: "What rational agents lack is the particular form of moral sensibility that underlies the desire to engage in fair cooperation as such, and to do so on terms that others as equals might reasonable be expected to endorse. I do not assume the reasonably is the whole of moral sensibility; but it includes the part that connects with the idea of fair social cooperation."

5   Compare Jaggar (1994:286), who argues that such responsibility would entail a communal right to approve or reject abortion in any given instance, such that the woman would lose her sole right to decide as her voice became equal to, but not weightier than, that of any other member of the community. Ironically the "attempt to guarantee the conditions in which each woman's right to decide about abortion would become a real option results in the achievement of conditions in which she no longer has that right."

1. Thick and Thin

1   U.S. Constitution, clause 1, amendment I (1791).
2   As categories, "thick" and "thin" do not exhaust all forms of normativity. One might argue, for example, that normativity includes the category of amoral rules. I would stress (and in later pages show) that thin normativity does not mean the absence of all moral norms whatsoever, nor is it otherwise immune to moral considerations and thus amoral.
3   Compare Ely 1980.
4   Drawing on the situations of Muslim immigrant communities and their relationships to state and society in France, Germany, and England today, I develop this possibility in Gregg 2003b. I propose a "normatively thin proceduralism" that "brackets" thick differences and concentrates on thin sharings. Proceduralism of this sort can motivate participation in political community by generating "correct" results; by accommodating a system of majoritarian rule; by emphasizing participants' *interests* over their *identities*, and then urging compromise among competing *interests;* by employing techniques such as "balancing" the interests of individual members with those of the group, or "bracketing" differences, or reducing normative complexity; by providing its own grounding, in this way "solving" the problem of the lack of ultimate or exterior foundations for political community today; and by pursuing a modus vivendi in the sense of mutual *accommodation* rather than *agreement* on substantive matters. But it cannot accommodate fanatic or absolutist groups, and persons unable to identify their needs and articulate their aspirations except in thick terms. It can, however, bring into a proceduralist social order members of the community now disinclined to participate in it. In the case of immigrants, it can discourage or at least mitigate fundamentalism in a variety of ways.
5   Williams develops this distinction at a linguistic level regarding the difference between thick and thin, suggesting that social integration in modern societies requires thin concepts much more than traditional societies did (to the extent they ever did). One normatively thin concept is formal legal "right," as in a "right to free expression." Williams contrasts this concept with normatively thick concepts that seem to be "specific" or "substan-

tive"—such as "treachery or cowardice or promise" (1995:184); "lie, brutality, gratitude" (1985:140) or "courage" (ibid., 129–130). Williams (ibid., 129) claims that thick normative concepts often "express a union of fact and value. The way these notions are applied is determined by what the world is like (for instance, by how someone has behaved), and yet, at the same time, their application usually involves a certain valuation of the situation, of persons or actions." Even "if the grasping of truths under thick ethical concepts provides some content for . . . [a general social] structure, it still remains . . . to a considerable extent local" (1995:208). Thick ethical concepts "belong" to participants, not to the outsider (such as the observer), in the sense that the participants' belonging to the corresponding culture renders their practice of it "authentic" or "definitive" as a source of information. The "extent to which a society uses . . . [thin] as opposed to thick concepts is partly a historical question, . . . [with] important social implications" (ibid., 191 n. 7). Williams (1985:145) distinguishes between practicing a culture and observing others practice it: the observer can still understand thick ethical concepts in which he or she cannot participate as a member. Consider the "situation in which vocabulary is affected by the speaker's . . . [sex], [where] we can both understand why the observer is barred from saying just what the locals say, and we can also see that he is not barred from recognizing that what they say can be true."

6   In a sense I develop in chapter 3.

7   In a sense I develop in chapter 2.

8   The limits of social integration in this model would lie in dogmatic communities that practiced exclusiveness to the point of an intolerance incompatible with generalized community.

2. Social Integration within Cosmopolitan Societies

1   Etzioni (1996:257) similarly attempts to relativize liberalism and communitarianism in terms of each other, toward a combined commitment to "moral order that is basically voluntary, and to a social order that is well balanced with socially secured autonomy." Yet in that process he reaches a conclusion opposite mine, namely, the need for and desirability of "correcting" contemporary liberal democratic society by constructing for it a "strong normative edifice" (ibid., 218) or a normatively thick structure.

2   Here I reword role theory in sociology. My point is that roles are less given or consensual, less standardized or uniform, than one might assume, in part because they are something akin to clothing: different persons wearing the same clothing are not thereby the same person, even as a certain similarity is created (especially in the case of uniforms, such as a nun's habit or a soldier's uniform, which emphasize the wearer's membership

in a very specific collectivity at the significant diminution of individual personality or identity). Even the nun or the soldier performs, as nun or as soldier, a specific role over which she or he has some influence. A role is something of a compromise between a template provided by society and the unique individual who more or less interprets it. Further, I am suggesting that social roles do not instantiate some kind of social consensus as to what the norms guiding this or that role are. Some roles may be internally conflicted; some may concentrate social conflicts. I agree with Giddens (1994:117) that society reproduces itself through the practices of individuals, not through the roles individuals perform. In other words, roles do not exhaustively determine practices, rather the uniqueness of the individual performing a role exceeds any standard description of the role. The role, then, is not what Parsons (1967a:11) calls the "primary point of direct articulation between the personality of the individual and the structure of the social system." Integral to performing any social role is what Garfinkel (1967:117) calls "ad hocing," which refers to considerations the performer makes in adapting a particular role to the myriad situational contingencies in which any role performance is situated. One must constantly improvise to make a job description work. Like rules, role prescriptions are not self-interpreting: "*ad hocing* practices are used . . . to recognize what the instructions are . . . talking about."

3   Conversely, where people seek cooperation in daily life, there the resort to legal codes and courts of law can only disturb cooperation, as an act of hostility. Here to cross the threshold of law is often to terminate the relationship (compare Luhmann 1978:68).

4   Luhmann (1994:30) points out how the same process holds true for morality itself, understood as a functional system: "Morality accepts its own retreat in moral terms and relinquishes the right to intervene in the options maintained by . . . [other] functional systems." "Moralization" as a pejorative term then refers to the inappropriate application of moral criteria, namely, beyond moral spheres.

5   Walzer's approach to political theory has elements of both thick and thin normativity. I agree with Walzer (1994:6) that, "[i]n moral discourse, thinness and intensity go together, whereas with thickness comes qualification . . . , complexity, and disagreement." But the ellipsis here marks one spot where my position differs from Walzer's; it marks the place on his list of a most doubtful characteristic of thickness, namely "compromise." Thick communitarianism is often incapable of compromise given its construction out of thickly normative commitments. My alternative makes compromise more likely precisely because it avoids normatively thick commitments.

6   Whereby Parsons's (1964:98) conception of social integration is normatively thinner than Durkheim's in its emphasis on the functional differen-

tiation of the individual in terms of the multiple roles he or she plays, and in terms of the multiple communities he or she inhabits simultaneously: "an actor may be a member of as many collectivities as he has roles — there is no inherent limitation to that number. With regard to personnel of collectivities [,] . . . while some may be completely separate with no overlap, others overlap, with some members in common, others not, while still others are related as more and less inclusive collectivities. Thus in this country residents of a town or city are also residents of a state, and in turn also of the United States; they thus have the role of 'citizen' in each of these three levels of governmental organization, that is, are members of all three collectivities." On this view, social solidarity is always very much less than total or complete; the individual is bound to roles and communities only relatively.

7   Habermas (1985:1044) regards individuation and sociation as the two (complementary) aspects of morality, from which the normative principles of justice and solidarity spring.

8   Localism is not parochial by definition; some local conventions may be suitable for generalization.

9   Because of the contextual and contingent nature of shared understandings, the thin normativity that informs them cannot be derived as somehow necessary, acontextual, a priori principles.

10   Greater sharings, not complete sharings. I propose thin communitarianism precisely for normatively fragmented societies. Under democratic arrangements, majoritarian understandings trump minoritarian ones in the formation of public policy, whereby the minoritarian understandings nonetheless enjoy legal protections that guarantee the right of freedom of conviction, expression, assembly, and the right to continue attempting to convince others of their merit. If a social and political system is so constructed that today's minorities can become tomorrow's majorities, then it may legitimately enforce majoritarian understandings in the face of minoritarian dissent.

11   And, says Walzer (1994:4), "reveals itself thinly only on special occasions, when moral language is turned to specific purpose."

12   The merit of merit-based norms is defined intersubjectively, in the sense of a rational, fallibilistic agreement among the participants that is always open to challenge and to replacement by alternative definitions where that challenge is rationally plausible to a majority of the participants.

13   Which is why one feature of normative thinness — particularity — need not be in tension with another: rationality. Particularity refers to context-dependent collective understandings, and rationality refers to grounds for their acceptability. The fact that a given understanding is shared by a majority of the population does not provide the rational grounds for its acceptability. Thus a rationally unacceptable understanding remains unac-

ceptable even if a majority shares it. Here we see what it means to say that the "sharedness" of rationally acceptable shared understandings is normatively thin, not thick. We then see why normatively thin understandings differ from the normatively thick ones defended by Hegel and Oakeshott.

14   Despite what for this sentence is the unfortunate antonymic relationship between the words "thin" and "wide."

15   Here, too, my position differs from that of Walzer (1997:89), and for the same reason specified in note 5. One finds in Walzer's generally thin approach occasional residues of normative thickness, as in his argument that a "fellowship of strangers would be at most a momentary grouping, existing only in opposition to some standing community," for "unless we experience sameness in some strong form, we cannot even recognize otherness. . . . If there were no such community, there would be no such fellowship." Not so: a "fellowship of strangers" can be sustained as long as that fellowship satisfies basic needs and interests of the participants, and in diverse societies that satisfaction cannot include the wholesale elision of normative differences among the participants. Rather, satisfaction of basic needs and interests will proceed in ways that respect, or at least bracket, these differences. Thin communitarianism is an argument for the viability of long-term, politically and culturally satisfactory relationships among strangers (among others). Again, Walzer (ibid., 88) insists that the "politics of difference, the ongoing negotiation of group relations and individual rights," requires "common identity and standard behavior." Not so: a politics of difference in no way presupposes fixed identities or normed behavior, as fixed points in terms of which political concessions and changes are made. On the contrary: a politics of difference may well involve the forging of new identities and the rethinking of heretofore unquestioned behavior. A fluid conception of identity and norms is a further important distinction between thin normativity and thick.

16   The empirical plausibility of distinguishing between societies of greater and societies of lesser normative homogeneity does not require, empirically or logically, what is probably a fiction anyway: a society that, normatively, is completely homogenous.

17   I explore this self-induced fragmentation in chapter 5 with respect to efforts in law and public policy to defeat intersections of sexism and racism, or sexism and class difference. Fragmentation occurs here with the generation of unintended consequences.

18   Even if the extent of agreement that any approach can attain is, in any given case, an important feature of its functional capacity.

19   Analyzed by authors from Parsons to Luhmann as the "problem of double contingency."

20   By Giddens (1994:81) and Alexander (1988:284), for example.

21   Here I substitute the word "group" for Goffman's term "team." Goffman

(1959:104) defines a team as a "set of individuals whose intimate co-operation is required if a given projected definition of the situation is to be maintained. A team is a grouping, but it is a grouping not in relation to a social structure or social organization but rather in relation to an interaction or series of interactions in which the relevant definition of the situation is maintained." In this way Goffman distinguishes a team from a group in one respect: cooperation within a team serves strategic, manipulative goals, which, to be effective, requires self-presentation on the team's part that conceals these goals and conceals cooperation toward achieving them. In fact, groups may have teams within them: "Teams may be created by individuals to aid the group that they are members of, but in aiding themselves and their group in this dramaturgical way, they are acting as a team, not a group" (ibid., 106). Teams, then, are simply strategically deceptive groups. Two points follow. First, Goffman conceives of social interaction collectivistically. While this hardly makes him a communitarian, it provides something of a base for my appropriating—against the grain—Goffman's notion of strategic interaction as a counterintuitive form of communitarianism, one better suited than liberalism to dealing with the demands of increasingly heterogeneous political communities. Second, because I construct social groups with regard to their politically strategic relationships to other social groups, my substitution of "group" for "team" has a certain if limited plausibility. The substitution retains Goffman's concern with strategic orientation even as it drops his insistence on the conspiratorial nature of that orientation.

22   One might characterize Gauthier's theory of morality as a kind of modus vivendi. Gauthier (1986:103) suggests morality as a regime of rationally required constraints that are empirically possible "if the constraints are generated simply by the understanding that they make possible the more effective realization of one's interests, the greater fulfillment of one's preferences, whatever one's interests or preferences may be." Morality then has no basis in emotional affect, and moral members of a community or society can be normatively unconcerned with one another. Indeed, concern and constraints would damage rather than facilitate interaction. Even in "circumstances that preclude the harmony of equilibrium and optimality under free activity which the market affords" (ibid.), a morality characterized by mutual unconcern is still possible "as a set of constraints on the pursuit of maximum utility that every rational person must acknowledge" (ibid., 103–104). In fact each individual has a rational, if selfish, interest simultaneously in urging others to uphold social conventions and rules for the good of all members, yet in flouting the conventions and rules him- or herself. After all, norm violators can benefit from norm violation only if others heed the norms he or she violates. In this way the violators are always dependent on the heeders; precisely the violator of con-

straints must logically be one of the greatest proponents of constraints. As we have seen, and shall see again in the remaining pages, thin communitarianism can accommodate such ambivalences—indeed, is itself marked by some of them.

3. Social Integration of Diverse Communities

1   Compare Mead 1967:154: The community or group that gives the "individual his unity of self may be called 'the generalized other.' The attitude of the generalized other is the attitude of the whole community." I am arguing that generalized community is the generalized other of the various concrete communities insofar as it enters into the experience of each concrete community: "in the case of such a social group as a ball team, the team is the generalized other in so far as it enters—as an organized process or social activity—into the experience of any one of the individual members of it" (ibid.). Mead offers the example of team sports: "Each one of his own acts is determined by his assumption of the action of the others who are playing the game. What he does is controlled by his being everyone else on that team, at least in so far as those attitudes affect his own particular response" (ibid.).

2   Where "harm" is defined from the perspective of generalized community.

3   I agree with Singer (1999:62): "Each of us belongs to indefinitely many communities, large and small, organized and unorganized, some more and some less central to our sense of self and of our own identity. Communities overlap and intersect in indefinitely many ways, and a given community (or segment thereof) may be a subcommunity of any number of more inclusive communities. Communities need not be localized. The intellectual community, its subcommunity of historians, typify communities that transcend geographic and linguistic boundaries and are dispersed through many other communities." "Communities can belong to more inclusive communities and, conversely, can also incorporate subcommunities" (ibid., 65).

4   The individual need not stand closer to generalized community than to his or her concrete community, or vice versa. But she or he could, for various reasons. Greenawalt (1988:258) offers one reason why one might be closer to one's concrete community while still a full member of generalized community. He argues that the "claim that citizens and legislators should rely exclusively on secular grounds . . . invites religious persons to displace their most firmly rooted convictions about values and about the nature of humanity and the universe in a quest for common bases of judgment that is inevitably unavailing when virtually everyone must rely on personal perspectives. The product of serious efforts by religious people to be model liberal citizens of the sort recommended would necessitate a frus-

trating alienation of their whole persons from their political characters. Rather than asserting any exclusivity for nonreligious reasoned judgment, sensible thought about a model of liberal democracy focuses mainly on domains of liberty and a more constrained commitment to shared premises and forms of reason. . . . [L]iberalism demands a high degree of tolerance, not the tolerance of indifference, but the tolerance of a sympathetic mutual understanding of the place that religious premises occupy in the life of serious believers and of the dangers to those of different beliefs if religious convictions and discourse overwhelm the common dialogue of rational secular morality."

5 The notion of generalized community is one not of normative neutrality but of normative minimalism. Where most political theories treat minimalism (and neutrality, for that matter) individualistically—most prominently in political liberalism—I transpose the problem to a higher level: to the relation of a general community to its component subcommunities. Here the issue of normative minimalism returns with some force. It is not just an abstract issue but also a vital empirical problem, often with historical dimensions (as I show in a range of examples).

6 For both examples, compare Bauböck 1994.

7 Compare Mead 1967:134: The "attitude of the other toward himself, that the individual is able consciously to adjust himself to that process."

8 Compare ibid., 138: "For he enters his own experience as a self or individual, not directly or immediately, not by becoming a subject to himself, but only in so far as he first becomes an object to himself just as other individuals are objects to him or in his experience; and he becomes an object to himself only by taking the attitudes of other individuals toward himself within a social environment or context of experience and behavior in which both he and they are involved."

9 Even a concrete community that became severely isolated from all other communities would still relate to itself in ways it once had related to other communities. The isolated community would respond to itself in the way another community would respond to it because it has "internalized" the other communities in an abstract and general sense: it has "internalized" its relationship to other communities such that it can assume the same relationship to itself. It thus takes the "attitude of the other" toward itself. A community able to do so no longer needs other concrete communities to become an object to itself. A community that had never had contact with other communities—probably an anthropological fiction—would not, on this account, be a "community." On the other hand a community that, say, after centuries of isolation somehow forgot its earlier contact with other communities, would still be a "community" in my sense, because—like persons placed in solitary confinement for the remainder of their lives— it could still relate to itself as other communities once related to it. By

analogy a human who somehow grew to maturity with no human contact whatsoever would not be a human in any sense other than the biological. Of course, such a person—who likely is impossible—might still be regarded as possessing an innate dignity and right to be treated as any socialized person. But such a regard would be predicated on the isolated person's potential for socialization, through which she or he could become a human in a social sense.

10   Compare ibid., 138: "The individual experiences himself as such, not directly, but only indirectly, from the particular standpoints of other individual members of the same social group, or from the generalized standpoint of the social group as a whole to which he belongs."

11   Compare ibid., 132: "Mentality . . . simply comes in when the organism is able to point out meanings to others and to himself. This is the point at which mind appears, or . . . emerges. . . . [w]e are dealing with the relationship of the organism to the environment selected by its own sensitivity."

12   This example is inspired by Taylor's (1992) discussion of *diversité profonde.*

13   Most but not all. I discuss two possible exceptions in later pages: first, special or enhanced rights vis-à-vis the national government for the concrete communities of indigenous minorities threatened by cultural extinction; second, fewer rights vis-à-vis the national government for concrete communities intolerant of other (tolerant) concrete communities.

14   Compare Mead 1967:162–163: "The structure . . . on which the self is built is this response which is common to all, for one has to be a member of a community to be a self. Such responses are abstract attitudes, but they constitute just what we term a man's character. They give him what we term his principles, the acknowledged attitudes of all members of the community toward what are the values of that community. He is putting himself in the place of the generalized other, which represents the organized responses of all the members of the group. It is that which guides conduct controlled by principles, and a person who has such an organized group of responses is a man whom we say has character, in the moral sense."

15   Compare ibid., 164: "We cannot have rights unless we have common attitudes."

16   Compare ibid., 134: "by means of reflexiveness—the turning-back of the experience of the individual upon himself—. . . the whole social process is . . . brought into the experience of the individuals involved in it."

17   Compare ibid., 163: "self-consciousness refers to the ability to call out in ourselves a set of definite responses which belong to the others of the group." Again, the person "taking one role must be ready to take the role of everyone else. . . . He must know what everyone else is going to do in order to carry out his own play. He has to take all of these roles. They do not all have to be present in consciousness at the same time, but at some

moments he has to have three or four individuals present in his own attitude . . . These responses must be, in some degree, present in his own make-up" (ibid, 151). "In the game . . . there is a set of responses of such others so organized that the attitude of one calls out the appropriate attitudes of the other" (ibid.). "What is essential to communication is that the symbol should arouse in one's self what it arouses in the other individual. It must have that sort of universality of any person who finds himself in the same situation. There is a possibility of language whenever a stimulus can affect the individual as it affects the other" (ibid., 149).

18 Compare ibid., 163–164: "We cannot be ourselves unless we are also members in whom there is a community of attitudes which control the attitudes of all."

19 Whereas some concrete communities may be constituted by the ascriptive characteristics of their members (for example, Christians, or married women, or Asian Americans—or married, Christian, Asian American women), generalized community cannot be predicated on such characteristics. Or we might say that, to the extent generalized community is so predicated, it is less than a generalized community, in ways described, for example, by Smith (1997:470–471): "U.S. citizenship laws have always expressed illiberal, undemocratic ascriptive myths of U.S. civic identity, along with various types of liberal and republican ones, in logically inconsistent but politically effective combinations; and . . . we should expect this to be the case. The founders of the United States did indeed define and construct their new nation in accord with Enlightenment doctrines of individual liberties and republican self-government more than any regime before and most since. . . . And the principles and institutions that those early elites adopted have contributed in many ways to movements that eventually achieved greater liberalization and democratization of the U.S. than the founders ever anticipated. But from Thomas Paine's identification of European-descended American men as the new chosen people of the Protestant God, to the Federalists' and the Whigs' Anglophilic nativism, to the Jeffersonian and Jacksonian doctrines of scientific racism, to the stark evolutionary theories of racial and gender hierarchies during the Gilded Age and the Progressive Era, U.S. leaders always fostered a sense of what made Americans a distinct 'people' that relied in part on inegalitarian ascriptive themes. The history of U.S. citizenship policies demonstrates incontrovertibly that the legal prerogatives of the majority of the domestic population through most of the nation's past have officially been defined in conformity with those ascriptive doctrines, at least as much as purely liberal and republican ones. And many examples, like the reductions in the rights of African-Americans from the Revolution to the 1850s, and from Reconstruction to the Progressive years, as well as the new restrictions imposed on married women in 1855, Asian-Americans in the late

nineteenth century, and homosexuals in the twentieth, all indicate that neither the possession nor the fresh achievement of greater equality can guarantee against later losses of status due to renewed support for various types of ascriptive hierarchy."

20   Compare Habermas (1994:138), who refers to the individual's "assent to the principles of the constitution within the scope of interpretation determined by the ethical-political self-understanding of the citizens and the political culture of the country." What Habermas calls the "principles of the constitution" are, in my terms, generalized community, as is what Habermas calls the "ethical-political self-understanding of the citizens." Because each generalized community presumably has a constitution and political culture in some respects different from the respective constitutions and political cultures of other generalized communities, generalized communities confront one another as concrete communities. The generalized community for the class of generalized communities might be formed in part by international covenants. But the analogy is weak insofar as the capacity of a particular generalized community to sanction any concrete community within it has very limited correspondence on the international level. War efforts that unite a variety of countries, as in the two world wars, often confront the efforts of other coalitions of countries. This constellation poses the question: Which coalition is the true generalized community for all participants, on both sides of the battle line? Any answer can be offered only from within one or the other coalition, and such self-regarding answers easily can be self-serving. The United Nations might be thought a plausible candidate for the generalized community of the class of generalized communities, but, like international law, it often depends on the cooperation of the relevant parties for its determinations to obtain. Such cooperation cannot be coerced and often is not forthcoming.

21   The legal rights generated in generalized community apply to all concrete communities; in this sense they are "generalizable." Generalized legal rights cannot obtain unless they find recognition in the various concrete communities. A theory of rights requires a "politics of recognition" that protects the integrity of the individual in the life contexts in which his or her identity is formed. The generalizable rights of generalized community protect the integrity of the individual not only as an individual with rights over against any concrete community; they also protect the integrity of the individual as a member of his or her concrete community, in his or her identity as a product of a (politically and legally) nongeneralizable way of life.

22   The normatively thin generalized community is capable of some sensitivity toward the thick normativities of the various concrete communities. Consider for example the claim that "[w]hen the Supreme Court and Con-

gress imposed a uniform national principle of racial nondiscrimination on the South, they did not destroy the functions of local communities. Rather they opened new opportunities for citizen participation in local public life. Localism was not suppressed; it was set free from the stifling effects of a racially exclusive definition of community. The redefinition has been limited to the community's public life. The Congress has not sought to invade the privacy of homes or of intimate associations, even for the purpose of eradicating racial discrimination, nor has the Supreme Court been inclined to pursue any such objective. The one kind of community that has been displaced by federal civil rights law is the community that seeks to operate an all-white preserve in the public arena" (Karst 1989:187).

23   Taylor (1994:38) speaks of "assimilation" as the "cardinal sin against the ideal of authenticity."

24   As is sometimes argued in terms of multiculturalism, feminism, ethnonationalism, and critical race theory, among other contemporary approaches to difference.

25   Of course, a generalized right or presumption cannot wholly capture the entire value of any given concreteness. But recognition of any concrete community, by generalized community or by other concrete communities, does not presume to do so.

26   Smith (1997:508 n. 5) might seem to contradict himself as he finds "ascriptive Americanism" to be "liberal" where it offers accommodation from a particular standpoint, from the standpoint of a particular type of concrete community. He speaks of theologically motivated communities whose "inclusiveness" is based on religious convictions not shared by all but which the community in question patronizingly extends even to those persons who do not share them: "ascriptive views can undergird universalistic, egalitarian civic positions, as when religious believers esteem the sacredness of all humanity, indeed all creation, on the ground that everything equally comes from God. Despite their ultimate theological moral ascriptiveness, the fact that such egalitarian views always urge civic inclusiveness and treat national citizenships as legitimately alterable political memberships makes them effectively liberal and consensual in regard to citizenship laws. Hence I subsume them under liberalism." If such a concrete community offered accommodation to nonmembers on condition of their accepting the community's faith, or coerced assimilation to the community's cultural way of life, it would be dogmatically intolerant. If it made no such condition, it would not be dogmatic in its actions toward other concrete communities, even as it regarded them as wrong-headed or otherwise afflicted with false consciousness. Political tolerance in the sense of generalized community is a question of behavior, not belief—insofar as belief does not issue into intolerant or otherwise exclusionary behavior toward other concrete communities.

27 Rights that obtain within any given concrete community—informed by
that community's thick normativity—cannot be granted within generalized community. They would be quite impossible there, inasmuch as generalized community rejects thick normativities and privileges no concrete
community. Thus the Catholic Church's right to excommunicate an apostate member does not derive from generalized community and cannot be
exercised there or in any concrete community other than the Church.

4. Solidarities, Understandings, Identities

1 No one of these systems is "reducible to terms of one or a combination
of the other two. Each is indispensable to the other two in the sense that
without personalities and culture there would be no social system and so
on around the roster of logical possibilities" (Parsons 1964:6). While each
of these systems is autonomous from the others, together they can be used
to analyze three dimensions of every social behavior. From this perspective, "an individual [social] action is not possible" but "can only exist in
connection with other actions and thus takes the form of a system" (Luhmann 1982:52).

2 Which presupposes that the social roles people play are constituted by
a harmony of normative expectations; that whole societies agree con-
sensually on the nature and definition of these expectations; and that
social structures tend toward (dynamic) equilibrium and orderly social
change. By contrast my approach shows that even as aspects of solidarity,
shared understandings, and individual identities fit together and function
together, such cooperation doesn't preclude significant tension, even conflict, among them.

3 This distinction differs from, but might be compared with, Habermas's
(1987:118) analysis of the development of the European modern age, which
distinguishes between nonnormative and normative forms of social integration. Nonnormative are "mechanisms that stabilize nonintended interconnections of actions by way of functionally intermeshing action consequences," where the "integration of an action system is established"
by a "non-normative regulation of individual decisions that extends beyond the actors' consciousness." Normative forms of social integration are
"mechanisms for coordinating action that harmonize the *action orientations* of participants," where the "integration of an action system is established by a normatively secured or communicatively achieved consensus"
(ibid.). Unlike Habermas, I am not concerned to distinguish between the
basically normative behavior of humans and the basically nonnormative
functions of social structures such as the economy or the bureaucracy.
Rather, I distinguish between human behavior that is strongly normative
and behavior that is only weakly normative. By means of this distinction

I identify some robust possibilities for social integration in liberal democratic societies despite their significant normative heterogeneity.

4   Compare Rawls 1993.

5   As long as that worldview will admit some allegiance to thin norms, such as constitutional guarantees to every citizen's right to freedom of speech.

6   And hold no normatively thick beliefs inconsistent with this notion of justice. Compare Rawls 1993:202.

7   Compare Smelser and Alexander 1999:13. In a related sense, what Parsons (1964:126) calls the inherent "diffuseness of political power" does not defeat the capacity of power to unite disparate individuals and groups where groups and individuals can be integrated into collective responsibility, such that power becomes fused with collective responsibility.

8   Consequently Parsons (1964:328) considers having a "common belief system shared by ego and alter . . . as important as that the beliefs should be adequate to reality outside the particular interaction system."

9   Compare Garner 1994:220–221.

10 In distinction to Braybrooke's (2001) conception of natural law.

11 This claim finds support across a range of authors of divergent social visions. For Luhmann (1982) and Rawls (1993), solidarity does not require morality, no more than political agreement among a citizenry requires shared comprehensive worldviews. Here we have thin normativity. Parsons (1977) discusses ways of conceiving of thin normativity as less solidary. Hayek (1976:111) shows how thin normativity is irreconcilable with solidarity in the sense of "unitedness in the pursuit of [some] known common goals." Normatively thick ends are not necessary for the integration of the individual's activities into an order, nor are they a necessary condition of social peace and stability.

12 Information technologies, such as computers and telecommunications, as well as businesses involved in their management and provision, deal with a commodity whose value (if it is not privileged information) is realized not in hoarding but only in its rapid and unrestricted release and exchange, exchange in ever changing environments by ever widening webs of participants. As institutions become thinner, so too do the relationships that carry them.

13 Thus at one local level, "[n]eighborhoods, as territorially defined communities, also have porous boundaries that permit looser connections to be maintained. Spending social evenings with neighbors has declined in recent decades, but spending time socializing with friends outside one's neighborhood has increased. Easier transportation and a more mobile population are the reasons for this change. Most people report that they know people at work better than those in their own neighborhoods. Friendships can be formed around temporary or specialized interests, rather than being embedded in the neighborhood" (Wuthnow 1999:29).

14   Compare Luhmann 1982:8.

15   Of course, the political potential of this conception depends on wide-spread participation in local political communities. Today such participation can only be an aspiration.

5. Political Judgment about Indeterminate Legal Norms

1   I cannot here take into account the increasing diversity among ethno-methodologists with respect to choice of both problem and method (see Maynard and Clayman 1991:386). Nelson (1994:324–324 n. 3) also observes "fragmentation within ethnomethodology, which now threatens to call the possibility of developing a coherent description of ethno-methodology into question. That is, classical ethnomethodology seems at times to be on its way to becoming the only kind of coherently describable ethnomethodology given the increasingly diverse and inconsistent ethnomethodological positions being espoused—or rather, given the increasingly separate articulation of discordant positions once held simultaneously in classical ethnomethodology." Nor can I take into account the far greater variety among jurisprudential approaches. But for the purposes of my thesis, these distinctions are immaterial. This foreshortened approach provides for clarity of exposition yet represents a degree of over-simplification. That degree is tolerable insofar as my distinctions within a small range are representative.

2   *Roth v. United States*, 354 U.S. 476 (1957). The First Amendment reads in part: "Congress shall make no law respecting an establishment of religion, or prohibiting the free exercise thereof; or abridging the freedom of speech, or of the press."

3   *Trop v. Dulles*, 356 U.S. 86 (1958). The Eighth Amendment reads: "Excessive bail shall not be required, nor excessive fines imposed, nor cruel and unusual punishments inflicted."

4   Beyond ethnomethodology, Derrida (1990:961) observes the practical impossibility of strict compliance in the related area of judicial opinions. He claims that "each [judicial] decision is different and requires an absolutely unique interpretation, which no existing, coded [norm] can or ought to guarantee absolutely" and that a decision can be "just and responsible" only if it both conforms to existing law and also justifies it anew or re-affirms its principle.

5   And that across a broad philosophical range, including authors as diverse as Dworkin 1977, Frankfurter 1970, Holmes 1968, Kress 1989, Posner 1990, Singer 1984, Smith 1992, Stick 1986, Tushnet 1991, Unger 1984, West 1990, and Williams 1990.

6   See Halkowski 1990, Hilbert 1981, Maynard 1985, Maynard and Clayman 1991, and Watson 1978.

7   My emphasis; author's emphasis deleted.

8   To distinguish between exogenous and endogenous underlying principles is not necessarily to deny the existence or possibility of underlying principles as such.

9   Among the presuppositions of pragmatism I count the following: rejection of a correspondence theory of truth; the claim that, even if truth itself is immutable, our estimation of it can only be variable; the notion that we estimate a belief as "true" if it proves to be a successful guide to action; the conviction that knowledge in moral and nonmoral situations is not sharply distinct, nor are the respective knowledge gathering procedures by which people control their environment; and the view that no inquiry whatsoever provides infallible results. This particular list is inspired by Posner (1990:28), although it is hardly original but rather broadly representative of the pragmatist movement. Elsewhere (Gregg 1997) I show that a pragmatist notion of jurisprudence asserts the absence of ultimate foundations for knowledge and morals and the necessity of drawing on local standards to render law determinate. And I show that it allows for a nonparochial form of localism; for legal critique that is more than idiosyncratic, arbitrary, and subjective; for a viable notion of autonomy of the group and individual vis-à-vis legal institutions; for law without mass delusion; and for a notion of justice as singular, not plural, and more than simply authority.

10 See Luhmann 1989:137 n. 2.

11 Luhmann (1985:288) nicely captures this circularity: "restrictions are only ever possible as restrictions of freedom, and . . . freedom itself emerges as a result of its restrictions." Again, "legal decisions are valid on the basis of legal [norms], although (even because!) [norms] are valid on the basis of decisions. Regulation and implementation presume each other reciprocally as granting validity" (ibid., 285).

12 Contrary to Kress 1989, Singer 1984, and Stick 1986.

13 347 U.S. 497 (1954).

14 347 U.S. 483 (1954).

15 In *Plessy v. Ferguson* (193 U.S. 537), decided in 1896 and overturned by *Brown*, Justice Harlan's dissent contains two different theories, which frame the argument in *Brown*. On the one hand, Harlan claims that "[o]ur Constitution is color-blind," therefore that race is never a permissible criterion of classification by the government. This proposition is not contained in the Fourteenth Amendment, which states in part that "[n]o State shall make or enforce any law which shall abridge the privileges or immunities of citizens of the United States; nor shall any State deprive any person of life, liberty, or property, without due process of law; nor deny to any person within its jurisdiction the equal protection of the laws." On the other hand, Harlan claims that "there is no caste here," that is, impermis-

sible is not necessarily a law that adverts to race but rather one that subordinates one race to another. Both *Plessy* and *Brown* address laws that treat different races symmetrically (preventing whites from certain kinds of association with blacks wherever they prevent blacks from the same kinds of association with whites). Of course, formal symmetry obscures material asymmetry: preventing blacks from attending white public schools is preventing blacks from enjoying materially better facilities. Consequently the second of Harlan's two theories has no practical purchase unless it looks beyond the formal symmetry to discern the asymmetrical or unequal intent or consequences of the law in question. Justice Warren, delivering the Court's opinion in *Brown*, does just that: "In approaching this problem, we cannot turn the clock back to 1868 when the [Fourteenth] Amendment was adopted, or even to 1896 when *Plessy* was written. We must consider public education in light of the [Fourteenth Amendment's] full development and its present place in American life throughout the Nation. Only in this way can it be determined if segregation is public schools deprives these plaintiffs" of equal protection.

16   For example, Garfinkel's (1996:18) claim that the "properties of indexical expressions are witnessable only locally and endogenously."

17   Jayyusi 1991:235. See also Maynard and Clayman 1991:399 and Sacks 1990.

18   See, for example, Bandyopadhay 1971 and Coulter 1973, 1979.

6. Political Judgment about Competing Cultural Values

1   Bourdieu (1990:90) offers an interesting example of the difficulty faced by an adherent of one value system attempting to understand him- or herself from the perspective of another: "as soon as he reflects on his practice, adopting a quasi-theoretical posture, [the adherent] loses any chance of expressing the [full] truth of his practice, and especially the truth of the practical relation to the practice. Academic interrogation inclines [the agent] to take up a point of view on his own practice that is no longer that of action, [yet] without being that of science, encouraging him to shape his explanations in terms of a theory of practice that meshes with the juridical, ethical or grammatical legalism to which the observer is inclined by his own situation. Simply because he is questioned, and questions himself, about the reasons and the *raison d'être* of his practice, he cannot communicate the essential point, which is that the very nature of practice is that it excludes this question," that it normally excludes the question or perhaps that it always does.

2   Reduction is one of many kinds of barrier. A different barrier falsely projects a theory of *x* onto *x* itself, in the sense of mistaking a model of reality for reality itself, such as confusing a grammar's description of a language with part of the way competent speakers actually use the language;

or reifying the "reasonable man" who in some legal arguments stands in for actual human beings.

3   Even as Bellah (1970:245) argues that "we can translate, painfully and tentatively, between different realms of reality without reducing the language of one to the language of the other," he sees Weber (to whose work I shall turn momentarily) as someone who conveys the "feeling that the scientific observer cannot finally take seriously the beliefs he is studying even though he must take seriously the fact that beliefs have profound social consequences" (ibid., 250).

4   Freud's (1961:32) opinion that religion, as the "attempt to procure a certainty of happiness and a protection against suffering through a delusional remolding of reality," is a form of mass delusion, is unlikely to be shared by religionists, as Freud recognizes: "No one, needless to say, who shares a delusion ever recognizes it as such" (ibid.). And the religionist who rejects Freud's interpretation likely will not share Freud's own estimation of the psychoanalytic approach.

5   Destutt de Tracy first developed the notion of "ideology" that was to figure so prominently in Marx's analysis of religion.

6   Represented by such works as Lessing's *Erziehung des Menschengeschlechtes* (1980), Kant's *Die Religion innerhalb der Grenzen der bloßen Vernunft* (1914), and Hegel's *Vorlesungen über die Philosophie der Religion* (1983).

7   The Enlightenment should not be constructed as a monolithic movement without internal ambiguity, ambivalence, or tension. The rationalism of the Enlightenment, its rejection of the nonrational, and its expectation that religion, as something nonrational, would disappear with the ineluctable spread of reason, finds clear expression in Marx's analysis of religion. From Feuerbach (1841) Marx adopts the idea that religion merely "reflects" the human being: in any act of religious consciousness, the subject of religion actually refers to itself, to the human subject thinking religiously. The object of religion is nothing other than the subject of religion: the human being him- or herself. But Marx (1982:171) goes beyond Feuerbach, beyond this identity of subject and object, to argue that religion also reflects the material circumstances of human suffering: "Das *religiöse* Elend ist in einem der *Ausdruck* des wirklichen Elendes und in einem die *Protestation* gegen das wirkliche Elend. Die Religion ist der Seufzer der bedrängten Kreatur, das Gemüt einer herzolsen Welt, wie sie der Geist geistloser Zustände ist. Sie is das *Opium* des Volkes." In a society emancipated from alienation, religion will not be necessary or even possible and will disappear of itself. Yet no less rationalist is Durkheim's (1886:69) approach, which does not expect religion to disappear: "Tant qu'il y aura des hommes qui vivront ensemble, il y aura entre eux quelque foi commune. Ce qu'on ne peut prévoir et ce que l'avenir seul pourra décider, c'est la forme particulière sous laquelle cette foi se symbolisera." "There is

something eternal in religion, namely, the faith and the cult" (Durkheim 1965:478).

8 On whom I draw not only as a major theorist but also as a significant interpreter of his classical predecessors, Weber and Durkheim in particular.

9 While Parsons (1954:205) here refers directly to Bronislaw Malinowski, in the following sentence he claims that Durkheim (1965) "went farther than Malinowski in working out the specific character of this difference." What he explicitly says of Malinowski, then, he implicitly means of Durkheim as well.

10 Compare Parsons 1954:211.

11 Sica (1988:228) even claims that for Weber the "'real kernel' of life rest[s] in the other than rational."

12 Rationality itself might seem to be relative and perspectival, inasmuch as rationality and irrationality each defines the boundary of the other. On this view, to question the boundaries of the one is necessarily to question those of the other.

13 Which may be part of a "civil religion" (compare Bellah 1970:168–169; 1973).

14 On this view symbols are the most fundamental of cultural forms, namely "collective representations" serving not only the integration of society but its very reproduction (compare Bellah 1970:251).

15 As Parsons (1967b:87) himself notes, only in a limiting case is science a purely individual, isolated activity; ordinarily it is socially organized. As such, it is oriented and dependent on the general values of the society and culture of its time. But Parsons is not claiming what Bellah (1970:246), for his part, claims: that science, if true, is true for reasons not solely scientific, but, like religion, for irrational reasons as well: the "great symbols that justify science itself rest on unprovable assumptions sustained at the deepest levels of our consciousness."

16 In Marx 1982a, but also in Marx and Engels 1930.

17 As in Marx 1974.

18 According to Wuthnow (1992:105–106), nonidentity in the sense of social fragmentation and overcomplexity is fertile ground for religion today: "Many religious beliefs and practices remain much in evidence, contrary to simpler predictions that have envisioned a simple decline in religious vitality. These beliefs and practices may have retained their vitality through accommodations to the contemporary cultural situation. In becoming more oriented to the self, in paying more explicit attention to symbolism, in developing a more flexible organizational style, and in nurturing specialized worship experiences, American religion has become more complex, more internally differentiated, and thus more adaptable to a complex, differentiated society." Wuthnow (1998:170) also notes how fragmentation and overcomplexity needn't defeat faith: "spirituality also

exists in the complex and fragmented arena of contemporary society. Commuting, dual careers, and busy family schedules have added complexity to many people's lives, often making it hard for them to find community (or to see the relevance of community), but spiritual practice remains possible in the midst of these challenging circumstances."

19 For Durkheim and Parsons, the internalization of normative culture does not imply a conformist attitude toward social expectations within a given social context (compare Münch 1988:129). With socialization, internalization implies the adoption of universalistic normative ideas that allow the individual to critically distance him- or herself from concrete social expectations. In Durkheim's (1974:59) formulation: "To love one's society is to love this ideal, and one loves it so that one would rather see society disappear as a material entity than renounce the ideal which it embodies."

20 Compare Parsons 1967b:90.

21 Although the notion of "sharing" immediately raises questions of relativism: is "truth" defined solely with regard to the values of a particular group? Is "truth" relative only to the group, and not between groups? Does the possibility of sharing require some objective standard of knowledge, for example on the argument that humans establish objectivity not through deductive reasoning or empirical proof but through the justification of a choice of standards, such that objectivity means agreement among the contending parties that their disputes will be judged according to the same standard? Compare Alexander 1982:114–115.

22 Given variations in institutionalized values, in the grounds of meaning, and in the interests of individuals in rewards for "acceptable" conduct.

23 Compare Parsons 1967b:91.

24 Similarly, legal professionals who share similar educational backgrounds, religious beliefs, political orientations, and professional experience will tend to interpret legal texts convergently, tending to agree on the premises for judicial decision. Under these circumstances, says Posner (1990:202–203), the law would appear (and, in a sense, even *is*) objective and impersonal. But Parsons (1967b:90) argues that the social scientist cannot share the values of the culture and society he or she studies, that otherwise he or she would be condemned to solipsism.

25 The role of the state, as society's organ of consciousness, would then be to "organize the cult, to be the head of it and to ensure its regular working and development" (Durkheim 1958:70).

26 By similar reasoning Bellah (1970:252–253) argues that religion is "true": "If we define religion as that symbol system that serves to evoke . . . the totality that includes subject and object and provides the context in which life and action finally have meaning, then . . . as Durkheim said of society, religion is a reality *sui generis*. . . . [R]eligion is true. This is not to say that every religious symbol is equally valid any more than every scientific

theory is equally valid. But . . . since religious symbolization and religious experience are inherent in the structure of human existence, all reductionism must be abandoned."

27   In Bellah's (1970:252) words; see Parsons, "Culture and the Social System," in Parsons 1961.

28   But unlike Marx, Weber does not subscribe to a unilinear philosophy of history driven by the unfolding of human reason: the rationalism of world mastery is neither without alternatives nor exclusively the result of free choice. This particular historical process had to assert itself in a struggle against other forms of cultured existence and was indebted to a chain of circumstances that in part were the unintended results of intentional action: "One can in fact . . . rationalize life in terms of fundamentally different basic points of view and in very different directions. 'Rationalism' is a historical concept which encompasses a world of antitheses" (Weber 1958a:77–78).

29   Compare Mestrovic 1988:100.

30   Parsons (1967b:90) makes a related point by claiming that social scientists must differentiate their role from that of all other participants in their culture and society. Only in this way can scientists attain the perspective necessary to differentiate cultural elements essential to their scientific purpose from irrelevant elements. Yet Parsons (1967c:152) also claims that every social theory is relative to the society in which it is developed, because the "*selection* of problems to which answers are given is a function of the values of the society in which such knowledge arises and becomes significant." Yet "selection in this sense must be carefully distinguished both from a secondary type of selection and from *distortion*, which is . . . always present, but which analytically must be attributed to quite a different order of factors" (ibid.).

31   Geertz (1966:644–645) similarly avoids reductionism by allowing for the autonomy of competing value systems. Humans construct the realities in which they live through the use of symbols, which convey meaning and are created, objectified, and internalized through social interaction. As a symbol system, religion is rooted in social processes, and religious symbols are directed to the cultural problem of the meaning of human existence in its broadest terms. Yet while psychological, political, and economic concerns influence how these tasks are performed, religion cannot be reduced to them. Through symbolism, religion integrates contexts of everyday life with larger contexts of meaning, establishing "powerful, pervasive, and long lasting moods and motivations in men by . . . formulating conceptions of a general order of existence and . . . clothing these conceptions with such an aura of factuality that . . . the moods and motivations seem uniquely realistic" (ibid., 643).

32   The notion of relativism is hardly of recent historical vintage, as some sup-

pose, but an integral part of the Western cultural heritage since the Sophists. Multiculturalism in theory and practice also followed the military campaigns of Alexander the Great, the military and cultural magnification of the Roman Empire, and the cultural and religious trends carried first by Christianity's spread and subsequently by Islam's as well. These trends included the Arab Caliphate, which briefly ruled from Spain to Samarkand in the name of Islam, and the Eastern Roman Empire of Byzantium, which lasted until 1453.

33   Habermas (1984:115) identifies several of these procedures and standards with the claim that the meaning of an utterance consists in the reasons that can be offered for it, and that to understand the meaning of an utterance is to know the conditions of its validity: to "understand an utterance in the paradigm case of a speech act oriented to reaching understanding, the interpreter has to be familiar with the conditions of its validity; he has to know under what conditions the validity claim linked with it . . . would have to be acknowledged by the hearer. But where could the interpreter obtain this knowledge. . . ? He can understand the meaning of the communicative acts only because they are embedded in a context of *action* oriented to reaching understanding."

7. Political Judgment as Ideology Critique

1   I adopt this definition given my interest (developed in later pages) in the relationship between ideas and material interests. Alternative definitions are many, including (1) the denial of contradictions between private appropriation and socialized production, as in the claim that economic conflict is nonpolitical; (2) where the "interests of dominant groups are bound up with the preservation of the *status quo*," "forms of signification which 'naturalize' the existing state of affairs" (Giddens 1994:195); (3) the repression of groups and individuals by the "culture industry," a powerful, rationalized structure that pacifies (compare Tar 1977) through television networks and other forms of mass culture, through "administered . . . nonspontaneous, reified, phony culture rather than the real thing" (Jay 1973:216). Not ideological, on the other hand, are claims that "certain questions are so fundamental that to insure their being rightly settled justifies civil strife" (Rawls 1993:152), because the element of distortion or concealment or camouflage is absent.

2   Like the preceding generation of critical social theorists (for example, Horkheimer [1974]), Habermas picks up on Weber's (1980:10) distinction between *Wertrationalität* and *Zweckrationalität*, between formal and substantive rationality. Critical theory understands formal rationality as "instrumental reason," oriented to the most efficient, effective realization of given ends without concern for the nature, desirability, or legitimacy of

those ends. "Instrumental reason" facilitates domination and the interests behind domination. Formal rationality is in fact a kind of irrationality, in the sense of a force repressing individuals instead of liberating them, thwarting their needs and desires rather than satisfying them, impoverishing communities instead of enriching them, "dummifying" people instead of enlightening them: in short, serving ideology rather than its critique. Noninstrumental is self-reflective reason, reason that can reflect on the admissibility of its goals. Capacity for critique resides in the latter.

3   Even as thin critique rejects the materialist philosophy of history intended by Marx and Engels (1930:50) in the sentence preceding the one I quote: "What else does the history of ideas prove, than that intellectual production changes in character in proportion as material production is changed?" Thin critique rejects any philosophy of history as a normative thickness.

4   In its normative thinness it differs from feminist "standpoint epistemology," as described by Harding (1986:148): "A feminist epistemological standpoint is an interested social location ('interested' in the sense of 'engaged,' not 'biased'), the conditions for which bestow upon its occupants scientific and epistemic advantage. The subjugation of women's sensuous, concrete, relational activity permits women to grasp aspects of nature and social life that are not accessible to inquiries grounded in men's characteristic activities. The vision based on men's activities is both partial and perverse—'perverse' because it systematically reverses the proper order of things: it substitutes abstract for concrete reality; for example, it makes death-risking rather than the reproduction of our species form of life the paradigmatically human act." Harding not only criticizes the repression of "relational" orientation to other persons; in a normatively thick commitment, she privileges it over alternatives. For Hartsock (1983:292), the "activity of a woman in the home as well as the work she does for wages keeps her continually in contact with a world of qualities and change. Her immersion in the world of use—in concrete, many-qualitied, changing material processes—is more complete than [a man's]. And if life itself consists of sensuous activity, the vantage point available to women on the basis of the contribution to subsistence represents an intensification and deepening of the materialist world view and consciousness available to the producers of commodities in capitalism, an intensification of class consciousness." In a normatively thick commitment, Hartsock privileges "sensuous activity" over abstract activity (even if in an analysis that itself is abstract not sensuous). "Women also produce/reproduce men (and other women) on both a daily and a long-term basis. This aspect of women's 'production' exposes the deep inadequacies of the concept of production as a description of women's activity. One does not (cannot) produce another human being in anything like the way one produces an object such as a chair. . . .

Helping another to develop, the gradual relinquishing of control, the experience of the human limits of one's action . . . [refer to child-rearing
activities more often done by women than men]. The female experience
in reproduction represents a unity with nature which goes beyond the
proletarian experience of interchange with nature" (ibid., 293). Hartsock
privileges one form of production over another, as if, for example, the social contributions of childless adults was necessarily less than that of any
parent as such. In these ways Harding and Hartsock advance normatively
thick preferences.

5   Geertz is speaking of adjudication, not critique, but his point applies to
critique as well.

6   "The under-valuation of low-wage women's jobs is an integral part of the
hierarchy that organizes work and locates class boundaries. These processes are visible primarily as gender-neutral bureaucratic practices or
as professionalization. The documents and procedures that structure the
processes are expressed in abstract, genderless terms. Women as well as
men may be those who organize bureaucratic measure and strive for pro-
fessionalism. . . . In the process, it is unnecessary to evoke images of special
female capacities or incapacities to perpetuate the hierarchical location
and the low wages of women's sex-segregated jobs; only an appeal to the
rational and the reasonable is needed" (Acker 1989:222).

7   I develop an alternative to cognitive parochialism in my theory of "enlightened localism" (Gregg 2003).

8   McGuire and Reskin (1993:499–500) found that "Black women shared
the penalties imposed on white women and black men. Being female
cost both white and black women authority and earnings. Along with
white women, black women suffered a depreciated payoff for education,
seniority, and authority. Although women averaged less education and
tenure than men, employers' propensity to regard men's credentials more
highly than women's allowed men to capitalize on these differences. Black
women also lost authority and earnings because of their color. The dis-
counted rate at which employers rewarded black women's seniority with
authority was more than the sum of the separate effects of their race and
sex. For both sexes, being black reduced private-sector workers' earnings."

9   On the other hand, "Married black women have always disproportion-
ately worked in the labor force as compared with white women. Although
black women also encounter a sexual division of labor in the home, their
response to it grows out of their own history of working as domestics for
white women" (Eisenstein 1994:201).

10 Sex and class intersect in other configurations as well: "The bar dykes
were/are largely working-class in background, and their world is working-
class. The academic feminists were occasionally of working-class background, but more usually they were middle-class white women. They

had read feminist theory and literature, they possessed the mobility that allows one to think of oneself as freely choosing one's world, and the bar world was not the one they would choose. In the bars, there were/are still butches and femmes, although there was an increasingly large group defying this dichotomy. There were/are women who work with men and don't seem to mind, who have male friends, who aspire to the American dream of secure prosperity. The middle-class women who hoped to show them the limited vision of their dreams and the need for radical self-definition and action were rebuffed, and hurt by the rejection. These women, then, were a source of confusion for feminist lesbians. In one sense, they were more 'truly' lesbian than those who came to it later, through feminism; they just were, inescapably, lesbian. On the other hand, they seemed to have less overt concern for feminist ideals; they seemed to want to just live their lives, to be left alone. They had a community, in the bars, but the lesbian feminists wanted more. So the question is, where do these women fit in the lesbian feminist community" (Phelan 1989:66).

11   See, for example, *Mississippi University for Women v. Hogan* (458 U.S. 718 [1982]), which sustained by five votes to four a male applicant's challenge to Mississippi's policy of excluding men from the MUW School of Nursing. Founded in 1884 and the oldest state-supported all-female university in the United States, MUW claimed its policy compensated for discrimination against women.

12   The relevance of sexual difference is less clear in other areas. For example, can women be excluded from combat without violating sexual equality? Are laws that criminalize abortion sexually discriminatory?

13   Equally ideological for Lukács (1976:135) is the experience of reification (a concept he develops from Marx's notion of the fetishism of commodities, an experience of consciousness, yet an experience based in the material conditions of a specific kind of society): "man in capitalist society confronts a reality 'made' by himself (as a class) which appears to him to be a natural phenomenon alien to himself; he is wholly at the mercy of its 'laws,' his activity is confined to the exploitation of the inexorable fulfillment of certain individual laws for his own (egoistic) interests. But even while 'acting' he remains, in the nature of the case, the object and not the subject of events."

14   Gramsci (1997:994) distinguishes "quel momento che in politica si chiama dell' egemonia, del consenso, della direzione culturale," on the one hand, from, on the other, "dal momento della forza, della costrizione, dell'intervento legislativo e statale o poliziesco." Hegemony is the power of ideas to shape consciousness, a kind of moral leadership over subordinate groups. It lies in the ruling class's cultural leadership of and control over the masses. While Gramsci (1975:461) concedes that "il fatto dell'egemonia presuppone che si tenga conto degli interessi e delle ten-

denze dei reggruppamenti su cui l'egemonia verrà esercitata, che si formi un certo equilibrio," his approach remains elitist, paternalistic, and anti-participatory.

15   In this form the "community exercises control over the conduct of its individual members because the "social process or community enters as a determining factor into the individual's thinking" (Mead 1967:155).

16   Expressiveness is not a form of passivity or dependency, and an expressive person can also act instrumentally, even as expressiveness is biased toward treating people as ends not means: "Expressiveness does not mean simply expressing emotion in an unpatterned way. Women, in this culture at least, are provided with patterned ways of expressing and negotiating socio-emotional subtleties in interaction. . . . Women may resonate with, respond to, cope with, and even define emotion for others, but this is hardly the same as being emotional. Expressiveness then is an integrative skill" (Johnson 1988:54).

17   To be sure, the social sphere is not unproblematic: thus "working mothers have higher self-esteem and get less depressed than housewives, but compared to their husbands they're more tired and get sick more often" (Hochschild 1989:4). Be that as it may, many women are in no position to choose between a life in the mainstream of social life.

18   Evidently "husbands use their earnings to 'buy' out of sharing in household tasks, while wives use their earnings to 'buy' increased participation by their husbands," even as the "effects are very small" (Goldscheider and Waite 1991:137).

19   Compare Fudge and MacDermott 1991:282 as well as England 1992:304.

20   In Bourdieu's (1990:132) sense, for example, that "by giving the same value to all holders of the same certificate, thereby making them interchangeable, the educational system minimizes the obstacles to the free circulation of cultural capital which result from its being incorporated in particular individuals . . . It makes it possible to relate all qualification-holders . . . to a single standard, thereby setting up a unified market for all cultural capacities and guaranteeing the convertibility into money of the cultural capital acquired at a given cost in time and labor. . . . From then on, relations of power and dependence are no longer established directly between individuals; [rather, now] they are set up . . . among institutions, . . . among socially guaranteed qualifications and socially defined positions, and through them, among the social mechanisms that produce and guarantee both the social value of the qualifications and the distribution of these social attributes among biological individuals."

21   For example, a program aiming to "eliminate the disincentives to family formation in the existing . . . program (which in many states disallowed payments if a man resided in the house) by subsidizing the low-wage labor of black males and paying benefits to working-poor households," yet cal-

culating benefits on family size but also on "family rather than individual income so that a woman's right to benefits depended on her husband's income. Beyond a certain point, additional earnings to the household (and most likely the woman's would be seen as supplementary given the higher earning power of men) would reduce the family payment" (Quadagno 1990:26).

Coda

1   Or if approval and censure did depend on the ends that actions serve, Hayek (1976:111) continues, the "forces for intellectual progress would be much confined. However much the existence of agreement on ends may in many respects smooth the course of life, the possibility of disagreement, or at least the lack of compulsion to agree on particular ends, is the basis of the kind of civilization which has grown up since the Greeks developed independent thought of the individual as the most effective method of advancement of the human mind."

SELECTED BIBLIOGRAPHY

Acker, Joan. 1989. *Doing Comparable Worth. Gender, Class, and Pay Equity.* Philadelphia: Temple University Press.

Alexander, Jeffrey. 1982. *Theoretical Logic in Sociology.* Vol. 1: *Positivism, Presuppositions, and Current Controversies.* Berkeley: University of California Press.

———. 1983. *Theoretical Logic in Sociology.* Vol. 3: *The Classical Attempt at Theoretical Synthesis: Max Weber.* Berkeley: University of California Press.

———. 1988. *Action and Its Environments.* New York: Columbia University Press.

Bandyopadhay, Pradeep. 1971. "One Sociology or Many: Some Issues in Radical Sociology." *Sociological Review* 19:5–29.

Bauböck, Rainer. 1994. *Transnational Citizenship: Membership and Rights in International Migration.* Aldershot, U.K.: Edward Elgar.

Beahrs, John. 1996. "Ritual Deception: A Window to the Hidden Determinants of Human Politics." *Politics and the Life Sciences* 15:3–12.

Bellah, Robert. 1970. "Between Religion and Social Science." In *Beyond Belief: Essays on Religion in a Post-Traditional World,* 237–259. New York: Harper and Row.

———. 1973. Introduction to *Emile Durkheim on Morality and Society.* Chicago: University of Chicago Press.

Benhabib, Seyla. 1989. "Autonomy, Modernity, and Community." In *Zwischenbetrachtungen: Im Prozess der Aufklärung,* edited by Axel Honneth, Thomas McCarthy, Claus Offe, and Albrecht Wellmer, 373–394. Frankfurt: Suhrkamp.

Bittner, Egon. 1967. "The Police on Skid-Row: A Study of Peace Keeping." *American Sociological Review* 32:699–715.

Bourdieu, Pierre. 1990 [1980]. *The Logic of Practice.* Translated by Richard Nice. Stanford: Stanford University Press.

Boyle, James. 1985. "The Politics of Reason: Critical Legal Theory and Local Social Thought." *University of Pennsylvania Law Review* 133:685–780.

Braybrooke, David. 2001. *Natural Law Modernized.* Toronto: University of Toronto Press.

Carter, Stephen. 1993. *The Culture of Disbelief: How American Law and Politics Trivialize Religious Devotion.* New York: Basic Books.

Casanova, Jose. 1994. *Public Religions in the Modern World.* Chicago: University of Chicago Press.

Chodorow, Nancy. 1978. *The Reproduction of Mothering: Psychoanalysis and the Sociology of Gender.* Berkeley: University of California Press.

Cicourel, Aaron. 1995. *The Social Organization of Juvenile Justice*. New Brunswick: Transaction Publishers.

Cobble, Dorothy, ed. 1993. *Women and Unions: Forging a Partnership*. Ithaca: ILR Press.

Cohen, Jean, and Andrew Arato. 1992. *Civil Society and Political Theory*. Cambridge: MIT Press.

Collins, Patricia Hill. 2000. *Black Feminist Thought: Knowledge, Consciousness, and the Politics of Empowerment*, 2d ed., rev. ed. New York: Routledge.

Collins, Randall. 1989. "Toward a Neo-Meadian Sociology of Mind." *Symbolic Interaction* 12:1–27.

Coulter, Jeff. 1973. *Approaches to Insanity: A Philosophical and Sociological Study*. London: Martin Robertson.

———. 1979. *The Social Construction of Mind: Studies in Ethnomethodology and Linguistic Philosophy*. London: Macmillan.

Derrida, Jacques. 1990. "Force of Law: The 'Mystical Foundation of Authority.'" *Cardozo Law Review* 11:921–1045.

Destutt de Tracy, Antoine Louis Claude. 1817. *A treatise on political economy: to which is prefixed a supplement to a preceding work on the understanding, or, Elements of ideology: with an analytical table and an introduction on the faculty of the will*. Translation revised and corrected by Thomas Jefferson. Washington, D.C.: W. A. Rind.

Dews, Peter, ed. 1986. *Jürgen Habermas: Autonomy and Solidarity*. London: Verso.

Durkheim, Émile. 1886. "Les études de science sociale." *Revue philosophique de la France et de l'Etranger* 22:61–80.

———. 1887. "La Science positive de la morale en Allemagne." *Revue philosophique de la France et de l'Étranger*. 24, 33–58, 113–142, 275–284.

———. 1961 [1925]. *Moral Education. A Study in the Theory and Application of the Sociology of Education*. Translated by Everett K. Wilson and Herman Schnurer. New York: Free Press of Glencoe.

———. 1973a [1890]. "The Principles of 1789 and Sociology." Translated by Mark Traugott, in *Emile Durkheim on Morality and Society*, 34–42, edited by Robert Bellah (Chicago: University of Chicago Press, 1973).

———. 1973b [1898]. "Individualism and the Intellectuals." Translated by Mark Traugott, in *Emile Durkheim on Morality and Society*, 43–57, edited by Robert Bellah (Chicago: University of Chicago Press, 1973).

———. 1965 [1912]. *The Elementary Forms of the Religious Life: A Study in Religious Sociology*. Translated by Joseph Swain. New York: Macmillan.

———. 1947 [1893]. *The Division of Labor in Society*. Translated by George Simpson. Glencoe: Free Press.

———. 1958 [1937]. *Professional Ethics and Civic Morals*. Translated by Cornelia Brookfield. Glencoe: Free Press.

———. 1963 [1897]. *Incest: The Nature and Origin of the Taboo.* Translated by
Edward Sagarin. New York: Lyle Stuart.

———. 1974 [1926]. *Sociology and Philosophy.* Translated by D. F. Pocock.
New York: Free Press.

———. 1982 [1897]. "Marxism and Sociology: The Materialist Conception of
History." Translated by W. D. Halls, in *Durkheim: The Rules of Sociological
Method and Selected Texts on Sociology and Its Method,* edited by Steven
Lukes, 167–174. New York: Free Press.

Dworkin, Ronald. 1977. *Taking Rights Seriously.* Cambridge: Harvard
University Press.

Eisenstein, Zillah. 1994. *The Color of Gender: Reimaging Democracy.* Berkeley:
University of California Press.

Elster, Jon. 1992. *Local Justice: How Institutions Allocate Scarce Goods and
Necessary Burdens.* Cambridge: Cambridge University Press.

Ely, John Hart. 1980. *Democracy and Distrust.* Cambridge: Harvard University
Press.

England, Paula. 1992. *Comparable Worth.* New York: Aldine de Gruyter.

Etzioni, Amitai. 1996. *The New Golden Rule: Community and Morality in a
Democratic Society.* New York: Basic Books.

Feffer, Andrew. 1990. "Sociability and Social Conflict in George Herbert
Mead's Interactionism." *Journal of the History of Ideas* 51:233–254.

Feuerbach, Ludwig. 1989 [1841]. *The Essence of Christianity.* Translated by
George Eliot. Buffalo: Prometheus.

Finnis, John. 1993. *Natural Law and Natural Rights.* Oxford: Oxford
University Press.

Fish, Stanley. 1989. *Doing What Comes Naturally.* Durham: Duke University
Press.

———. 1993. "On Legal Autonomy." *Mercer Law Review* 44:737–741.

Frankfurter, Felix. 1970. *Felix Frankfurter on the Supreme Court: Extrajudicial
Essays on the Court and the Constitution.* Edited by Philip Kurland.
Cambridge: Harvard University Press.

Freud, Sigmund. 1961 [1930]. *Civilization and Its Discontents.* Translated by
James Strachey. New York: W. W. Norton.

Fudge, Judy and Patricia McDermott, editors. 1991. *Just Wages. A Feminist
Assessment of Pay Equity.* Toronto: University of Toronto Press.

Fuller, Lon. 1969. *The Morality of Law.* Rev. ed. New Haven: Yale University
Press.

Gabaccia, Donna. 1994. *From The Other Side: Women, Gender, and Immigrant
Life in the U.S., 1820–1990.* Bloomington: Indiana University Press.

Garfinkel, Harold. 1967. *Studies in Ethnomethodology.* Englewood Cliffs:
Prentice-Hall.

———. 1968. Oral contributions. In *Proceedings of the Purdue Symposium on
Ethnomethodology,* edited by R. J. Hill and K. S. Crittenden. Institute

Monograph Series no. 1. Institute for the Study of Social Change, Purdue University.

———. 1988. "Evidence for Locally Produced, Naturally Accountable Phenomena of Order, Logic, Reason, Meaning, Method, etc. in and as the Essential Qiddity of Immortal Ordinary Society (I of IV): An Announcement of Studies." *Sociological Theory* 6:103–109.

———. 1996. "Ethnomethodology's Program." *Social Psychology Quarterly* 59:5–21.

Garner, Richard. 1994. *Beyond Morality*. Philadelphia: Temple University Press.

Gauthier, David. 1986. *Morals by Agreement*. Oxford: Oxford University Press.

Geertz, Clifford. 1968. "Religion as a Cultural System." In *The Religious Situation*, edited by D. Cutler, 639–688. Boston: Beacon Press.

———. 1973. "Thick Description: Toward an Interpretive Theory of Culture." In *The Interpretation of Cultures*, 3–30. New York: Basic Books.

———. 1983. *Local Knowledge: Further Essays in Interpretive Anthropology*. New York: Basic Books.

Giddens, Anthony. 1994. *Central Problems in Social Theory*. Berkeley: University of California Press.

Gilligan, Carol. 1982. *In a Different Voice: Psychological Theory and Women's Development*. Cambridge: Harvard University Press.

Goffman, Erving. 1959. *The Presentation of Self in Everyday Life*. New York: Doubleday.

———. 1967a. "On Face-Work." In *Interaction Ritual*, 5–45. Garden City: Doubleday.

———. 1967b. "Where the Action Is." In *Interaction Ritual*, 149–270. Garden City: Doubleday.

———. 1969. *Strategic Interaction*. Philadelphia: University of Pennsylvania Press.

———. 1983. "The Interaction Order." *American Sociological Review* 48:1–17.

Goldscheider, Frances and Linda Waite. 1991. *New Families, No Families? The Transformation of the American Home*. Berkeley: University of California Press.

Gramsci, Antonio. 1975 [1948–51]. *Quaderni del Carcere*, vol. 1. Torino: Giulio Einaudi.

Gramsci, Antonio and Tatiana Schucht. 1997. *Lettere 1926-1935*. Torino: Giulio Einaudi.

Greenawalt, Kent. 1988. *Religious Convictions and Political Choice*. New York: Oxford University Press.

Gregg, Benjamin. 1997. "Democracy in Normatively Fragmented Societies." Review of Jürgen Habermas, *Between Facts and Norms*. In *Review of Politics* 59:927–930.

———. 2003. *Coping in Politics with Indeterminate Norms: A Theory of Enlightened Localism.* Albany: SUNY Press.

Gregg, Benjamin. 2002. "Proceduralism Reconceived: Political Conflict Resolution under Conditions of Moral Pluralism," *Theory and Society* 31:741–776.

Habermas, Jürgen. 1970 [1968–69]. *Toward a Rational Society. Student Protest, Science, and Politics.* Translated by Jeremy Shapiro. Boston: Beacon Press.

———. 1973. "Self-Reflection as Science: Freud's Psychoanalytic Critique of Meaning," in *Knowledge and Human Interests*, 214–245. Translated by Jeremy Shapiro. Boston: Beacon Press.

———. 1975 [1973]. *Legitimation Crisis.* Translated by Thomas McCarthy. Boston: Beacon Press.

———. 1984 [1981]. *Theory of Communicative Action.* Vol. 1: *Reason and the Rationalization of Society.* Translated by Thomas McCarthy. Boston: Beacon Press.

———. 1985. "Moral and Sittlichkeit: Hegels Kantkritik im Lichte der Diskursethik." *Merkur* 39:1041–1052.

———. 1987 [1981]. *Theory of Communicative Action.* Vol. 2: *Lifeworld and System: A Critique of Functionalist Reason.* Translated by Thomas McCarthy. Boston: Beacon Press.

———. 1994. "Struggles for Recognition in the Democratic Constitutional State." In *Multiculturalism*, edited by Amy Gutmann, 107–148. Princeton: Princeton University Press.

———. 1995. "Citizenship and National Identity." In *Theorizing Citizenship*, edited by Ronald Beiner, 55–82. New York: SUNY Press.

———. 1996 [1992]. *Between Facts and Norms: Contributions to a Discourse Theory of Law and the Democratic State.* Translated by William Rehg. Cambridge: MIT Press.

———. 1998. *On the Pragmatics of Communication.* Edited by Maeve Cooke. Cambridge: MIT Press.

Halkowski, Timothy. 1990. " 'Role' as an Interactional Device." *Social Problems* 37:564–577.

Harding, Sandra. 1986. *The Science Question in Sociology.* Ithaca: Cornell University Press.

Hart, H. L. A. 1961. *The Concept of Law.* Oxford: Clarendon Press.

Hartsock, Nancy. 1983. "The Feminist Standpoint: Developing the Ground for a Specifically Feminist Historical Materialism," in Sandra Harding and Merrill Hintikka, eds. *Discovering Reality: Feminst Perspectives on Epistemology, Metaphysics, Methodology and Philosophy of Science*, 283–310. Dordrecht: Reidel.

Hayek, F.A. 1976. *Law, Legislation and Liberty.* Vol. 2: *The Mirage of Social Justice.* Chicago: University of Chicago Press.

Hegel, Georg Wilhelm Friedrich. 1983 [1832]. *Vorlesungen über die Philosophie der Religion.* Hamburg: Felix Meiner.

———. 1996 [1821]. *Elements of the Philosophy of Right.* Translated by H. B. Nisbet. Cambridge: Cambridge University Press.

Hilbert, Richard. 1981. "Toward an Improved Understanding of 'Role.'" *Theory and Society* 10:207–226.

Hobbes, Thomas. 1985 [1651]. *Leviathan.* London: Penguin Books.

Hochschild, Arlie. 1989. *The Second Shift. Working Parents and the Revolution at Home.* New York: Viking.

Hollinger, David. 1995. *Postethnic America.* New York: Basic Books.

Holmes, Oliver Wendell. 1968. *The Common Law.* London: Macmillan.

Horkheimer, Max. 1974 [1944]. *Eclipse of Reason.* New York: Seabury.

Husserl, Edmund. 1977 [1931]. *Cartesianische Meditationen. Eine Einleitung in die Phänomenologie.* Hamburg: Felix Meiner Verlag.

Jaggar, Alison. 1994. *Living with Contradictions: Controversies in Feminist Social Ethics.* Boulder: Westview Press.

Jay, Martin. 1973. *The Dialectical Imagination.* Boston: Little, Brown.

Jayyusi, Lena. 1991. "Values and Moral Judgment." In *Ethnomethodology and the Human Sciences,* edited by Graham Button, 227–251. Cambridge: Cambridge University Press.

Johnson, Miriam. 1988. *Strong Women, Weak Wives: The Search for Gender Equality.* Berkeley: University of California Press.

Kant, Immanuel. 1914 [1793]. "Die Religion innerhalb der Grenzen der bloßen Vernunft," in *Kant's gesammelte Schriften,* edited by the Königliche Preußische Akademie der Wissenschaften, vol. 6, 1–202. Berlin: Georg Reimer.

Karst, Kenneth. 1989. *Belonging to America: Equal Citizenship and the Constitution.* New Haven: Yale University Press.

Kress, Ken. 1989. "Legal Indeterminacy." *California Law Review* 77:283–337.

Kuhn, Thomas. 1970. *The Structure of Scientific Revolutions.* Chicago: University of Chicago Press.

———. 1992. *The Trouble with the Historical Philosophy of Science.* Cambridge: Department of the History of Science, Harvard University.

Kymlicka, Will. 1989. *Liberalism, Community, and Culture.* Oxford: Oxford University Press.

Larmore, Charles. 1987. *Patterns of Moral Complexity.* Cambridge: Cambridge University Press.

Lasch, Christopher. 1986. "The Communitarian Critique of Liberalism." *Soundings* 69:60–76.

Lessing, Gotthold Ephraim. 1980 [1780]. *Die Erziehung des Menschengeschlechts.* Bern: Peter Lang.

Lind, Michael. 1995. *The Next American Nation.* New York: Free Press.

Lovibond, Sabina. 1983. *Realism and Imagination in Ethics.* Oxford: B. Blackwell.

———. 1989. "Feminism and Postmodernism." *New Left Review* 178:5–28.

Luhmann, Niklas. 1978. "Soziologie der Moral." In *Theorietechnik und Moral,* edited by Niklas Luhmann and Stephan Pfürtner, 8–116. Frankfurt: Suhrkamp.

———. 1982 [1977]. "The Differentiation of Society." In *Differentiation of Society,* 229–260. New York: Columbia University Press.

———. 1985 [1972]. *A Sociological Theory of Law.* Translated by Elizabeth King and Martin Albrow. London: Routledge and Kegan Paul.

———. 1989. "Law as a Social System." *Northwestern Law Review* 83:136–150.

———. 1994. "Politicians, Honesty and the Higher Amorality of Politics." *Theory, Culture and Society* 11:25–36.

———. 1995 [1984]. *Social Systems.* Translated by John Bednarz and Dirk Baecker. Stanford: Stanford University Press.

Lukács, Georg. 1976 [1922]. *History and Class Consciousness.* Translated by Rodney Livingstone. Cambridge: MIT Press.

Margalit, Avishai. 1996. *The Decent Society.* Cambridge: Harvard University Press.

Marx, Karl, and Frederick Engels. 1930 [1848]. *The Communist Manifesto.* Translated by Eden and Cedar Paul. London: Martin Lawrence.

———. 1962 [1932]. *Die deutsche Ideologie,* in *Karl Marx Friedrich Engels Werke,* vol. 3. Berlin: Dietz Verlag.

———. 1974 [1867]. *Das Kapital. Kritik der politischen Ökonomie.* Berlin: Dietz Verlag.

———. 1982a [1844]. *Zur Kritik der Hegelschen Rechtsphilosophie. Einleitung,* in *Karl Marx / Friedrich Engels Gesamtausgabe,* part 1, vol. 2, 170–183. Berlin: Dietz Verlag.

———. 1982b [1928]. *Ökonomisch-philosophische Manuskripte,* in *Karl Marx / Friedrich Engels Gesamtausgabe,* part 1, vol. 2, 325–438. Berlin: Dietz Verlag.

Maynard, Douglas. 1985. "How Children Start Arguments." *Language and Society* 14:1–30.

———. 1996. "Introduction of Harold Garfinkel for the Cooley-Mead Award." *Social Psychology Quarterly* 59:1–4.

Maynard, Douglas and Steven Clayman. 1991. "The Diversity of Ethnomethodology." In *Annual Review of Sociology,* vol. 17, edited by W. Richard Scott and Judith Blake, 385–418. Palo Alto: Annual Reviews.

McGuire, Gail and Barbara Reskin. 1993. "Authority Hierarchies of Race and Sex." *Gender and Society* 7:487–506.

Mead, George Herbert. 1967 [1934]. *Mind, Self, and Society.* Chicago: University of Chicago Press.

Mehan, Hugh, and Houston Wood. 1975. *The Reality of Ethnomethodology.* New York: John Wiley and Sons.

Mestrovic, Stjepan. 1988. *Emile Durkheim and the Reformation of Sociology.* Totowa: Rowman and Littlefield.

Minow, Martha. 1990. *Making All the Difference: Inclusion, Exclusion, and American Law.* Ithaca: Cornell University Press.

Morgan, Leslie. 1991. *After Marriage Ends: Economic Consequences for Midlife Women.* Newbury Park: Sage.

Mullings, Leith. 1994. "Images, Ideology, and Women of Color," in Maxine Zinn and Bonnie Dill, editors, *Women of Color in U.S. Society.* Philadelphia: Temple University Press:265–289.

Münch, Richard. 1988 [1982]. *Understanding Modernity: Toward a New Perspective Going Beyond Durkheim and Weber.* Translated by S. Minner, N. Johnson, G. S. Silverberg, R. Schilling, and S. Kahlberg. London: Routledge Nelson.

———. 1994. "Ethnomethodological Positions on the Use of Ethnographic Data in Conversation Analytic Research." *Journal of Contemporary Ethnography* 23:307–329.

Nelson, Christian. 1994. "Ethnomethodological Positions on the Use of Ethnographic Data in Conversation Analytic Research." *Journal of Contemporary Ethnography* 23:307–329.

Oakeshott, Michael. 1984. "Political Education." In *Liberalism and Its Critics,* edited by Michael Sandel, 219–238. Oxford: Basil Blackwell.

Parsons, Talcott. 1937. *The Structure of Social Action.* New York: McGraw-Hill.

———. 1954. "The Theoretical Development of the Sociology of Religion." In *Essays in Sociological Theory,* rev. ed.: 197–211. New York: Free Press.

———. 1961. "Introduction" to Part 4, "Culture and the Social System," in Talcott Parsons, Edward Shils, Kaspar Naegele, Jesse Pitts, eds., *Theories of Society. Foundations of Modern Sociological Theory,* vol. 2:963–993. New York: Free Press of Glencoe/Macmillan.

———. 1964. *The Social System.* Glencoe: Free Press.

———. 1967a. "Durkheim's Contribution to the Theory of Integration of Social Systems." In *Sociological Theory and Modern Society,* 3–34. New York: Free Press.

———. 1967b. "Evaluation and Objectivity in Social Science: An Interpretation of Max Weber's Contributions." In *Sociological Theory and Modern Society,* 79–101. New York: Free Press.

———. 1967c. "An Approach to the Sociology of Knowledge." In *Sociological Theory and Modern Society,* 139–165. New York: Free Press.

———. 1977. *The Evolution of Societies.* Englewood Cliffs: Prentice-Hall.

Phelan, Shane. 1989. *Identity Politics: Lesbian Feminism and the Limits of Community.* Philadelphia: Temple University Press.

Pollner, Melvin. 1991. "Left of Ethnomethodology: The Rise and Decline of Radical Reflexivity." *American Sociological Review* 56:370–380.

Posner, Richard. 1990. *The Problems of Jurisprudence.* Cambridge: Harvard University Press.

———. 1999. *The Problematics of Moral and Legal Theory.* Cambridge: Harvard University Press.

Quadagno, Jill. 1990. "Race, Class and Gender in the United States Welfare State: Nixon's Failed Family Assistance Plan." *American Sociological Review* 55:11–28.

Rawls, John. 1993. *Political Liberalism.* New York: Columbia University Press.

Rhoades, John. 1991. *Critical Issues in Social Theory.* University Park: Pennsylvania State University Press.

Rhode, Deborah. 1989. *Justice and Gender: Sex Discrimination and the Law.* Cambridge: Harvard University Press.

Roberts, Dorothy. 1998. "The Meaning of Blacks' Fidelity to the Constitution." In *Constitutional Stupidities, Constitutional Tragedies,* edited by William Eskridge and Sanford Levinson, 226–234. New York: New York University Press.

Rorty, Richard. 1989. *Contingency, Irony, and Solidarity.* Cambridge: Cambridge University Press.

Sacks, Harvey. 1990. *Lectures on Conversation, 1964–1972.* Oxford: Basil Blackwell.

Savage, Stephen. 1981. *The Theories of Talcott Parsons: The Social Relations of Action.* New York: St. Martin's Press.

Scalia, Antonin. 1989. "Originalism: The Lesser Evil." *University of Cincinnati Law Review* 57:849–865.

Seidman, Steven. 1999. "Contesting the Moral Boundaries of Eros." In *Diversity and Its Discontents: Cultural Conflict and Common Ground in Contemporary American Society,* edited by Neil Smelser and Jeffrey Alexander, 167–189. Princeton: Princeton University Press.

Sica, Alan. 1988. *Weber, Irrationality, and Social Order.* Berkeley: University of California Press.

Simmel, Georg. 1950a [1917]. "Individual and Society in Eighteenth- and Nineteenth-Century Views of Life." In *The Sociology of Georg Simmel.* Translated and edited by K. H. Wolff, 58–84. New York: Free Press.

———. 1950b [1908]. "The Negative Character of Collective Behavior." In *The Sociology of Georg Simmel.* Translated and edited by K. H. Wolff, 396–401. New York: Free Press.

———. 1950c [1902–3]. "The Metropolis and Mental Life." Translated by H. H. Gerth and C. Wright Mills. In *The Sociology of Georg Simmel.* Translated and edited by K. H. Wolff, 409–424. New York: Free Press.

———. 1997 [1902]. "Contributions to the Epistemology of Religion." In *Essays on Religion.* Translated and edited by H. Helle and L. Nieder, 121–133. New Haven: Yale University Press.

Singer, Beth. 1999. *Pragmatism, Rights, and Democracy.* New York: Fordham University Press.

Singer, Joseph. 1984. "The Player and the Cards: Nihilism and Legal Theory." *Yale Law Review* 94:1–70.

Smelser, Neil, and Jeffrey Alexander. 1999. "Introduction: The Ideological Discourse of Cultural Discontent." In *Diversity and Its Discontents: Cultural Conflict and Common Ground in Contemporary American Society,* edited by Neil Smelser and Jeffrey Alexander, 3–18. Princeton: Princeton University Press.

Smith, Adam. 2000 [1776]. *The Wealth of Nations.* New York: Modern Library.

Smith, Barbara Herrnstein. 1988. *Contingencies of Value: Alternative Perspectives for Critical Theory.* Cambridge: Harvard University Press.

———. 1992. "The Unquiet Judge: Activism without Objectivism in Law and Politics." *Annals of Scholarship* 9:111–133.

Smith, Rogers. 1997. *Civic Ideals. Conflicting Visions of Citizenship in U.S. History.* New Haven: Yale University Press.

Stick, John. 1986. "Can Nihilism Be Pragmatic?" *Harvard Law Review* 100:332–401.

Strom, Sharon. 1992. *Beyond the Typewriter: Gender, Class, and the Origins of Modern American Office Work, 1900–1930.* Urbana: University of Illinois Press.

Sudnow, David. 1965. "Normal Crimes: Sociological Features of the Penal Code in a Public Defender Office." *Social Problems* 12:255–276.

Tar, Zoltan. 1977. *The Frankfurt School: The Critical Theories of Max Horkheimer and Theodor Adorno.* London: Routledge and Kegan Paul.

Taylor, Charles. 1975. *Hegel.* Cambridge: Cambridge University Press.

———. 1985. *Philosophy and the Human Sciences.* New York: Cambridge University Press.

———. 1992. "Convergences et divergences à propos des valeurs entre le Québec et le Canada," in *Rapprocher les Solitudes. Écrits sur le Fédéralisme et le Nationalisme au Canada,* 179–214. Sainte-Foy: Les Presses de l'Université Laval.

———. 1994. "The Politics of Recognition." In *Multiculturalism,* edited by Amy Gutmann, 25–73. Princeton: Princeton University Press.

Toland, John. 1984 [1696]. *Christianity Not Mysterious.* New York: Garland.

Tönnies, Ferdinand. 1957 [1887]. *Community and Society.* Translated by C. P. Loomis. East Lansing: Michigan State University Press.

Tushnet, Mark. 1991. "Critical Legal Studies: A Political History." *Yale Law Journal* 100:1515–1544.

Unger, Roberto. 1984. *Passion: An Essay on Personality.* New York: Free Press.

Vogel, Lise. 1993. *Mothers on the Job. Maternity Policy in the U.S. Workplace.* New Brunswick: Rutgers University Press.

Wallwork, Ernest. 1972. *Durkheim: Morality and Milieu*. Cambridge: Harvard University Press.

Walzer, Michael. 1994. *Thick and Thin: Moral Argument at Home and Abroad*. Notre Dame: University of Notre Dame Press.

———. 1997. *On Toleration*. New Haven: Yale University Press.

Watson, D. R. 1978. "Categorization, Authorization, and Blame Negotiation in Conversation." *Sociology* 12:105–113.

Watson, Graham. 1994. "A Comparison of Social Constructionist and Ethnomethodological Descriptions of How a Judge Distinguished Between the Erotic and the Obscene." *Philosophy of the Social Sciences* 24:405–425.

Weber, Max. 1949 [1904]. " 'Objectivity' in Social Science and Social Policy." In *The Methodology of the Social Sciences*, translated and edited by E. A. Shils and H. A. Finch, 49–112. New York: Free Press.

———. 1958a [1904-5]. *The Protestant Ethic and the Spirit of Capitalism*. Translated by Talcott Parsons. New York: Scribner's.

———. 1958b [1915]. "The Social Psychology of the World Religions." In *From Max Weber: Essays in Sociology*, translated and edited by H. H. Gerth and C. W. Mills, 267–301. New York: Oxford University Press.

———. 1980 [1922]. *Wirtschaft und Gesellschaft. Grundriss der verstehenden Soziologie*. Tübingen: J.C.B. Mohr.

———. 1993 [1922]. *The Sociology of Religion*. Translated by Ephraim Fischoff. Boston: Beacon Press.

Weitzman, Lenore. 1985. *The Divorce Revolution: The Unexpected Social and Economic Consequences for Women and Children in America*. New York: Free Press.

West, Cornel. 1989. *The American Evasion of Philosophy: A Genealogy of Pragmatism*. Madison: University of Wisconsin Press.

West, Robin. 1990. "Relativism, Objectivity and Law." *Yale Law Review* 99:1473–1502.

Wieder, D. Lawrence. 1974. *Language and Social Reality: The Case of Telling the Convict Code*. The Hague: Mouton.

Williams, Bernard. 1985. *Ethics and the Limits of Philosophy*. Cambridge: Harvard University Press.

———. 1995. *Making Sense of Humanity*. Cambridge: Cambridge University Press.

Williams, Joan. 1990. "Culture and Certainty: Legal History and the Reconstructive Project." *Virginia Law Review* 76:713–746.

Wilson, Bryan. 1982. *Religion in Sociological Perspective*. Oxford: Oxford University Press.

Wuthnow, Robert. 1988. "Sociology of Religion." In *Handbook of Sociology*, edited by N. J. Smelser, 473–509. Newbury Park: Sage.

———. 1989. *The Struggle for America's Soul: Evangelicals, Liberals, and Secularism*. Grand Rapids: W. B. Eerdmanns.

————. 1992. *Rediscovering the Sacred: Perspectives on Religion in Contemporary Society.* Grand Rapids: W. B. Eerdmans.

————. 1998. *After Heaven: Spirituality in America Since the 1950s.* Berkeley: University of California Press.

————. 1999. "The Culture of Discontent." In *Diversity and Its Discontents: Cultural Conflict and Common Ground in Contemporary American Society,* edited by Neil Smelser and Jeffrey Alexander, 19–35. Princeton: Princeton University Press.

Young, Iris Marion. 1986. "The Ideal of Community and the Politics of Difference." *Social Theory and Practice* 12:1–26.

Zelizer, Viviana. 1999. "Multiple Markets: Multiple Cultures." In *Diversity and Its Discontents: Cultural Conflict and Common Ground in Contemporary American Society,* edited by Neil Smelser and Jeffrey Alexander, 193–212. Princeton: Princeton University Press.

Zimmerman, Don. 1970. "The Practicalities of Rule Use." In *Understanding Everyday Life: Toward a Reconstruction of Sociological Knowledge,* edited by Jack Douglas, 221–238. Chicago: Aldine.

Zimmerman, Don, and Melvin Pollner. 1970. "The Everyday World as a Phenomenon." In *Understanding Everyday Life: Toward a Reconstruction of Sociological Knowledge,* edited by Jack Douglas, 80–103. Chicago: Aldine.

Zinn, Maxine Baca. 1994. "Feminist Rethinking from Racial-Ethnic Families," in Maxine Zinn and Bonnie Dill, editors. *Women of Color in U.S. Society,* 303–314. Philadelphia: Temple University Press.

INDEX

Benjamin Gregg

is Associate Professor of Government

at the University of Texas

at Austin.

Library of Congress Cataloging-in-Publication Data

Gregg, Benjamin.
Thick moralities, thin politics : social integration
across communities of belief / Benjamin Gregg.
p. cm.
Includes bibliographical references and index.
ISBN 0-8223-3081-4 (cloth : alk. paper)
ISBN 0-8223-3093-8 (pbk. : alk. paper)
1. Communitarianism.   2. Social justice.
3. Social policy—Moral and ethical aspects.
4. Religion and politics.   I. Title.
HM758.G74   2003
307—dc21   2002152608